Praise for Striding Rough Ice

"Gary Wright has produced a warm and authentic tribute to his life in hockey, one that is both unique yet also familiar to those of us who have been blessed to follow a similar path. It is detailed and it is entertaining. A true hockey book by a true hockey guy."

—Joe Bertagna, former ECAC Hockey and Hockey East Commissioner, author of *Late in the Third*

"In *Striding Rough Ice*, Gary Wright shares the wisdom he garnered while growing up in a family of educators, playing and coaching a sport he is passionate about. With detail and humor, he describes the joy of team, the nuances of hockey, and the value of perseverance. Written in an enjoyable and engaging way, the book is both a coaching and a history lesson. But, most of all, it's a real hockey read."

—Bill Beaney, coached a record-setting eight NCAA D3 hockey national championships at Middlebury College

"During my years at AIC, Coach Wright showed me how much he cares about people first, and you can see that in his portrayal of the people and players that he writes about. Coach made a career of inspiring others with the utmost integrity and moral compass. His anecdotes and amazing recall of events bring the reader right into the rink."

—Eric Lang, former assistant at Army West Point, and current NCAA D1 Atlantic Hockey championship coach at American International College

Striding Rough Ice

Striding Rough Ice

*Coaching College Hockey and
Growing Up in the Game*

Gary Wright

Rootstock Publishing

Montpelier, VT

First Printing: October 2022

Striding Rough Ice, Copyright © 2022 by Gary Wright

All Rights Reserved.

Release Date: October 11, 2022

Softcover ISBN: 978-1-57869-100-5
Hardcover ISBN: 978-1-57869-109-8
eBook ISBN: 978-1-57869-110-4

Library of Congress Control Number: 2022905791

Published by Rootstock Publishing
an imprint of Multicultural Media, Inc.
27 Main Street, Suite 6
Montpelier, VT 05602 USA

www.rootstockpublishing.com

info@rootstockpublishing.com

Interior and cover design by Eddie Vincent, ENC Graphic Services
(ed.vincent@encirclepub.com)

Author photo by Caleb Kenna
Cover photo by Craig Houtz / courtesy of AIC.
Back cover photos courtesy of Proctor Academy Archives (left) and UVM Athletics (right).

For permissions or to schedule an author interview, contact the author at:
garywright2121@gmail.com

Printed in the USA

For Spencer and Nancy, my parents. Dad introduced me to the great game of hockey, and Mother inspired me to write this book.

And for my siblings and my seven nieces and nephews: Zoe, Spencer, Zelie, Rosalie, Alex, Connor and Forrest.

Hockey Coach
for Gary

He shuffles across the ice behind his team,
chin high, though one can see the ticking throat
above the loose orange tie. Today is
the big game with Army; cadet-gray forwards
ram in two quick goals—the stands are
a rearing horse! And I, his mother, am trying

to hold on to the reins. The coach now is
quiet behind the bench; I want to call
down but he won't have it. He chews on a pencil
as though the slow grind of jaw might dredge
up a winning tide. I think of his father,
my former husband: hockey coach, in love

with his work but afraid of the word "love"—
we married without it—the word, that is,
but we're better friends, for all that. I picture
the coach in the locker room, urging on
an eager team, warning the boys to stay out
of the box, avoid a power play that could

bring on a rival's goal. My son badly wants
the win, and so do I. I try not to think
of defeat, though losing is part of the game—
one mother's sorrow, it seems, is another's
joy. A drum roll resounds on the ice
and the lads morph into a pack of dogs,

spinning the puck into the net to tie the game!
While later, down in the parking lot, a light
rain drips from the coach's brow, and freezes
into a wreath on the glittering hair. I try to say
it was a good game, this tie, "and you must
be proud of your team." But he doesn't want

the equivocation. I rub his back quickly
before he can pull away and the words escape:
"Hey, man, you've earned a point for that tie!"
He smiles, then draws the circle around
the self that neither of us knows how to cross
and follows his players back onto the bus.

—Nancy Means Wright

Chapter 1

West Point Weekend

The buzzer sounds, ending regulation with the score tied 2–2 at Army West Point. Tonight is Game 2 in our best-of-three 2016 Atlantic Hockey first-round playoff series with the Cadets. We lost 5–0 last night and now we need a goal to win in sudden-death overtime. For those of us on the American International College (AIC) bench, it's score first, or our season is over.

But unlike the regular season in college hockey when teams remain on their benches for two minutes before playing a five-minute sudden-death overtime frame that often ends in a tie, playoff rules are different. Both teams will return to their respective locker rooms for a fifteen-minute intermission, then we will come out and play a twenty-minute period, more if necessary. There has to be a winner.

Our coaching staff huddles in the hallway outside the visitor's locker room at Tate Rink. My assistants, Mike Towns and Steve Wiedler, each offer some input, but our discussion is brief—before overtime we aren't looking to say too much to the team. The old adage "Too much analysis is paralysis" is in play. We have prepared hard for this series, but we don't want to overcoach. Guys need the freedom to make plays. Mike and Steve, however, will generally be close by the locker room area if brief discussion with a team member is necessary.

We all enter the room about five minutes before our team is to return to the ice. Our players sit intently on benches along three walls, their faces flush and sweaty. I begin to talk:

"The green line starts, and we will continue to roll green,

yellow, and red. We'll let you know if we insert the blue line. We have to play short-shift hockey with our goalie at the far end. This also allows us to hem Army in their zone, so they can't change. We must be assertive and go for the goal, but not at the expense of our defense, because we know winning in OT is about two-way hockey. We've shown great guts to come back from being down 2–0 tonight, and remember we beat them twice in overtime this season, so let's go do it again."

I head to the bench with about two minutes to go, and our team follows Army out to freshly made ice with a minute left on the clock. Shortly after, the starters are positioned for the faceoff with the scoreboard clock hanging above center ice now showing twenty minutes, and the referee drops the puck. Portly Army play-by-play announcer Nikolai Busko, who further fortifies his natural exuberance during games by chugging on a large jug of Coke infused with Red Bull energy drink, makes the call:

> "Army wins the faceoff back to Ryan Nick, who passes to Kozlak on the far wing. Kozlak skates and fires a long shot on the AIC net. Murray gloves the puck down and holds for a faceoff to his left in the AIC zone. Faceoff is won by AIC back to Johnny Mueller, who wraps to the far side, and McBride retrieves the puck and starts up ice from the right wall. He dumps into the left corner of the Army zone. Orszulak retrieves the puck for AIC, and now Christian fires the puck behind the Army net to the far side and it's kept in by Johnny Mueller at the point. Mueller shoots. It's redirected at net-front by Christian. Bryant Christian scores. AIC wins!"

Teammates on the ice mob Christian, and instantly our bench empties as players scramble to join the celebration, while scores of Army fans sit silent. With a deciding game tomorrow night, it's a joyful celebration, but suitably brief. Then our players proceed to center ice as our staff shakes hands with Army head coach Brian Riley and his assistants, Zach McKelvie and Eric

Lang. We are respectfully sober as we meet up with them, but underneath I am at once relieved and thrilled we have won.

Turning to join our team in the handshake line, I can feel myself on slippery ice. With the overtime ending so quickly at the thirty-second mark, the ice has hardly been skated on. As a result it's slick, with limited traction. The fact that I'm a candidate for hip replacement only adds to my stability challenges. Moving toward center ice, my feet suddenly start to slip from under me, and I barely regain balance. More worried about making a fool of myself than getting hurt, I frantically freeze in place. Fortunately the Army players skate over to me to shake hands. That finished, I cautiously shuffle toward the bench. Safely off the ice, I can feel my heart beating faster than it did in overtime.

It's a happy postgame locker room. We have won in dramatic fashion and extended the series. There's a lively shared-accomplishment, sing-in-the-showers feeling energizing the room. Captains and others voice random thoughts aloud:

"Nice job in net, Mugsy."

"Way to go boys, but it doesn't mean much if we don't win tomorrow."

"We've got a big Game 3 coming up, so let's take care of ourselves tonight."

All their points are good. I wait a minute and signal for our players' attention to congratulate them on the win, to acknowledge the play of goaltender Alex "Mugsy" Murray, and to tell them that they deserve to celebrate for a little while, but that we all know we have unfinished business tomorrow night. They nod. They already know.

Alex Murray is one of those players whose comic relief can keep a team loose. In November, we beat a strong Robert Morris team 3–2 on the road. As the bus left the rink after the game, Alex yelled from his seat in the back, "Hey, Coach, we forgot the two points," meaning he hoped we'd have the driver honk the horn twice to indicate the two points we received for the win.

I stood up and said to Alex, who had recently forgotten to bring his practice jersey on the road, "We aren't going to forget those two points, and I hope you won't forget your practice jersey again." More laughs broke out on the bus. It was the full-throated laughter that accompanies a big win. Alex got it all started.

As we pull into the hotel parking lot, it's exciting to know we'll be staying another night. Had we just lost, we'd be here to pick up our stuff and head home to Springfield, Massachusetts. One option I didn't consider was packing everything on the bus before we left for the rink today, so that if we lost, we could head straight back. That would have sent a bad message to the team. Our guys file off the bus, and blond-haired Bryant Christian pauses near my front seat and says, "Coach, thanks for those nice comments about me in that article."

"Glad to do it," I answer.

In the *New England Hockey Journal*, I had mentioned how Bryant is such a smart and dependable hockey player, and how growing up in a prominent hockey family likely contributed to his on-ice innateness.

Our playoff series with Army this weekend involves individuals from two of America's most famous hockey families. Bryant's dad, Ed, played at North Dakota, and his grandfather Bill Christian and uncle Roger Christian both played on the 1960 Olympic gold-medal team in Squaw Valley, California. His uncle Dave Christian was a member of the 1980 Olympic team that famously beat the Russians and then won the gold medal in Lake Placid. Christian hockey sticks, produced by Bill and Roger, were a popular stick for many years. Jack Riley, father of Army coach Brian Riley, was the head coach of the 1960 Olympic team, where he coached Bill and Roger. His four sons, Jay, Mark, Rob, and Brian, all played Division I college hockey. Army has, remarkably, been led by a Riley since 1950, starting with Jack, who was followed by Rob and now Brian.

On the ride from the rink to the hotel, I jotted down some notes and discussed various team matters, particularly lineup considerations, with my assistants. We won, so there will likely be few, if any, lineup changes for tomorrow's contest, but the final decision will be made after Mike and Steve watch tonight's game film late into the night. For me, it will be an easier end to the evening. I open the door to my hotel room about 11 p.m., and log onto collegehockeystats.net to look at other playoff box scores. I also check emails. And there it is, an email sent about an hour ago from Nancy Means Wright, my eighty-eight-year-old mother, under the subject line, "Yay Yay Yay":

> I can hardly believe this—a goal in the first 30 seconds of OT! Good for Christian! And Austin and Johno. AIC played so much better tonight—like its old self—(except for the penalties) . . . Anyway, I'm thrilled. So now you've a playoff

game tomorrow which you can surely WIN! Very, very exciting,
and you and your team deserve this so badly. You must be
overjoyed, Gary. Of course you've more work ahead of you
tomorrow, so don't let the lads get overtired. Or yourself.
With love and admiration,
Mother

My mother lives in Middlebury, Vermont, and is an accomplished writer,
having written over twenty books, many of them mystery novels. Recently
she published a book of her poems called *The Shady Sisters*. Most of her
pursuits are of a scholarly nature. She's also a big AIC hockey fan, not
because she's necessarily a fan of hockey or any sport, but because I coach
the team. She follows us passionately and watches or listens to our games on
the Internet. Usually, I get an email from her after a game. Sometimes it's
cheering me on after a loss, other times it's a congratulatory note when we've
won. The fact that my career win/loss record isn't great doesn't deter her. She
provides continuous, unsolicited, and unconditional love and support as only
a mother can.

As I climb into bed, I receive an 11:47 p.m. text from Adam Pleskach, a
former AIC player who skates for the Tulsa Oilers in the East Coast Hockey
League. Recruited by Mike Field, one of my former assistant coaches, Adam
was a captain and three-time Atlantic Hockey All-Conference performer.
His freshman year he was on the All-Rookie Team. He scored 114 career
points, which is significant considering we've only had one other hundred-
point scorer since becoming an NCAA Division I program in 1998–99.
Adam can flat-out score, and he's one of the hardest-working, tooth-and-
nail competitors I've ever coached. He's also a great leader. Tomorrow during
our game day meeting, I will share his inspiring text with the team.

Whatever the outcome of a game, falling asleep afterward is difficult.
You'd think it would be the other way around, but sleep after a win is
even more elusive for me. Maybe it's because we don't win enough, so that
winning becomes magnified, or perhaps it's so exhilarating that it tops the
disappointment of defeat. The fact is I am happy and energized by our win
and the challenge that awaits us tomorrow in Game 3. So tonight, I toss and
turn in bed, playing the game over and over in my mind.

I awake on Sunday morning and head to the hotel's complimentary breakfast buffet. The bus is about to leave for an optional game-day skate at Tate Rink. Steve and a few players are aboard. For most teams a game-day skate is an abbreviated practice that allows for free ice at the end. We also had morning skates on Friday and Saturday. Friday was a mandatory session and yesterday was optional. However, guys not in the lineup were expected to participate. We tried to discourage our team members from practicing this morning since this is our third straight day of competition, but some guys didn't want us to cancel the available ice. As a coach, it's hard for me to say no to players who wish to skate more, so I relent. I'm not exactly sure who's on the bus now, but I'm certain it includes David Gandara.

David is a senior forward and one of our assistant captains. He's a Native American from Canyon Lake, California, and a member of the Morongo Tribe, where his dad is a tribal leader. David is a third- or fourth-line–type player, with a top-line commitment. He has won the Wally Barlow Fitness Award, which goes to the winner of our fitness test, for three straight years. He's a bear in the weight room, the energizer bunny on every shift, and a rink rat.

Today, the team will get together for a pregame meal at 1:45 p.m. combined with a fifteen-minute meeting and film session. Mike and Steve will run most of the meeting and show a few film clips from last night's win geared toward helping us in tonight's game. The clips will be instructive and positive. Usually they include areas where we can make a systemic adjustment. I'll say a few words at the end. I'm fortunate to have Mike Towns and Steve Wiedler as assistants. They are both talented individuals who work extremely hard and have bright futures in coaching. We have a reputation for moving a lot of our assistant coaches to other college coaching positions, and those two are among the best assistants I've had.

During our week of practice prior to this playoff series, my assistants presented each team member with a scouting report. It included bullet points on Army's power play and penalty kill, defensive zone coverage, forecheck, etc. Film clips were used to show these and other areas of their play. Moreover, the team viewed footage of our two overtime wins versus Army back in December. That film was also used as positive reinforcement. Despite our sweep, Army is the higher playoff seed and they were a hot team down the stretch, plus we're on the road. At our practices, Mike and Steve each ran a daily "beat Army" drill. One point of emphasis on their scouting report is that Army will pressure our defense hard during the breakout, so Steve created a two-part beat Army drill called Breakout vs. Black Knights Pressure.

Mike directs our penalty kill and I run the power play. Recently, I challenged him to make our penalty kill better. Mike pushed back at the beginning, possibly because the challenge involved some nagging on my part. I especially wanted him to practice the PK with greater urgency, so our players win battles early before our opponents' PP sets up. He responded and developed some intense drills. Our penalty kill units were out before practice a few days ago, working feverishly on 200-foot clears and exiting the zone. Entering tonight's game, we have killed off nineteen of our opponents' last twenty power plays. Mike put me in my place and I love it.

In addition to the Army scouting report, I chipped in with a somewhat lighter handout that was placed in each team member's notebook before Wednesday's practice. These notebooks are kept in their locker room stalls, and Ben Hodgkins, our equipment manager, puts the latest handout in the front of each notebook. I generally write something like this several times a season, and always before a playoff series. In this one, the first letter in each sentence is enlarged acrostically to spell out *Beat Army @ Tate*. It goes as follows:

Buck up and play playoff defense.
Effort. Energy. Execution. // Compete. Commit. Communicate. Comport. Courage.
Army rushes fast—allow minimal odd man rushes and no 3v1s or 2v1s.
Take the Check to make the play.

Attack the net and raise the Warriors.
Reputations are made on great playoff performances.
Move your feet and be fleet on Army's big ice sheet.
Your effort, attitude, and discipline mostly defines you.

Tough tips and net-front traffic is terrific.
As always, PP/PK play wins games.
Two hands on your stick. Body on Body and Stick on Puck will

bring you lots of luck.

Everyone makes plays: win battles, clutch goals, awesome assists, defensive stops, big saves, win draws.

There's a fine line between preparing and being over prepared for an opponent. Some coaches are big believers in scouting reports and others depend on them to a lesser degree. Regardless of one's philosophy on scouting, most coaches subscribe to the idea that focusing on the play of their own team is more important than obsessing over an opponent, because too much focus on the other team can stifle preparation and performance. We're fairly balanced in this area, but we still lean toward getting our own group ready to compete. We emphasize an "If it is to be, it's up to me" mentality from our team members, assuming it's within a team concept. That makes the player more accountable for his play.

Before heading into our meeting and meal, Steve tells me he noticed something unusual at the morning skate when observing a few minutes of Army's session. Their starting goalie, Parker Gahagen, and assistant coach Zach Mckelvie were re-creating the goal Johno May had against Gahagen in Game 2. McKelvie would play the part of Johno, come down the right side and shoot from the outside. Then they'd talk about it. The sequence was repeated a few more times. Steve wondered if the goal was getting into Gahagen's head or what. I'm not sure what to think in this case, but my belief is that goaltenders willing to attack their weaknesses head-on are often mentally tougher. An example would be a goalie eager to learn by watching film of bad goals scored against him, as opposed to another who's reluctant to watch. My preference is the former. In any event, I do know Parker Gahagen is a good goalie and has been clutch for the Cadets.

Our players are excited and confident following last night's game. There's a fun feeling in the room. They listen attentively as Steve says, "When we play our game the right way, get back above pucks on O-zone turnovers, and have good net-front defense, we put ourselves in a position to win."

Mike talks about how, "We played with a ton of grit last night, which gives us an opportunity to take this program to the next step." They show film clips and end with Austin Orszulak's power play goal, Johno's game-tying score, and finally Bryant's overtime winner. I finish the meeting by reading Adam Pleskach's text from the night before:

Hey coach, it's Adam Pleskach. Huge win tonight. Pass this on to the guys if you wish. Tell them: don't let a comeback effort like that be for nothing. Don't let the days on the track with the ninety-degree heat be for nothing. A lot of character was shown and now that's over. Today is a new day. Everyone be a leader in your own way. Everyone play the role you were recruited for. If you don't know, ask. This needs to be a step forward for the program. Don't take a shift off. I had a lot of good times in college but I'd give them up for more playoff wins. Take care of it. "Come To Play. Make Plays. Keep Playing."

The bus leaves at 3:45 p.m. for the forty-minute drive to Army. As usual, no one is late. When Shawn Walsh coached at Maine, he had a saying, "Maine hockey waits for no one," and apparently there were occasions where players and even an assistant coach were left behind in Orono. There's no word whether Shawn himself was ever late, but it would have been interesting to see. We usually get a hotel closer to the arena we are playing at, but the Atlantic Hockey office does the bookings during the playoffs, and they have placed us in the Holiday Inn Express in Fishkill, New York. The 3:45 p.m. departure will get us to Tate Rink at about 4:30 p.m. or so, in plenty of time for a 7:05 p.m. faceoff.

It's plenty of time for players, but a long wait for coaches. I often sit in the bus until about 5:45 p.m., while our guys go through their pregame routines. Army only allows the bus to be parked next to the rink for a short time, so after dropping the team and support staff off, we drive to a lot behind the famed Michie Stadium, where Army has played football since 1923. I'm joined by several players not dressing for the game. They sit toward the back and I stay in my seat up front across from the bus driver. There is always some awkwardness about this arrangement. Except for Ryan Polin, a promising freshman defenseman who reinjured a sprained ankle in Friday night's game, and two guys recovering from surgery, the others are healthy scratches. They want to play badly, and it's disappointing for them to not play in any game, much less a game of tonight's magnitude. Ultimately, my position as the head coach is to be the final arbiter as to who plays. The decisions can be hard as they can make for unhappy players. When it was determined Ryan's injury was likely season ending despite his heroic efforts to play, we had to dress another defenseman for last night's game. I consulted with my staff, especially Steve, since he directs our defensive corps. It was a choice between Carson Grolla and rangy Wade Schools. They are both competent defensemen and close in ability. Steve suggested Wade, because Carson can get caught out of position defensively. I signed off on Steve's pick. Wade played well last night.

Sound carries with few people on the bus. I'm focused on tonight's game, but I do overhear sophomore forward Bailey More announce, "John Micheletto, the UMass coach, just got fired." Many coaches cringe when they hear this kind of news, especially guys like myself, who struggle to win consistently. This one hits pretty close to home. The fact that UMass is right up the road in Amherst will put me more in the crosshairs of my detractors. It's not as bad as professional sports, but college coaches are often let go when they don't win enough. UMass plays in Hockey East, a stronger league than Atlantic Hockey, but both leagues are Division I and John has bravely agreed to play us annually, despite the inherent risk that we will pull a semi-upset and beat them. Last year we did. We won 3–2 at the Mullins Center.

I look over the line charts for both teams. We're staying with the same lineup, mainly because we won. Army's lineup also remains unchanged. Familiarizing myself again with their lines is important. I change the forwards and Steve runs the Ds. He will again match defensemen Derek Henderson and Andrew DeBrincat against Army's top line of CJ Reuschlein-Tyler Pham-Conor Andrie. Derek is a prototype defensive defenseman, who consistently competes. Even this morning at the light game-day skate, he approached Steve to work on some defensive details. Andrew is a diminutive defenseman, but he's highly skilled, tough, and reliable.

Mike works with our forwards in addition to the penalty kill. He also tracks the Army changes. Our No. 1 and No. 2 power play units involve forwards from all different lines, so the shift following an AIC power play can make us vulnerable if our opponent comes out with their top players. As a result, we send out our three most dependable, non-PP forwards from the red and blue lines. They are almost their own kind of special team. Tonight, it's Gandara-Rodgers-Douglas. They may only get called on a couple of times, but we're counting on them.

I've been coaching college hockey for a long time. Five years as an assistant at Maine, and this season is my thirty-second as the head coach at AIC.

Like all coaches and athletes, I look forward to the games, and my game demeanor is usually calm, but I'm anxious and nervous before they start. You would think that after all these years, I would be calmer beforehand. But that's not the case. I worry about how our team will play, if I will make the right coaching decisions, if we'll take bad penalties, and if the officials will over-call the game. I worry about how our goaltending will hold up because, as legendary Boston University coach Jack Parker once said, "If they don't call it hockey, it should be called goaltending."

A *Good luck tonight* text arrives from my girlfriend, Cindy Bolger, at 4:57 p.m. Her comforting gesture has become part of my pregame routine. After tying Bentley 2–2 in our last regular season game, she texted, *Congrats on the point.* Cindy is a pharmacist and competitive runner who didn't know much hockey before meeting me, but her text indicates that she's learning the lingo and knows that teams get two points for a win and one for a tie. When we first met, I doubt she knew the difference between a point and a point shot.

A little later I remind Gilberto Gonzalez, our bus driver, to bring the bus back outside the rink about 9:15 p.m. and then I take the short walk down the hill and over a small footbridge to the Holleder Center, which houses the 2,650-seat Tate Rink. At the front entrance of the building is an outdoor terrace-like area, which includes a plaque bearing a quote from Army West Point grad General Douglas MacArthur. It reads, "Upon the fields of friendly strife are sown the seeds that, upon other fields, on other days, will bear the fruits of victory." The line reflects MacArthur's interest in athletics and its lasting benefits. I always glance at it during my pregame pass by.

I stop by the locker room briefly. Guys are starting to get dressed following a dynamic team warm-up in the mezzanine area. Others are getting taped or treated by our head athletic trainer, John Culp. A few of the faster dressers remain out in the stands, likely engaged in some form of mental imagery while taping their sticks. Headphones for listening to music are a popular pregame item. There's a quiet purpose in the room but for a bit of light chatter. With a half hour until we take the ice for warm-ups, I head out into the stands and sit down. Soon, I'm joined by Brian Riley and Eric Lang, who have spotted me from across the ice. Coaches often meet up before games, but generally only the first game of a series, so conversing before three games is unusual, but our relationships are close. Eric played for me and several years later came back as a graduate assistant coach. Brought up in the Bronx, which isn't exactly a hockey hotbed, Eric has made himself into an excellent coach and superb recruiter. He is also a close friend. Brian is among my favorite coaches. He has the game in perspective, yet he's still a staunch competitor.

"Well, here we are again," Brian says as he takes a seat.

"Yes," I say with a grin, "and this third game does make things interesting, although it's extra stress for us coaches. When your brother Rob was coaching the Springfield Falcons, he told me one of his biggest adjustments was playing three straight games on weekends."

We agreed that this arrangement is difficult, especially as a regular season scheduling strategy in the American Hockey League. Playing back-to-back games most weekends in college hockey is intense enough. Fortunately, we only have to play three straight if a playoff series warrants it—like tonight.

I remind Eric of what he told me before Friday's Game 1, that his wife, Chris, whom I know well from Eric's time coaching at AIC, doesn't want either of our teams to lose. I tell him that it's nice she feels that way, but I bet she'll be cheering for him and Army tonight.

"I'm not so sure about that," he says, and we all laugh.

The three of us discuss last night's game and other league playoff scores. We quip about how these longer days in early March indicate that a less hectic spring is not far behind, when our year-round jobs won't include games, practices, team travel, and the constant preparation that accompanies these activities. Mostly, though, this talk between congenial coaching colleagues offers a brief respite from the seriousness of the night. In about forty minutes Game 3 will start, and we'll do everything we can to beat each other.

Our staff enters the locker room eight minutes before game time. I start by reminding everyone of the importance of short support (getting open near the puck carrier), moving our feet on the large ice surface, and staying out of the box. And then finish with this:

> "Guys, we are totally prepared to beat Army again tonight, and this rubber match is our time to shine. You've all played hundreds of hockey games in your lives, so you've been in situations like this before—and succeeded. It will take great effort and a desire to compete. That means 'bodies up and bodies back' at all times. No shortcuts. And, I'll remind you

how Adam Pleskach ended his text with our AIC Hockey slogan: 'Come To Play. Make Plays. Keep Playing.'"

I leave the room to a spirited vocal reaction and the sharing of encouraging words between our players. In three minutes the team will meet out in the hallway and, then, led by starting goaltender Alex Murray, twenty-one determined AIC hockey players dressed in yellow, black, and white uniforms will head out onto the big ice sheet to battle Army.

Officials Eric Ernst and Ken Gates come over to our bench for the usual handshake, following the national anthem, which has obvious significance at Army West Point. As such, we always remind our players to stand still and straight for the anthem out of respect for the Cadets. (Furthermore, Brian Riley once told me that his players came out flying in a game because they were offended by an opposing team that fidgeted during the anthem.) We had Ernst and Gates in Game 1 on Friday night. They did a decent job letting players play without calling unnecessary penalties, so I'm fine having them again. After greeting the Army staff, the officials skate to center ice and drop the puck. It's game on.

Well into the first shift, we ice the puck under pressure. The Cadets change and we can't because of the icing. We're already tired at the ensuing faceoff and again we're hemmed in and scrambling. Seconds later, the red goal light flashes and their fans erupt. It's a minute and a half into the game and Army's Christian Pomarico has his first goal of the season. The action continues, and Austin Orszulak has a good chance from the slot, but they carry the play and we are chasing. Then they score back-to-back goals near the end of the period. This isn't good.

The period ends and I follow our team into the locker room to quickly acknowledge the obvious: that we're in a hole, and it won't be easy, but there's lots of time left, so let's regroup, toughen up and get back in the game. Our staff then meets in the hallway. Usually, I take notes as my assistants talk, but I can't now because athletic trainer John Culp is trying to get a piece of lead out of my eye. Absurdly, during the period as I pressed a mechanical pencil on paper while taking notes, the lead snapped into my eye. John tried to get it out as I followed the play, but I became impatient, and we agreed to wait until the break. Now, he still can't get it, so he flushes my eye and the piece disappears.

"I can't believe this whole thing," I say to John. At this point, I tell Steve that he'll have to address the team shortly. He's a fresh voice, so I might have asked him or Mike to talk anyhow. As my assistants head back into the room, John is still looking to confirm that the lead is no longer in my eye. We never find it.

We start out better in the second period. Still, they have the edge in play and Alex has to bail us out with big saves. He makes a nice stop from the slot on Nick Decenzo, and induces the dangerous Tyler Pham to miss the net as he walks in alone. Our staff provides constant encouragement on the bench, but we don't seem to have the legs, whereas Army skates with energy and purpose. We gut it out, however, and neither team scores in the period.

Our third period play is good at times, but we aren't sustaining enough offensive pressure to bridge the 3–0 deficit. And we continue to get outshot. Importantly, there is no quit in us, and I wouldn't expect anything different. They score with two minutes left to make it 4–0. At the last shift the game is essentially over, and I send our four seniors out. This is a longstanding tradition that teams often do during their last game. We end up having a strong shift in the waning seconds with our goalie pulled. David Gandara hustles for a point-blank shot just outside the crease; Chris Porter makes a diving poke check at the puck. Moreover, Derek Henderson finishes his career with a strong game, and Brandon Lubin, as I tell him, might have had his best game of the season. As in life, it's important to finish strong, even if you're experiencing a downer like tonight.

The room is filled with disappointment, almost sorrow, as I begin to say a few words to our team, which also includes the guys who haven't dressed for tonight's game:

> "This is difficult for us, just as it will be for almost every other playoff team in college hockey, because most teams end their season with a loss. Last night we courageously gave ourselves the opportunity to compete tonight. Now, suddenly our season is over. It hurts and it should, because you guys really care. We also appreciate Chris, David, Derek, and Brandon, who played their last college game tonight for AIC. It's sad now, but in time, you'll have special memories of your career."

A rather moving moment a few minutes later involves Steve Wiedler and senior Derek Henderson. Their relationship has been close, with Steve being Derek's position coach. They hug, and fighting back tears, Derek says, "Thanks for helping me so much."

I hang out in the hallway by myself, and then Bruce Marshall stops by. As the site administrator, he asks for my opinion on tonight's officials, and I tell him the officiating was fine. He doesn't stay long because he senses my disappointment. We've had a long relationship after competing for twenty-five years when Bruce coached at UConn. We both have close family members who attended Middlebury College. His grandparents had a place on Lake Dunmore in Vermont, where my family has a camp. Plus, his brother, Jon, lives in Springfield, Massachusetts. In addition to our profession and some similar interests, we have these other things in common.

I run into Helen McKibben. Her son, Jacob Caffrey, is one of our goaltenders. Jacob rarely plays, yet Helen comes all the way from Maryland for most of our games. She either drives or flies. Despite Jacob's lack of game action, she is a loyal supporter of our team. I let her know how much that's appreciated. I don't tell her what I've been thinking about for a while now, which is that I regret not giving Jacob another start during the regular season. He had one start against Princeton in January, a game we lost 1–0. He played well, which should have earned him another game, but I felt safer going with Alex Murray down the stretch. Alex is good, but he's not so good that it wouldn't have been smart to take another look at Jacob.

The time is 10:30 p.m., and we've been on the road for a half hour. We should be home just after midnight. My assistants and I spoke when we first boarded the bus, otherwise, it's pretty quiet up front. In fact, it's a subdued bus overall. I rehash the weekend in my mind and think about what could have been. How, with a win tonight, we, and not Army, would be playing Holy Cross next weekend. That would be great for our program, and perhaps for my own job security. There's nothing like a reveling ride home with the boys after a big road win, especially playoff wins. But that's not happening tonight. Our season is over, and the loss has left us feeling like roadkill as we roll along.

I think about our seniors, how players graduate every year, and how decades later most alumni hockey players reflect back nostalgically on college and their college hockey careers as being among the best years of their lives.

If guys could gain that perspective when in college, they'd probably enjoy the experience even more, as opposed to worrying about things that aren't so important. I think, too, about the good group of returning underclassmen, and that Dom Racobaldo, one of our top defensemen and a captain who missed the entire season as a medical red shirt, will return next year.

Somewhere in back of me, I hear the voice of Seth Dussault, a member of our support staff with a rather disheveled appearance. Sometimes after a loss, I have to ask Seth to keep it down, as he's usually involved in an animated hockey discussion. Seth broadcasts our home games, and this weekend is helping John Hanna from the sports communications office. A grad of our college, he loves AIC hockey, which we all appreciate. He's also a huge fan of the NHL and AHL. When he wrote for the *Yellow Jacket* student newspaper, the sports section would be full of articles on hockey and other school sports, all penned by Seth. He doesn't own a car and is known to walk nearly three miles to his part-time supermarket job. He's one of those unique people who help make college hockey great.

"Are you OK staying awake up there?" I ask Gilberto, leaning forward in my seat. "Yes, I'm fine," he says. "That's good," I answer, and relax back into the seat. The easy motion of the bus has a soothing effect, and I close my eyes, although not really to sleep. The playing season may be over, but when you're a head coach, there's more to think about during the dark drive home to Springfield.

Chapter 2

The Pond at Proctor

I and my three siblings, Lesley, Donald, and Catharine, grew up on the campus of Proctor Academy in Andover, New Hampshire, where both my parents worked. Spencer Wright, my father, taught history and economics, and was also the athletic director and coached varsity hockey and football. My mother, Nancy Means Wright, taught French and directed the Proctor Players, the school's theater group. Our parents were initially dorm parents in two different dormitories and, eventually, as the family expanded, we lived in single-family faculty homes.

Our family resided at Proctor Academy during the school year from the early 1950s to the early 1970s and enjoyed our summers and school vacations in Cornwall, Vermont, at the only home my parents owned. Andover was a town of a thousand residents, and all of us kids attended the local elementary school. Before grades 1–8 consolidated into the old Andover High School, I completed first through third grades in a two-room schoolhouse—not quite as romantic as attending a one-room school, but still "old school."

Proctor Academy was a prep school playland—at least that's the way it felt in my youth. I skied on the school's slope, played football, baseball, and lacrosse with my friends on the athletic fields, and romped in the gym. We played tennis on the school courts, and fished down the street at the "Beaver Dam." It was a three-minute walk to the trails that explored Ragged Mountain and led to the Proctor Cabin. And, most importantly, there was a hockey rink right on campus, for hockey was far and away my favorite sport.

Hockey was revived at Proctor by my father in 1955. (The school had a team in the 1930s, coached by future headmaster Lyle Farrell.) The outdoor rink was constructed with pine boards and homemade nets on what was essentially a temporary four-month winter pond. A stream ran across a semi-swampy area before running through a culvert under the campus. Near where the water went underground, a large sheet metal plate was fitted to dam up the stream each November, and the swamp became a pond. When it froze, it became a rink. To me, it might as well have been Madison Square Garden.

I was introduced to skating when I was four, and by the time I reached the age of eight in the early 1960s, I started to hoof it down to the rink almost every day there was skateable ice. About this time, I stopped skiing to focus more on hockey. I loved the game and my heroes played on the Proctor team. I knew them all by name. They wore green and white uniforms, so green became my favorite color. Riding the bus to an occasional away game was a huge thrill. It was the beginning of my million bus miles. The bus seemed big and powerful, and the ride was "really neat," especially with the whole team on board, and me sitting up front with my dad. I thought the postgame box lunches were the perfect meal. However, it's doubtful the players' enthusiasm for the food matched mine.

Another benefit of riding the bus to away games was pregame warm-ups. I'd bring my skates, gloves, and stick, and skate with the Proctor players. I didn't fully participate in the drills, but moved around handling the puck, while occasionally taking a shot on net. Sometimes the players would even exchange a pass or two with me. One time when we played an away game against Hanover High School in the old Dartmouth Rink, I was out near the red line during warm-ups when an opposing player growled, "What are you doing out here, kid?" I didn't answer, but bolted to the bench and started untying my skates. My father asked why I got off the ice. I told him they didn't want me out there.

"Who doesn't want you out there?" he demanded.

"The guys on the other team," I said, although only one player had actually said anything.

"I've heard enough," my father said, "Now get back out on the ice." I returned to the warm-ups, but stayed clear of the center ice area.

The Proctor pond supported the regulation "rink" and the adjacent "small rink," which was about the size of a neutral zone. It was where we kids skated when the Proctor varsity or junior varsity teams practiced or played home games. During varsity games, I'd alternate between watching the game and playing with my pals. Eventually the school fielded a third reserve team (sometimes called the Scrappers) and they practiced on the small rink. Considering many of the reserve players had never played hockey before, it wasn't a bad spot for them. Except for the end boards of the regulation rink, which bordered one side, the small rink had no boards, only snowbanks from shoveling and plowing. For the reserves and some of my friends with stopping challenges, the piled snow softened crash landings.

In addition to the boards surrounding the rink, it had a chicken-wire backstop at the small rink end to protect skaters and fans. Saving pucks was also important, as the rink, like the small rink, was usually surrounded by snowbanks. Unless the snow surface had a hard crust, errant pucks sank into the snow and often couldn't be recovered until the snow melted. For several years in the 1960s, Ernest Sherman, the assistant headmaster who lived next to the rink, went around gathering pucks in the spring. Unlike people who collect lost golf balls, he gave them all back.

There were no formal youth hockey organizations around when I was growing up. The closest program existed in Concord, New Hampshire, about a half hour away, and my parents never considered enrolling me in it. Instead, I played pickup games, or "shinny," as these activities were sometimes called. Often the games were played with my invited friends and schoolmates. I was their link to the rink. My siblings and I ran all over campus like we owned the place. Our house was a gathering spot for kids around town because of the vast sports opportunities at Proctor, so they were used to visiting us and using the athletic facilities. My mother, who valued quiet to pursue her academic interests, wasn't always happy about this arrangement, but she took one for the team. Or maybe I should say, took one for her kids.

We typically played on the small rink after school and on weekends, and usually there would be six or seven of us runny-nosed kids participating. This included Donald, and sometimes Lesley. Lesley was feisty, sort of like Lucy in right field, and didn't take guff from anybody. Catharine was younger and would join us later in the decade. Curiously, my father ground down the toe picks from Lesley's white figure skates, so they became kind of a hybrid hockey-figure skate. In those days girls rarely wore hockey skates— or played hockey, for that matter. Close friends like George Martin, Bert and Lynn Kelsey, Ernie Blake, Evan Snyder, John Maguire, and Jon Randall were among the regulars. We were a ragtag group. None of us wore full equipment, although a few of us had hockey gloves. Some of my friends even played in their shoes. "Always wear a hat to help protect your head if you fall on the ice," my father would say. Today that rationale probably wouldn't fly.

We occasionally used a ball in place of a puck. A ball allowed for shot blocking, lifting, and acrobatic goalie saves. We either played with two nets or half court with one net, where the team making a defensive stop had to skate out to a prearranged spot about forty feet from the net before turning back to attack on offense. However many nets we used, it was a possession game, or, considering our shaky skillsets, the intent was to possess the puck. It's unlikely we had ever heard the term "dump," which was a good thing in retrospect. "Lifting," as in lifting the puck, wasn't allowed considering our lack of equipment. Due to the competitive nature of the games, this resulted in disagreements. The team scored on might yell, "No goal. That's a lift."

"No, it wasn't a lift," the scoring team usually insisted. Whoever won the argument prevailed. There was no coach, referee, or replay machine on the scene.

Parents weren't around much either. Other than my father, who was often at the rink anyway, we rarely saw anyone's parents. Dad supported our hockey pursuits, but never pressured us. At most, he gave us positive pointers. Donald and I skated at our own initiative. Only later in my career did I observe pushy parents. My mother's main concern was our academics. She attended most home games when I eventually skated for Proctor, and corrected papers while watching us play.

If my friends didn't want to skate, or if they escaped the cold by heading back to their heated homes, it was no matter. I'd go it alone and work on various aspects of my game, such as stickhandling with my sawed-off Northland Pro hockey stick, skating figure eights to work on edges, and experimenting with different shots. Lifting the puck was a big objective at first. Over time, I tried to refine a variety of moves. Like a lot of young hockey players, I dreamed of performing heroic acts on the ice. I might have been skating solo, but my imagination kept me in good company as I deftly dribbled the puck, deking make-believe NHL defensemen, or shooting pucks past blue-jerseyed Holderness goalies. My dream of playing in the NHL had a bit of a pipe-dream feel to it, but I knew I would someday play for Proctor Academy.

And when that happened, the team I looked forward to playing the most was archrival Holderness. One season they beat my father's team 4–0 at their rink and a few weeks later the teams clashed at Proctor during Winter

Carnival. While watching the game, I saw a most unusual occurrence. Down 3–2 late in the game, Holderness pulled their goalie, only he didn't go to the bench to be replaced by an extra attacker—he was the extra attacker. Dave Hagerman, son of the Holderness headmaster, left his net and skated hard to the Proctor end. There he planted himself in front of our goaltender, Bill Prout. He continued screening him as Holderness pressed for the equalizer. It didn't happen. Proctor hung on and won 3–2. I was excited about the win and astonished about what I had just seen.

Fifty-five years later, I spoke with Dave Hagerman, who had spent his life in various aspects of prep school education, and he confirmed my memory of the event. (Dave's daughter, Jamie, won a hockey bronze medal in the 2006 Winter Olympics.) His coach, George "Rip" Richards, had instructed him to "get right in front of the Proctor goalie." It was a creative tactic that's no longer possible because goalies can't cross the red line. Dave also referred to our rink as a "pond" when we spoke, and he recalled sitting in a cozy car in his goalie equipment between periods of a cold contest at Proctor. We talked around a half century after one goalie screened another in a hockey game. I watched it with wonder then and I still can't quite believe what I witnessed.

Our family got a collie dog in the mid-1960s. My mother named her Hester, after Hester Prynne, of Nathaniel Hawthorne's *The Scarlet Letter*. Like the literary Hester, our Hester became a bit of a protagonist, at least on the Proctor hockey scene. She had a strong herding instinct, similar to most collies, and she was prone to barking. The rink, about a hundred yards from our house, proved to be a perfect-storm setting for Hester's loud antics. Part of the rink could be seen downhill from our house and when pucks struck the boards, they resounded in the quiet. Hester, like many Andover dogs during that era, was rarely leashed, so when she heard or saw action at the rink, she tried to get there. This could be problematic, because a hockey game seemed to be the ideal locale for her herding instincts. As a result, she tramped down a collie cow path atop the snowbanks, located just outside the boards.

We tried to keep Hester in the house when we headed out for a skate. If someone opening the door didn't pay attention, Hester blew right past them and hightailed it to the rink. Upon arrival, she'd bark with abandon. If my father coached from the bench during a game, or was on the ice at practice, he was basically helpless (and not happy about it) until a family member retrieved the dog. Sometimes that could take a while. In the meantime, if a game was being played, Proctor skaters and their opponents could expect a crazed collie, often just a few yards away, barking incessantly at them. It was total chaos. And when the puck moved, Hester moved with it, nearly knocking over spectators as she chased the play with dogged determination.

There were other challenges on the winter pond besides Hester. Ice quality depended on the weather. If it was cold out, the ice was hard and fast. If the weather warmed up, it turned slushy, making it difficult to handle the puck. A quick, deep freeze at the beginning of the season produced perfect see-through black ice. With various weather changes and resurfacings, eventually the black ice changed over. Outdoor ice conditions were erratic compared to inside rinks with a Zamboni. The maintenance staff plowed the rink with a tractor or snowblower, and a group of students my father called "engineers" helped resurface the ice. Frequently they used a hose, and other times they pushed around a fifty-five-gallon drum. A valve at the bottom of the tank attached to a horizontal pierced pipe drained water evenly onto the ice. Fixing cracks in the ice was also part of their job. I think my father called them engineers to pump them up.

Peter Williams, the elected school leader and captain of the 1962 team, recalled my father saying, "Williams, you are a committee-of-one to water the rink tonight." The temperature dropped below zero when he started flooding the ice after study hall. He remembers a pretty night with snow all around and a bright moon overhead, and a "low gulping sound" as the ice cracked and shifted in the cold. "I worked past lights-out in the dorms," he said, "I guess you could say I was breaking the rules with permission."

For players, especially those brought up in indoor arenas, the ice, and the outdoor winter weather, took getting used to; otherwise, it could hamper your game—and your attitude. Mental toughness was an asset. Like a quarterback who can throw a wet ball, or a golfer who plays well in the wind, you had to find a way to get it done under adverse conditions. Just like in life. Somehow, you had to skate with a strong stride and stickhandle smoothly on rough ice.

Lights were one of the rink's endearing features. Four light poles lined each side of the rink, and one pole lit the small rink. Previously only a single Buick headlight, left over from the earlier hockey era, hung from a nearby tree. The rink lights had to be turned on inside a locked room in the basement of the adjacent Shirley Hall, while the small rink light had a handy on/off switch right on the pole, allowing anyone to skate after dark. I flipped the switch regularly. It was especially nice at night when the lights illuminated both rinks, and the shining ice, framed by the tan-colored boards and winter whiteness of the surrounding snow, was beautiful to behold. I suppose it wouldn't be too much of a poetic stretch to say that those lights helped to light up my life.

Donald and I also played hockey in the house. This activity wasn't allowed by our parents, so games were held when they were away. We invented a combo hockey-soccer game, which took place in the living room. It was basically floor hockey with a softball-sized rubber ball that could also be kicked. In case our parents arrived home unexpectedly, we placed Hester in the hallway near the front door. She acted as sort of a sentry, since we knew her barking would alert us if our parents came home. The bark warning gave us seconds to stop the game and get things in order. We used a bookcase and the TV for goals since they were at opposite ends of the living room. I defended the larger bookcase, because I was bigger and older than Donald. He guarded the TV. One time, I took a shot and knocked over one of my mother's statues, a bust of William Shakespeare. Part of the nose got broken off. We blamed it on the dog.

Our on-ice games didn't just happen. We recruited players (a little like in college) by phone. Sometimes parents answered first and we'd be told "no" before even speaking to our friends. I'm sure Mrs. Snyder enjoyed having Evan play with us, but she often seemed slightly exasperated, answering, "Yes, Gary, Evan is here," in drawn-out fashion. (True, I did call all the time.) When Evan got to the phone, he usually said, "I'll play." Those were welcome words. Ernie Blake preferred hanging around his father's junkyard over skating; therefore, he was hard to get. Still, we hounded him enough that he joined us on occasion. Old friend Bill Wightman, who moved to Andover later on, still talks about the time "Ernie peed in front of the net while playing goalie." Apparently, he was trying to keep opposing players out of his crease.

As I neared junior high, I started to play in pickup games with the Proctor boys every Saturday night. When the school movie got over at 9 p.m. or so, large numbers of them rushed to the rink for a giant game of shinny. The chaotic all-campus games were played by hockey players and non-players alike. Sometimes there were as many as forty guys involved—with no one on the benches. These free-for-all games were loads of fun, even if I didn't touch the puck much. Competing against older guys, most of whom were either bigger or better than me, helped my game, considering I didn't play on an organized youth team.

One Saturday night I got in trouble when the Proctor Players performed onstage. I told my mother I'd leave the rink early to attend her play. In the meantime, I got involved in a pickup game with a few Proctor boys not attending the performance. I skated right through the play and later into the night. When I arrived home, my mother asked if I was at the play.

"No," I said, "We were playing 3-on-3, and I couldn't leave the game because it wouldn't be fair to the other guys."

"Nope," my mother said. "You told me you would be there and, besides, you go to all your father's hockey games, and yet you can't make it to my play." I almost told her I didn't go to all the away games, but decided it was best to shut up. The next year I was at the play.

I followed my father's teams throughout my youth. The Proctor varsity had no bigger fan than me. I celebrated their wins and lamented when they lost. Sumner Rulon-Miller, John Laundon, Dudley Clark, Peter Williams, and Lloyd Senno were among the top players in the early years. Senno started school after Christmas when he arrived in 1965. He scored four goals in his first game, a rarity at any time, much less one's initial game. Thrilled by his feat, I told my parents how awesome it was to have him on the team. My father nodded, but my mother said, "That's nice, but I wish he was off to a better start in my French class."

Years after, I met up with Lloyd when recruiting for AIC on the Cape. I brought up his four-goal effort and he told me that after the game my father walked by him and said, "Senno, we'll work on it." Puzzled, Lloyd asked his own father if he knew what that meant. "I have no idea," his dad answered, "but that's an unusual comment considering your performance." Lloyd also called his father after his first practice and said, "I can't believe we're playing on a pond."

I was astounded when I first witnessed players using curved sticks. Proctor had been playing football against Westmount High School, a team from the suburbs of Montreal, for a long time. Half the game was played under Canadian rules and the other half under American rules. The rivalry extended to hockey in the mid-1960s and during one of those years Westmount showed up with curved blades. Stan Mikita of the Chicago Black Hawks had recently been credited with inadvertently inventing the first curved stick, so with the Montreal Canadiens being nearby, it's likely the Westmount players became exposed to them early on.

The Proctor boys started curving their sticks and I followed suit. I put the stick blade in a pot of boiling water and then placed it under a door. Gripping the shaft end of the blade with two hands, I slowly lifted it up until I had the desired curve. A toe curve could be achieved by placing a lesser part of the blade under the door. At first, there were no restrictions on the size of the curve, but eventually parameters were set. None of this applied to me or my friends, though. I played with a big banana curve, taped with black Bull Dog Friction Tape, for some time. My shot became higher and harder, but control was another matter. And I kind of forgot about the backhand shot.

When I was in eighth grade, JV coach Wayne Curtis approached me mid-season about playing on his team. He said he spoke with my father and it would be OK for me to join the JVs, "even though you don't attend Proctor yet." This seemed far-fetched to me, but I was certainly interested. Mr. Curtis also said he thought I could help his team. It turned out faculty children could "possibly" participate on non-varsity teams under certain, albeit vague, circumstances. I began practicing soon after and wore full equipment for the first time. The only Proctor gear I had worn before was a green hockey sock with three white stripes—and I wore it as my favorite hat. It would be three years before I proudly owned a pair of CCM Tacks. I played six games as a third-liner. It was a big thrill to play on the JV team and to score a breakaway goal.

My freshman year at Proctor, I played on the JVs again, though now as a full-fledged team member. Chris Norris, a former Harvard player, coached the team. He also taught English. One of his college teammates was Tim Taylor, who became the longtime head coach at Yale, and the 1994 Olympic coach. Mr. Norris was young, and I liked the fact he had played in college. He exposed his players to new ideas about the game. I played football and baseball at Proctor as well, but I aspired to play college hockey. My being on the JVs made it clear there would be no partiality in my father's selection of varsity players.

The write-up under the picture of our JV team in the *Green Lantern* yearbook was quite philosophical:

Having frostbitten fingers, and shoveling a never-ending pile of
snow were part of the game, and part of the spirit that kept the
team going. A great deal was learned during this year's season,
the acquired skill and new knowledge will not be forgotten. They
will be the basic framework under which many of these players
will continue in their endeavors both in sports and in other walks
of life. For this help we would like to thank Mr. C. Norris.

Years later I contacted co-captain Jim Hoyt, a writer for the yearbook, to
see if he'd written that. He thought he had a hand in the content, but said, "I
can't be sure." He added, "Proctor was a huge gift to me and a life changer."

The varsity team won the Lakes Region Championship that year. Led by
John Gary, Jim Sherman, goaltender Dave Babbitt, and others, my father
earned his third league title. The season concluded with a unique arrangement
that pitted Proctor against top players from around the league. A spectator
bus brought interested students to the game and I, of course, was on the bus.
Proctor prevailed in a 4–3 thriller. It was an impressive win considering the
number of talented players represented by the other teams. We all chanted,
"We're number one." at the end of the game and I daydreamed about being
a varsity player.

Shoveling snow was indeed a part of the Proctor Academy hockey
experience, and all players, plus the engineers, got involved. We also cleared
the benches and penalty box areas. If the snowbanks became too big outside
the boards, we reduced them. The maintenance staff helped with a plow or
snowblower after snowstorms. Cleaning the ice with homemade scrapers
was a regular task. We would start down the middle of the ice, one after the
other, with our scrapers angled snowplow-like toward the side boards. When
we got to the other end, we'd head back the other way. The resultant piles
of snow were then shoveled over the boards. Shoveling wasn't much fun,
but it had to be done. Sometimes it felt like we spent more time shoveling
snow than shooting pucks. If there weren't enough engineers or spectators
to help scrape and shovel the ice between periods, we players might have
to help. When I came back for my first alumni game after graduating from
Proctor, I asked Chris Norris why Dean Jacobs, a fine player and former
varsity teammate of mine, didn't return for his junior year. "Dean didn't like
to shovel," he said. He was only half-kidding.

Proctor rented the Everett Arena in Concord when ice conditions were poor. The "Concord Arena," as we called it, was especially available on early weekday afternoons and was accessible to most teams in the league, so the arena could usually be reserved on short notice. We typically played there four or five times each season. For our team and others, driving to Concord to play in a modern indoor arena hardly seemed an inconvenience. Plus, the Zamboni saved us from the shovel.

I played two years of varsity hockey for my father. My mother was my French teacher, but I was better at hockey. At the time, Proctor played in the Lakes Region League with Berwick, Brewster, Holderness, New Hampton, and Tilton. My father often called the team captains, "El Capitan," a reference more to the three-thousand-foot vertical rock formation in Yosemite Valley, California, than to the original Spanish meaning. Otherwise, he called everyone else by their last name, including me, though he used my first name elsewhere. Accordingly, I called him "Dad" at home, but didn't really call him anything around the team. This was accomplished by facing him when I needed his attention. I was horrified whenever I mistakenly called him "Dad" in front of my teammates.

It can be a tricky proposition either playing for a parent, or coaching a child. If the son or daughter is a good player, people rarely suspect favoritism. When the individual is a more marginal performer and plays ahead of similarly skilled players, questions can arise. I was a decent player, so that wasn't an issue. Plus, I had great teammates, who were friends. I never criticized or ratted on a teammate at home, and my father never put me in that position. He treated me exactly like any other player, which is why he called me "Wright." And that was fine with me. Hockey was what I loved most, and I didn't need any parenting when we practiced or played, just a coach.

I skated with Frank Tripp and Ben Bradley during my first year on varsity, and "Stewie" Rapp replaced Ben the next season. Frank's brother, Tom, centered the first line. Tom Tripp was the team's best player, though our line easily equaled the first line. Frank was tough, could score, and was an adroit playmaker. He didn't skate as well as his six-foot-two brother, but he made plays. Ben Bradley, a crafty player, possessed notable hand-eye dexterity. Like me, he was a rink rat. Our young line had great chemistry, and I was disappointed when Ben left after only a year.

One time after practice Frank complained to me, "I know he's your father, but he makes me mad sometimes." I just nodded and moved along. The next day, he came up to me and apologized. "Don't worry about it," I said. "I get mad at him sometimes, too."

Hockey was a less structured game when I played for Proctor in the late '60s and early '70s. Systems were simpler. In some respects, that allowed for more player creativity. My father posted the practice plan at lunch in the student waiting area near the dining hall. A typical practice would involve a couple of quick passing/shooting drills to warm up, followed by 1-on-1s, 2-on-1s, 3-on-2s, and maybe some 5-on-2s and a Defensive Zone Coverage drill. We scrimmaged a lot. The D-zone was basically man-on-man, and if you were a winger like me, you better cover your opposing wing no matter what. Dad studied Lloyd Percival's seminal book, *The Hockey Handbook*, but he was not exposed to all of the publications, clinics, and Internet sites of today. Also, coaching hockey was only a part of his job description.

My redheaded, extroverted father had a quirky side. One season he had an inexperienced starting goalie named Steve Shapiro, whose in-game focus was apparently lacking. His solution was to have a manager stand behind the net continuously yelling things like, "Be ready, Steve. Here they come. Stay focused, Stevie. You're looking good," and so on. I'm not sure what effect it had on Steve's play, but it was a different tactic. Just before my second season playing for him, my father said, "You know, you can't play with hair that long." I didn't say much and he never mentioned it again. We had several guys with long hair, so maybe getting all of us to the barber wasn't worth the bother.

As Chris Norris once noted, "Spencer Wright is a master of the obscure response." He tells a story of when he asked my father, who was also athletic director, why he canceled his JV game when the weather conditions were ideal for hockey. Dad's answer: "It's snowing in Buffalo." (Buffalo is four hundred miles from Proctor.)

Another book my father owned was *Ice Hockey*, written by Thomas K. Fisher and published in 1926. Fisher coached at St. Paul's School, not far from Proctor. The book is dedicated to Hobey Baker, who went to St. Paul's before attending Princeton. The Hobey Baker Award is college hockey's version of the Heisman Trophy. It's a classic, historical book with accompanying photographs of St. Paul's games and instructional pictures taken in what appears to be a swamp. Fisher also lists important points for defensemen in the book, one of which was, "Yell 'shot' to wake up your goal-guard." I eventually asked my then-ninety-two-year-old father if Fisher's D point gave him the idea of having someone talk to Steve Shapiro during games. "I'm not sure if it came from that," he said, "but I know we needed to keep Shapiro focused."

In my second year on varsity, we played our usual two games with Holderness. The first was at our place on an unusually warm and sunny day, causing the ice to be soft and slow. (A prolonged thaw could sink the boards into the ice, causing a checked player to catapult into the snow.) Contests were often pushed back a couple of hours under those conditions, when the sun went down and the temperature cooled, but the game began at its scheduled 2 p.m. time. After a period of sloppy play, Holderness coach George "Rip" Richards stunningly pulled his team off the ice, ending the game due to "poor playing conditions." The ice was marginal, but Coach Richards may have been fussier because he was used to the Holderness Rink, which had outdoor artificial ice. After the game was canceled, a few of us headed back out to skate on the "unplayable ice."

Two weeks later we played a night game at Holderness. Our rivalry didn't need extra incentive, though the aborted game was still on our minds. Near the end of his pregame remarks, my father held up a puck and said, "Everything tonight—passing, shooting, forechecking, backchecking—comes down to how bad we want to own and command this object." After speaking, he left the locker room. Minutes later, team manager and head engineer Howard "Howdy" Rue walked in and surprised us by announcing, "I just found out their coach is a Marty-maintenance, so we can beat these guys." Howdy was still upset about Coach Richards taking his team off the ice that had been prepared by the engineers, and he was also referencing the fact that Richards was director of buildings and grounds at Holderness. There were some eye rolls in the room, although we joked about it later.

We strode onto the ice after hearing from Howdy, and shortly the game began. The crowd cheered and the dramatic setting was enhanced by the beams of light pole light that lit the night. The sound of pucks pounding the boards, and the on-ice scrapes of sticks and skates, cried out "hockey game" in the evening air. It was a great night to be a hockey player. Play went back and forth, and I scored a goal by passing to myself off the springy baseboards behind the net and then one-timing it from the slot. Years later, Doug Windsor, a former player, mentioned the goal in an email.

Our line got benched for indifferent defense at one point. "When you guys mature and start covering people, let me know and I'll put you back in," my father hollered. Soon, Frank asked me to say something to him. He may have thought I had a better chance as his son, but I wanted no such discussion because he was my dad, so I told Frank that he'd have to talk to him. Frank then told my father our line was ready to defend, and we got back on the ice. It wasn't enough. We were awarded the first game by forfeit when they left the ice, but this time the contest went three periods, and we lost a close game that we wanted to win badly.

The weather that night was mild, but it could get bitterly cold when we played. Subzero temperatures were common. Wearing long underwear and an extra sweatshirt under our jerseys kept us warmer. We wore headbands (or old jockstrap waistbands) beneath our helmets when the temps tumbled and it helped to wear a thin pair of gloves under hockey gloves. Our feet were especially vulnerable. We'd rub Cramergesic ointment on our toes to help keep them warm. Next was a pair of socks. Then, we put small plastic bags over our feet for insulation. The top of the bags stuck out of our skates. Still, our feet could get cold, and when our frozen toes started warming up afterward, they stung. A chilly wind not only reddened our faces, but skating upwind was taxing. A stiff breeze did offer some advantages: It generally blew the snow down to the end boards, making for better ice conditions overall, less scraping, and easier shoveling.

My passion for the sport overrode any cold-weather concerns I might have had. Plummeting temperatures never prevented me from skating. When I read Jack London's *To Build A Fire* in a Proctor English class, it reminded me of skating (and my spitting habit) at the rink. London wrote that the main character walking in the "tremendous cold" knew "that at fifty below, spittle crackled on the snow, but this spittle had crackled in the air." I don't know if it ever got that far below zero in Andover, but it came close enough.

One phenomenon that could occur during a bone-chilling freeze involved the puck. When we fired off our best Bobby Hull–like slap shot and the frozen practice puck hit the goal pipe just right, the rubber disk would split in half. It was always nice to have a few witnesses saying something like, "What a blast," or, "Get a picture of the puck," when a mighty shot and some luck resulted in a broken puck.

Dave Roper recalls the cold. He once played a game with "zero feeling in my hands," and said, "I remember Spence Wright, on the coldest of days, out there with very little clothing, seemingly immune to the cold." A three-sport athlete at Proctor, with flaming red hair to match my father's, Dave tells of the time he was playing linebacker and a mammoth fullback barreled toward him. He chose self-preservation by purposely missing the tackle. In a subsequent team film session, coach David Fowler rewound the play several times, and said, "Jeez, Roper, what were you thinking?"

"About the rest of my life," he replied.

My parents left Proctor after the 1970–71 school year to move into our Cornwall home near Middlebury, Vermont. Dad had roots in the area and Mom wanted to pursue her writing career. Hester went with them, which ended her career hounding and herding hockey players. I would still return for my senior year in the fall and live in the dorms for the first time as a Proctor student. I'd been selected as a floor leader in Cary House, where we lived when I was born. Donald would be an incoming freshman. This was made possible by David Fowler, who'd recently been appointed the new headmaster. Mostly to acknowledge my parents' twenty years of service, he allowed us to attend at almost no cost. It was an incredible gesture on his part. With the perspective of age, I've appreciated David Fowler's generosity even more.

Chris Norris, my former JV coach, was named the new varsity hockey coach and it was exciting to have him as my coach again. He was also my former English teacher. A big believer in skill development, he often told us, "It's a great feeling to let go a nice snap [wrist] shot," as he implored us to improve our shots. He himself had a potent shot, which was enhanced by a rapid sweep-snap stick motion that propelled the puck. One of his shooting drills, designed to fire the puck using only wrists and forearms, with no weight transfer or forward body lean, had us skating backward away from the net while shooting. Among other individual skills, he encouraged us to improve our outside edge utilization. I did a one-footed outside edge stopping exercise on my own almost every day.

Goaltending was a concern entering the season and Peter Emmons, a former JV defenseman, converted to that position. It's a move rarely made at such a high level, yet he played well. He didn't always look good stopping the puck, but he usually succeeded, mostly because his athleticism and competitiveness helped compensate for a lack of developed technique. With adjoining rooms in Cary House that overlooked the rink, we talked a lot of hockey during the season. I was the quarterback and he played center on the varsity football team, so our late-night talks started in the fall. Peter died in a car accident following his senior year. Dying young is a terrible thing.

My brother Donald played hockey on the JVs that year. He was a big Boston Bruins fan and we watched Bobby Orr score his iconic overtime goal to win the Stanley Cup in 1970. He got placed in mandatory study hall once for "uneven grades," an interesting description for subpar academics. Members of the faculty monitored the study halls. Donald listened to most of the Bruins broadcasts, so this presented a dilemma. He dealt with it by pocketing his transistor radio and running a small cable with an earpiece beneath his shirt and then up under his long unruly red hair to his ear. This allowed him to secretly listen to the play-by-play calls of Bob Wilson. He just had to suppress his delight when Orr, Esposito, or Hodge scored.

I had a case of uneven grades myself, but my first trimester senior grades proved to be an outlier when I made the honor roll. The distinction earned some privileges and allowed for more off-campus weekends. I assumed it also meant I didn't have to observe the evening study hours. One night I turned on the little rink light and went for a skate.

"Gary, what are you doing out there?" a voice called from the darkness. There was Don Burke, the assistant headmaster and academic dean, on the road above the rink.

"I'm on honor roll, so I'm just playing a little hockey," I said.

"I'm pleased you are on the honor roll, but that doesn't allow for other activities during study hours," he said, "so head back to your dorm." I turned off the light and quickly removed my skates. My self-designated scholarly skate had ended.

I remained a rink rat, though, and Donald and I were always on the ice. Many times, we played a Saturday afternoon game with our teammates and then skated again at night. Donald's roommate, Raymond "Bass" Smith, a member of the reserve team, and his JV teammate, John Caesar, who idolized Bobby Orr, frequently accompanied us. John even copied Orr's one-strand tape job. Bass was an African American from Harlem who played the bass guitar, thus his nickname. It was his first year playing hockey. He mostly ran on his skates and, because he couldn't stop, often ran into us. Our group of four, plus whoever else joined us, would play shinny or just shoot around. We played in all conditions and we usually had so much fun that falling snow might just as well have been confetti.

Proctor had a relatively strong hockey program in that era, and we were 10–7–1 my senior year. I was moved to center, now that the Tripp brothers had graduated, and I finished high among the league scoring leaders. The league kept standings, but not other statistics, so I never knew exactly where I stood. My parents drove over from Vermont to see the Lawrence Academy game and a few others. It was strange seeing my father watching me play from outside the bench area. I'm sure it must have felt different for him too.

My final goal tally didn't include two goals I scored in a snowstorm at Berwick Academy. (Mike Eruzione, best known as the captain of the 1980 Winter Olympics "Miracle on Ice" national team, starred there the next year.) It started snowing on our bus ride and by game time thick white flakes filled the air and blanketed the ice. Visibility was affected and the puck plowed mole-like through the powdery snow. I always skated in snowy conditions, so it didn't bother me as much. After the second period the refs and coaches conferred. Not a good sign. Then they canceled the game, despite a tie score. I doubt many players on either team agreed with the decision. As we left the ice, Mr. Norris introduced me to Pop Whalen, the Berwick coach, who competed against my father when he coached at Brewster.

"This is Spencer Wright's son." he said.

I said, "Hi," but that was about it. I was too mad about the game being canceled.

Other than the Berwick fiasco, I relished my last season at Proctor and I could feel myself becoming a better hockey player. I hoped it would be enough to continue playing the game. Mr. Norris proved to be a big advocate of me playing college hockey. Considering my worries about making it at the next level, his confidence in my abilities was reassuring. He sometimes started a sentence by saying, "One thing you'll love about college hockey . . ." His assumption that I would play at the next level made me feel better about my chances.

My mother called my dorm a few hours before a home game in February. A letter from the University of Vermont (UVM) had arrived in a large envelope, and she asked if I wanted her to open it or forward it to me. I told her to open it. There was a long pause, while the phone shook in my hand.

"You've been accepted," she cried out. "I'm so happy for you."

"Thanks, what a relief," I said, "so I'll plan a champagne celebration."

"No, Gary, you know better than that," she pleaded.

I assured her I was just kidding. Besides, my acceptance gave me a high in itself since UVM was my first choice.

Our season concluded a couple weeks later, which effectively ended my years of playing hockey for Proctor Academy, as well as many more years of skating and participating in pickup games. It had been a wonderful run, and I felt like Proctor had been the perfect place to grow up and play hockey. Graduation was still three months away, but the ice had melted on my hockey experience. Soon enough, I would be attending the University of Vermont and trying out for the team as a walk-on. My hockey career faced an uncertain future.

Chapter 3

Go Cats Go

Whe I entered the University of Vermont in the fall of 1972, the hockey program competed at the ECAC Division II level. It was a young program, as the school officially started the sport beginning in 1963. However, Vermont hockey had already emerged as a powerhouse, having won the ECAC championship in 1970, followed by two more playoff appearances, which included another championship game appearance in 1971. That year included a watershed win over Division I Harvard. Jim Cross coached the team. He played at Boston University and became the head coach in 1965–66. Home games were played on campus before large and loud capacity crowds of three-thousand-plus at Gutterson Fieldhouse. The team was enthusiastically supported by the student body and Burlington community alike.

The housing office placed me in Wright Hall, a coed dormitory located on UVM's Redstone Campus. Being an undistinguished member of the over-two-thousand-student freshman class, I can probably safely say the housing assignment was unrelated to my last name. Two hockey players, Herb Muther and Ken Yeates, lived in a room next to mine, and became close friends. Herb and Yeates, as we called him, were classmates and teammates at Kent School in Connecticut before entering UVM. Herb's family lived in Burlington for a while, and Yeates was from Dorval, Quebec. Yeates's older brothers, Jim and Ted, preceded him as UVM hockey players. Yeates gave me a nonsensical nickname, "Wrightbag," which stuck with me in college and beyond. Abbreviated monikers included "Bags" and "Bagger." I eventually outdistanced those nicknames, except when I saw old friends.

As a non-recruited player, I didn't have the security of knowing I had a spot on the roster, a feature afforded to a recruit. A walk-on candidate could be cut following the most cursory look. Moreover, most of the squad returned from the previous season. A couple of people had told Coach Cross about me, but I suspect that he only had a vague sense of who I was. In any event, I'd arrived at UVM with the dream of playing college hockey for the Catamounts. Realizing that the dream would be a tall order, I fretted about the upcoming tryouts.

The team held tryouts in October. As a non-recruited player, I had to try out in my own equipment. Having never played summer hockey, I didn't even own a pair of hockey pants, so Yeates loaned me an old blue pair of his. After skating once or twice, I entered Gutterson for the combination tryouts/first day of practice. All of us walk-on candidates dressed in the skate changing room. Shortly before the session began, someone said the team manager was sharpening skates, so I waited around to get mine done. Getting them sharpened at the last minute wasn't smart. I got on the ice late and only skated in the waning minutes of the warm-ups. It was all pretty crazy. Here I was, desperate to make the team against seemingly long odds, and I was showing up late, with almost no warm-up, on newly sharpened skates.

In addition to the returning players and recruits, about twenty-five of us tried out. After scrimmaging for fifteen minutes, Cross met with a line of non-recruited players following a shift. Seconds later, everyone was surprised to see three individuals exiting the ice. Cross had cut them. Then it happened again a few minutes later. It was scary, but I kept working hard—and holding my breath after each shift. Coach Cross pulled everyone together when the session ended, including four of us walk-ons who hadn't been cut. He told us to report to practice the next day, along with the rest of the team. He did not tell us we had made the team.

I skated in the upcoming practices, all the while dressing in the skate changing room with the other walk-on candidates. The practices were full of challenging drills, conducted at a much quicker pace than our Proctor practices. All the players seemed highly skilled to me. I felt self-induced pressure to produce at every practice, and at night, I worried about my worthiness to make the team. Still, I did some good things, and felt encouraged when other players occasionally stick-tapped my shin pads after a nice play. And then one day I collided with Fred Hunt, a standoffish senior and one of the team's top players. The impact sent me flying and I landed on the ice like a tossed octopus. "I'm sorry about that," I said. Remaining on his skates, Fred glared down at me and moved on. I got up quickly and moved on myself.

A week later, Coach Cross made an announcement at the beginning of a practice: "Today will be the last practice for those of you trying out for the team. You are all good players, but we have too many numbers out here and we have to move on. I appreciate your efforts to play for our team and you're welcome to try out again next year." Continuing to practice after hearing the bad news was hard. My focus was fogged and, for perhaps the first time in my life, practice seemed pointless.

Being cut was a big blow, yet with my long tryout I felt I had a fair opportunity to make the team. The idea of transferring crossed my mind, but I decided against it. Recruiting was less sophisticated back then, and there weren't many schools familiar with me. Plus, I loved the University of Vermont. It was where I wanted to be, even if my goal of playing college hockey had likely ended. Hockey was a big part of my identity, or so I thought, and not playing for UVM left a void in my life. I joined a team called the Highgate Flyers, who played in a six-team league within twenty-five miles of Burlington. The hockey was fun, but the non-Philadelphia Flyers clearly weren't my first choice.

I moved into Sigma Nu fraternity the following fall, after pledging my freshman year. Tom Rudkin, a former hockey teammate at Proctor, was a member and first encouraged me to join. Herb Muther also joined. Several hockey players resided in the house, as part of an overall membership of about sixty "brothers." Sigma Nu was not quite *Animal House*, but it wasn't to be confused with the local library either. Our fraternity was renowned for hosting postgame parties at a time when the drinking age was eighteen and alcohol laws were liberal. In fact, a bedsheet often hung below the scoreboard at Vermont hockey games announcing: SIGMA NU POST GAME PARTY—15 KEGS.

Years later, Jim Duffy, a former Sigma Nu brother and hockey player from the late 1970s, when speaking at a UVM hockey event hosted by the athletic department, spoke whimsically about playing at Gutterson in front of our fraternity banner: "I felt like I was playing for the Sigma Nu party sign." In Ken Dryden's book *The Game*, Canadiens player Rick Chartraw said something similar: "I don't play for money. I play for the party after."

Word came out that the hockey program intended to start a new JV team. I couldn't believe my good luck. I had planned to try out for the varsity again, but having been cut once, my chances weren't great. Now, with a JV team, I was positioned to possibly make the big team at some point. If not, I was still playing hockey at Vermont, albeit at a lower level. Coach Jim Cross appointed George Kreiner to coach the team. A former All-American defenseman at UVM, he served as a part-time assistant coach for Cross, and co-owned a local insurance agency. A physical D-man, Kreiner was known as "Crunch" and "Earthquake" during his playing career. He wasn't someone you wanted to run into on the ice.

JV practices were held at 6 a.m., not an opportune time for night-owl-leaning college students. A few guys from Sigma Nu played on the team, including Bill Coogan, the originator of the amusing term "Sub-Cats," used to describe the JV team. "Sub" referenced the secondary and substitute aspect of the team, and "Cats" was a widely used abbreviation for Catamounts. Participating on the Sub-Cats and playing a ten- to twelve-game schedule seemed promising. George Kreiner coached the UVM system, which added continuity should someone ascend to the varsity. "Play the system. Cross's system works and it's been proven time and time again," he often told us.

And suddenly, that happened to me in November when I got called up following a shoulder injury to Willie MacKinnon, a fellow Sigma Nu member and first-line center. He was on his way to an outstanding twenty-seven-goal senior season, despite missing several games. Willie, who had long flowing hair, was described as "stylish" when he appeared on the cover of the NCAA Ice Hockey Guide. (More than a few coeds on the UVM campus were interested in him.) The day of the call-up, Jim Cross said this about me in the *Burlington Free Press*: "We have really been impressed with his progress."

Practicing with the team proved to be a valuable experience and suggested I was playing well—and just might make it. I definitely didn't feel the same pressure as in tryouts the year before. This time, I had more security; failing to stick with the team would result in being sent down to the JVs, as opposed to being cut outright.

I returned to the Sub-Cats ten days later. Cross shared encouraging words before sending me down. He advised me to "keep working hard" and said he'd continue to follow my progress. As expected, I only skated in practices, not games. But that was OK with me; just practicing was an important step in itself. I now had to find a way to go back up and stay. I vowed to approach every practice like a game, every shift like overtime, and to stay out after practice whenever possible. Even though the opportunity basically benefited me, it indicated to my JV teammates that Cross was watching, and the same chance could be presented to them.

I remained with the JVs for the rest of the season. We were a bare-bones operation, having to supply our own equipment, except for jerseys and socks. Driving our rickety cars to games didn't exactly feel like the big time, but we were playing for UVM, and that felt good. Meanwhile, the varsity team won its second ECAC D-II title in a row, and third in the past five years. Ted Castle, Willie MacKinnon, and John Murphy were named All-Americans, and Cross was chosen Coach of the Year. The team finished 28–5, and went 9–3 against NCAA Division I opponents. The record versus Division I teams was further proof the University made the right decision to upgrade to D-I for the upcoming 1974–75 season.

The next season, I joined the Cats right from the start. After cutting me, Cross had decided to keep me. I was added to the roster with little fanfare and directed to move into the locker room with the rest of the squad. Coach Cross didn't say much to me about my new status, but it was fine with me. His actions spoke loud enough. Moreover, George Kreiner and one or two others who dealt with Cross, had hinted that my chances of making the team looked promising. I didn't show it, but I was delighted to be a Catamount.

Herb Muther and I walked to class one day soon after practices started, and he told me that he'd decided not to play anymore and was meeting with Cross about it after class. He asked me not to say anything until he had a chance to tell people. Herb said that he'd given it a lot of thought and didn't see things changing after not playing in any games the year before. As expected, his meeting with Cross went well. Herb and I were similarly skilled players and experienced the same lack of playing time. He decided to stop playing and I was still trying to dress for games. I could have queried him about quitting hockey and he could have questioned why I kept trying to play. But neither of us second-guessed the other. He made the right decision and so did I.

I occasionally rode to practice with senior defenseman Ted "Fast Eddie" Curtis, a frat brother. We got to practice fast, but I didn't always know if we would get there. Ted rarely waited at a red light. Instead, he steered his jeep off the road and onto a sidewalk or whatever, then drove past the light and back onto the road. He said it was OK to drive around a red light, but not through it.

I practiced on the fifth line, which some days consisted of four players rotating through. Having skated with the team previously, things weren't all new to me, but I still had much to learn. Despite graduating a strong senior class from the previous season, the team had a good group of returnees and a talented freshman class. The illustrious line of Tim O'Connell, a junior, and seniors Bill Koch and Rogie Mallette returned intact. They were the key unit as Vermont entered the NCAA Division I ranks as a member of the ECAC hockey league.

Tim O'Connell, or "Oakie," as everyone called him, had already emerged as an extraordinary player after just two seasons. He came from an athletic family, which included his father, Tommy, a former NFL quarterback, and brother, Mike, who played in the NHL and became the Bruins general manager. Oakie, a Buffalo Sabres draft pick, led the nation with forty-one goals in that first Division I year, and was named an All-American. The team captain his senior year, he eventually graduated as the program's all-time leading scorer. Twenty years later he was finally surpassed by Martin St. Louis, who went on to become a superstar in the NHL, and Eric Perrin. As good a person as he was a player, Oakie grew up saying to himself every night before bed: "Tomorrow I'm going to be a better hockey player than I was today."

It felt great to wear team-issued equipment and have my own stall in the locker room. The college also supplied bright red Titan sticks. They were fine with me because I was just happy to have free sticks. Some guys exchanged their Titans for other brands with Reggie Snow at Mills & Greer, a Burlington sporting goods store. Reggie played for the Burlington Braves, a local hockey team I played a few games with early the previous year. We later became teammates on the Mills & Greer softball team. Sometimes referred to as "Slapshot Snow," Reggie was known to rent ice by himself at area rinks, and fire off a few hundred 90-mph slappers. Many of them went high and wide.

Coach Cross addressed the stick issue one day at practice. We all knew he'd get mad if someone broke a stick in frustration, but this time he spoke to some of the complaints about having only one choice. Tapping his Titan on the ice, he said, "I don't have any complaints about this stick; it works fine for me." There were a few side glances as he spoke. Cross wasn't a player anymore and he wasn't exactly a sniper at BU.

Burlington percolated with excitement as the Division I era commenced. However, an uncharacteristic 2–7 start ended with a 5–2 loss to Saint Anselm. They were a middling Division II program, so the loss caused a degree of consternation. But not to worry, as the team responded with an old Catamount-like run, featuring seven straight wins. The streak included a win over powerful Cornell in the championship game of the Syracuse Invitational Tournament.

I still hadn't dressed for a game at this stage. When Cross announced the lineup at practice, it didn't affect the regulars as much, but it was a tense time for those of us on the bubble. I always stayed out late to work on my game after not hearing my name in the lineup, instead of sullenly exiting the ice. It also helped with conditioning. With the team averaging two games or more each week, there were fewer practices than in the preseason and less opportunity to skate. Despite all this, sticking it out wasn't an issue. I loved hockey, I had great teammates, practices were fun, and I liked Cross, even if he didn't play me.

Jim Cross was a most unusual person and coach. His interests included bird watching, classical music, and politics. He was a golfer, a tennis player, and a sailor. A fine baseball player himself, he coached the sport at UVM for a time. As the hockey coach, he espoused clean play and despised bad penalties. He even kept a unique player stat called GSWIB, which stood for "goals scored while in the [penalty] box." He became one of the first coaches in North America to adopt Russian and European hockey tactics and systems. A competitor, he always told us to skate right up to the center ice faceoff circle after being scored on. No head hanging allowed. He insisted we handle ourselves with class and treat other people with respect. "You are no better than anyone else," he would tell us players. Character was his chief concern, not dress codes and 1970s hair lengths. Art Kaminsky wrote an article in the *New York Times* headlined "Vermont a Small College, But It Plays 'Big' Hockey" where he said the Catamounts "lead the league in long hair and beards." I was one of those longhairs, but I wasn't contributing to any wins yet.

During the recruiting process, Johnny Glynne, who had shoulder-length hair and a beard, asked Cross "about playing with long hair."

"Some of the biggest assholes I know have crew cuts," Cross said. Johnny ended up committing to Vermont and developed into a skilled defenseman. He was known for his physical play and bomb from the point. Somewhat of a rebel, he could be a handful for Cross at times.

Long after retiring, Cross received an award at the American Hockey Coaches Association (AHCA) convention in Naples, Florida, in 2001. Bill Kangas, the head coach at Williams College, who played at Vermont, nominated him for the award. I attended the convention as the head coach at AIC. Bumping into Cross as we both walked to the banquet, I noticed a sales sticker attached to his pants. As I reached down to remove it, Cross said, "You know, I never was much of a fashion plate." Any former player would concur with that. I sat at his table alongside Kangas, George Kreiner, and others. Cross accepted the award, told a few quick stories and sat down. His remarks were nice, and they were funny, but I found myself wishing he said more, that he revealed more of himself. Many of the several hundred college coaches at the banquet knew little about Cross, and they could have benefited by hearing a few additional remarks from Jim Cross, one of the most interesting and enlightening coaches to grace the college game.

Cross blew his whistle at the beginning of a second semester practice and ordered us into the skate changing room. Meeting in this manner was rare. We filed off the ice and everyone sat on wooden benches facing our coach, who stood up front.

"Watch this," Yeates whispered, from where we sat in the back.

"What do you mean," I whispered back.

"You'll see," he said.

Moments later, Cross started to talk, and as Yeates hung his head, said, "The bad penalty that Ken Yeates took last night nearly cost us the game."

Following the initial seven-game winning streak, the season included another run of eight straight wins in February. We finished 24–12 overall and 14–6 in the ECAC, earning the No. 3 playoff seed. Providence College, seeded No. 6, came to Gutterson on March 4 for a single elimination quarterfinal game. Still not in the lineup, I joined 3,500 enthusiastic fans and watched the game from the stands. When the team staged a furious comeback from a 5–2 deficit with ten minutes left to win 7–5, the decibel level turned deafening as the crowd cheered and chanted "Go Cats Go."

March 4 was a Tuesday night, so the party involved fewer kegs, but it didn't deter students from pouring into Sigma Nu for the postgame party, and those revelers poured beer from a dozen kegs deep into the Vermont night.

The ECAC finals were held at Boston Garden on March 7 and 8, 1975. The semifinals featured Vermont vs. Boston University (BU) and Harvard vs. Cornell. Bill Koch's shoulder injury in the Providence game allowed Jack "Jocko" Clifford to move into the lineup. I traveled as the spare forward and we were roommates during the tournament. Jocko was funny and smart, and lived in Sigma Nu. He greeted friends as "Senator" and we called him that in return. He sold Miller beers for fifty cents out of a Coke machine in the fraternity house. And he wore his favorite "saltys" (sneakers) year-round. A golfer, he once hit balls off the roof of the house in an attempt to reach Waterman Building nearly 275 yards away. Some landed in the parking lot before bouncing against the building. His press guide bio curiously said this about his shot: "Prefers the off-wing and with his strong backhand (by far his best shot), he is very effective on the right side."

BU beat us on Friday night and Harvard handled Cornell. Over three thousand Vermont fans journeyed to Boston to watch the tournament, including Vermont Governor Tom Salmon. Playing in Boston Garden was a wonderful experience for the participating teams. At one point, we watched part of a Bruins practice run by coach Don Cherry. Considering his affinity for the Bruins, my brother, Donald, would have liked to be with us. Years later, Peter "Beek" Beekman, a Sigma Nu friend from college, remembered running into me in one of the massive Garden bathrooms. I don't recall it, but he swears I told him, "I've never seen so many urinals in my life." Growing up in a small town probably had something to do with my oddly provincial observation.

Back then the championship weekend included a consolation game. We played Cornell on Saturday afternoon. There were no lineup changes, so I watched the game from the stands. We beat Cornell 7–3, and garnered third place in the tournament, which BU won. The game presumably had more significance to us than to Cornell, considering it was our first season in Division I. In fact, ending up in third place out of seventeen teams during the regular season was a huge accomplishment and attracted widespread attention. Cross sent all the seniors, except for the injured Bill Koch, out for the final shift. Someone said Mrs. Curtis started to tear up when she saw her son, Ted, and the other seniors skate one last shift for the Cats.

I headed down to the locker room after the game ended. Upon entering the room, I ran into a euphoric Coach Cross. "You'll be a bigger part of it next year, Gary," he said as we shook hands. When you're in my position you don't forget that line. It provided incentive in the upcoming months as I prepared for my senior year.

Cross was again named Coach of the Year, only this time as a Division I coach. He received the prestigious award at a Boston area banquet after the season, wearing a black tuxedo and white Tretorn sneakers.

I stayed at Sigma Nu over the summer and lifted weights at the Burlington YMCA, where I worked as a camp counselor. I was goal-line thin and felt getting bigger and stronger would benefit my game. Lifting helped, but I wasn't necessarily a workhorse in the weight room. Strength and conditioning training was not widespread in hockey circles back then, like it is today. We had a weight room in the athletic complex, but the team didn't have a mandatory conditioning program. Many of us ran on the nearby Burlington Country Club course and played racquetball during the off-season. We also rented ice on our own at area rinks before practice started. Only a few guys worked out with weights during the season. The concept of "skating into shape" still prevailed in the mid-1970s, but the game was changing, and most college and professional teams had formal conditioning programs by the end of the decade.

We started practice in October for the 1975–76 season. The Green & Gold game was held in Rutland, Vermont, a short time later. It was basically an intrasquad affair played around the state each year. UVM Hockey received statewide attention and these games helped expose the team to more Vermonters. Growing the sport in Vermont was another objective. Rutland was forty minutes south of our Cornwall home, and my parents brought my grandmother to the game. We were close, and she hadn't seen me play since prep school. As we entered the ice for warm-ups, I heard someone frantically calling, "Gary! Gary!" It was my grandmother, and she was half-hanging over the chicken wire surrounding the rink. My parents knew not to carry on like that, but my grandmother obviously didn't. I gave her a no-look nod and skated on.

I felt encouraged when Cross commented on me in a *Burlington Free Press* article by Ted Ryan, the team's beat writer: "He was just an nth of a degree from playing last year. We dressed 12 forwards and he was the 13th. He's a pretty good hockey player."

Soon a couple of guys got sent to the JVs, where Donald now played as a freshman. That meant our team carried nine defensemen and just thirteen forwards. Plus, I was skating regularly on the fourth line. My chances of finally being in the lineup looked promising. Cross brought up Ed Barry from the JVs two days before we were to fly out for the season opening series with St. Louis University, which had a Division I program for nine seasons. Then I found out I wouldn't be making the trip; Ed and all the other forwards would be going, not me.

That night I called my mother to tell her how upset I was about not going to St. Louis. "I thought I was finally getting a chance to play," I said. "It seems like Cross will only dress me if he has no other choice. I don't usually complain, but now I feel like I've been screwed. I might quit, because it just doesn't seem worth it anymore."

Mother cautioned me to think it over during the weekend to ensure I made a rational decision, not an "emotional one." She wondered if I would regret my decision in the future, if leaving the team might hurt me if I decided on a coaching career. She said to call back if I wanted to speak with my father. I didn't call back, but I thought about what she said and other things, as well. Venting ended up being the biggest reason I called home. I was back at practice on Monday.

The North Country Thanksgiving Hockey Festival was scheduled the next weekend at Clarkson and St. Lawrence. The tourney actually featured games on three consecutive days, starting with St. Lawrence on Thanksgiving Day. When Cross announced the travel squad and the lineup for that game, I looked down at the ice and hoped hard. Moments later I heard my name in the lineup. It felt terrific. And it's a good thing I didn't quit. The contest was scheduled for the next day, but given the choice, I'd have thrown on my green-and-gold game jersey and played it right then.

It's unusual for someone to be playing their first collegiate game as a senior. Most players in that category have already been cut, or transferred, or decide on their own not to play anymore. Therefore, if a student-athlete dresses for twenty or so games in his or her career, those games are usually played during the individual's freshman and sophomore years. So when I walked into the visitor's locker room to get dressed for the St. Lawrence game, I was sort of a rookie-senior, and the uncertainty and first-game jitters I felt was a feeling my teammates experienced when they were considerably younger than me.

My first shift ended uneventfully, except for the fact it was my first shift. Cross rolled three lines and spotted our line. I found myself in a safety forecheck situation soon after. It was a UVM term for a 1-in, as opposed to a pressure forecheck, which featured 2-in and a weak side "decision-maker." We had wings-on-wings and their defensemen contained deep in the zone. As the 1-in, my job involved angling the puck carrier toward either boards, and to entrap him with the strong side wing. I had to stop and start if the puck changed direction. And not circle. (It was more of a stops-and-starts game than today.) I did that several times, harassing the puck carrier and causing a turnover. Cross stressed the hard work aspect of stops and starts, as opposed to "lazy circles," so teammates were excited when I got to the bench. It was an important start to my late-starting career.

I played all three games, which included contests with Clarkson and with Concordia, a Canadian team. Unfortunately, we lost all three, a rare occurrence for a program accustomed to winning. My overall performance was good but not spectacular and, frankly, I wasn't capable of being a star player in college. Players often think they're better than they are, which leads to unhappiness when ice time doesn't match expectation. Many players tend to evaluate themselves subjectively rather than objectively. Growing up as the son of a coach probably gave me a better perspective on my abilities. Whatever the case, I had to adjust from the comfort of being a productive player at Proctor, to my uncertain playing status at Vermont. This had been the situation all along at UVM, but now more than ever, I had to find a way to stay in the lineup.

Reinventing parts of my game was one way. At Proctor I was a skill player and a scorer and my defense was erratic. I became a big fish in a small pond. My college teammates were better than me, so that approach wasn't going to get me anywhere at Vermont. Thus, I focused on being noticed by doing the "little things," such as stopping and starting, winning 1-on-1 battles, being first in the corners, backchecking diligently, and making smart plays. When we practiced the power play, I competed hard as a penalty killer, all the while adhering to our PK system. Cross started throwing me over the boards in short-handed situations at the North Country tournament, so my practice approach paid off. I became a key killer, which helped define my role. Now it became harder for my coach to not dress me.

Two stations broadcast our games. Tom Cheek did the play-by-play for a Burlington commercial station. I still have a radio interview he did with me, which my parents recorded on an old cassette, while listening to the Brown game from our home in Cornwall. Tom moved on to become the original voice of the Toronto Blue Jays for twenty-seven years before cancer ended his career and his life. He called Joe Carter's 1993 World Series winning walk-off home run by saying, "Touch 'em all, Joe, you'll never hit a bigger home run in your life."

Student radio station (WRUV) also broadcast the games. Bill Newell did play-by-play and fellow Sigma Nu brother, Chris "Wally" Wallace provided analysis. An unusual five-minute "Vermont Farm Report" between periods occasionally accompanied the broadcast. The "Report" had a decided Vermont flavor, considering the state had "more cows than people" until 1963. Hosted by nondescript Joe Smith, who recited milk, sorghum, and alfalfa prices, along with remedies for calf constipation, the show also included an interview with Pee Wee Korvaleski, proprietor of the Vergennes Country Store, who peddled everything from grocery specials to appliances to off-the-wall advice. Unbeknownst to many of the listeners tuning in for a hockey game, the show was actually hosted by Newell and Wallace themselves, who assumed Vermont accents to stage the fictitious report.

In December, we played Norwich and Clarkson before packed crowds at Gutterson (now nicknamed "The Gut"). Norwich, an old Division II rival came in on Friday and Clarkson on Saturday night. Dave Taylor led Clarkson, where he had ninety-eight career goals, before scoring 431 times for the NHL's LA Kings. We won both games, although Oakie suffered a shoulder injury in the Clarkson game. It was a fabulous feeling to score my first goal against Norwich and then bang in another against Clarkson the next night. During warm-ups before the Clarkson game, I skated to the bench to change sticks. Cross stood there as he often watched warm-ups from the bench. He suddenly said, "Gary, you're really playing well. Keep it up."

"Thanks, I appreciate that," I replied.

Mark Twain once said, "I can live for two months on a good compliment."

I found out I could, too.

The ECAC Hockey Festival at Madison Square Garden highlighted our schedule. The event was held just after New Year's Day. My parents attended the games and my father, having lived in nearby White Plains, could hardly contain his excitement over watching us play at MSG. The tournament had an off day in the middle, and we practiced at the Rye Country Day School, where freshman defenseman Chuckie Stahlin played. We lost to Clarkson in the championship contest and beat the University of Pennsylvania in a semifinal game, when Cross told me, "Gary, you're better off using one move, not two," after I deked an opponent and a moment later turned the puck over trying to juke another. His plainspoken point was on point. I wasn't Andy Halford, Randy Koch, Michel Lebeau, or certainly Tim O'Connell, teammates with better skillsets.

Following our win over Penn, Cross said something to us players that I haven't forgotten, although I don't really know why, as it shouldn't have resonated with me back then like it does now after forty years of coaching. He said that Penn coach Bob Crocker looked decidedly downcast and ashen-faced as they shook hands after we defeated them in sudden death. The fact is the game can be especially hard on coaches, and losses can affect your livelihood.

Coach Cross announced a system change one day at practice. A radical, head-turning change might be a more apt description. He had been following the Russians since the 1972 Summit Series. Most of us watched the Super Series game between the Soviet Red Army and the host Montreal Canadiens on New Year's Eve. The two teams tied 3–3 in a classic matchup featuring many of the best players in the world, including goaltenders Ken Dryden and Vladislav Tretiak. Our team was familiar with the Russian style of play, and we knew Cross had an innovative view of the game, but we were otherwise blindsided by his insistence that we start performing like the Russians.

We began with regroup walk-throughs in the neutral zone. Forwards were told to not just skate our lanes; instead Cross ordered us to use all three lanes and interchange with our linemates laterally to support the puck carrier. Defensemen could also exchange positions with us. "You take my spot, I take yours," was the basic premise. If a center skated left to right to support the right defenseman and the RD kept the puck, the center could continue to the right boards area as the right wing filled the departed centers spot in the mid-lane area. If the RD passed to the LD, the right wing supported the LD in his temporary role as the new center. He might even change places with the left wing, depending on what the LD did with the puck. If the opponents pressed our defenseman, however, the wings posted up.

Cross adopted the general patterns from the Soviet system. He called it "weaving." Considering we'd mostly played straight-line hockey, this was new and disorienting. And with Cross shouting, "WEAVE! WEAVE!" repeatedly, and us skating in all directions while bumper-car crashing into each other, things got chaotic. This concept emphasized purposeful movement, not just moving to move, which former UCLA basketball coach John Wooden called "activity without achievement." We practiced this with great urgency for about a week and continued to a lesser degree after, to the extent there was some game carryover. Jocko Clifford, who worked at What Ales You, a popular bar with pictures of UVM hockey players on the wall, watched us weaving at practice one day. "What the hell was going on out there," he quipped, "with all that skating-every-which-way wackiness?"

Bill and Randy Koch were two of Vermont's finest players during that era, and they were popular teammates. I liked them both. At the start of the season, Bill came out with a book titled *A Guy Named Cross + A Place Called Vermont*. It was quite a feat for such a recent graduate. The book extolled the virtues of Coach Cross and the rise of the UVM Hockey program. Bill admired Cross, as Randy and their parents did. Their dad, H. William Koch Jr., had published several books and undoubtedly gave Bill guidance with his writing. (Even Randy, who was in an English class with me, offered near-brilliant insight during book discussions.) Mr. Koch seemed omnipresent, attending most games and various practices. He was friendly, and before our Boston College game in January he said my skating looked improved. I hoped he was right about that.

Ken Yeates ran into Mr. Koch at a game in Gutterson the year after we graduated. "It's pretty bad out there, isn't it," he said to Yeates, referring to the team's play. After six years of unbridled success, the Cats were experiencing their second straight season of .500 hockey, and it wasn't good enough for Mr. Koch. Randy, then a junior, also started to sour on Cross. By Randy's senior year when he became captain, things got worse and there was an alleged team vote to oust their coach. It went nowhere, because the UVM administration fully supported Cross, but it indicated the fragility of the coaching profession and the fickleness of not only fans but parents and players. Two years after practically knighting Cross in print, some of the Kochs had turned on him.

Our unadorned locker room in Gutterson was a split room with a shower area in between, where Cross dressed. My own stall space seemed like a mini-home away from home. In a sense, our stalls also served as front porches, because conversations were public. Back-and-forth banter, often accompanied by laughter, emanated from stall to stall. Meanwhile, we were all busy putting on our equipment. Before finishing with my shoulder and elbow pads, practice jersey, Jofa helmet, and gloves, I wrapped white tape mummy-like around the bottom of my hockey-sock-covered shin pads and the tendon guards of my prized CCM Super Tacks. After dressing, I'd grab two freshly taped sticks and race out to practice.

The locker room was located at one end of the rink, beneath the expansive student section, and before games we could hear the pounding feet of our classmates filling the stands. The room had a different feel on game nights. Conversation prevailed early, but everyone gradually turned contemplative. As the opening faceoff neared, teammates milled around and called out positive words. Then we headed onto the ice and into the bright lights, as the renowned UVM pep band played and college hockey's greatest fans rocked the rink to its rafters.

One night in late January, perennial power Boston University came to Gutterson sporting a 14–1 record. The Terriers won national championships in 1971 and 1972, and another in 1978. Future Olympians Mike Eruzione and Jack O'Callahan skated for them. Our record was 7–13–1 and three forwards were sitting out due to injuries. Cross assigned two defensemen to my line as a result of the injuries. I wondered if we'd be used as a unit against such a strong team. On the day of the game, Ted Ryan wrote in the *Burlington Free Press*, "The Terriers recently dismantled UNH and Brown and realistically should blitz Vermont tonight, unless BU suffers a letdown or UVM goalie Tom McNamara has the finest evening of his career."

Tom, nicknamed "Mac," did have a fine night in net, and we upset BU 5–1 as our fans went wild. BU coach Jack Parker even visited our locker room to congratulate us. It was the only game I ever dressed for and didn't play. Not even to penalty kill. After the game, Cross went merrily around the room, shaking everyone's hand. When he got to my stall, he paused and said, "Gary, I'm sorry, but I forgot all about you." His bluntness surprised me. But I knew the importance of staying detached from my ego.

Our student fans certainly recognized the enormity of the BU win, as they continued their noisy celebration at the Sigma Nu postgame party. Nearly a thousand of the revelers, a record crowd, which included Mac and most of our team, filled the frat house. The revelers guzzled draft beer, stood in long lines at the bathrooms, bumped into each other, and threw up on the floor. You had to shout to be heard. The fifteen kegs emptied just past midnight. Fraternity President "Beek" Beekman, charged with accepting the $1 admission fee, told the still-arriving latecomers that "there's wall-to-wall people and no more beer." It was such a momentous night, most of them came in anyway.

Before the Sigma Nu party, those rowdy students clustered with their classmates in Gutterson's student section. They were seated on long wooden benches that rose toward the ceiling, row after row. Down below, right behind the opposing net for two periods and UVM's for the other period, Jim "Rosa" Condos led loud cheers in a yellow sou'wester rain hat, and when he wasn't leading the signature "Go Cats Go" chant and other cheers, he heckled the BU goalie. Condos, a Sigma Nu brother, continued doing this even after graduating. He eventually became secretary of state. Only in Vermont.

Our goalie Mac was an ECAC All-Conference selection the previous season, and the New York Rangers drafted him. A fierce competitor in whatever athletic activity he engaged in, he also played club baseball at Vermont. Peter "Dud" Reynolds served as a backup, but he had several strong starts in his career. (His nickname came after eating Milk Duds on the bench.) Paul "Rat" Donovan acted as the team's third goalie. Peter aspired to be a dentist and Paul studied to become a doctor. Mac and Dud were competitors and close friends. They and Tom Colby have maintained a forever friendship.

Recently, Mac told me he still "shudders at the thought of the Clarkson hockey bell," which clangs with earsplitting loudness after a Clarkson goal. Interestingly, Ken Dryden, a Cornell grad, said something similar when commenting on "that damn bell at Clarkson."

We beat Penn the following Tuesday. I killed parts of every penalty and skated several shifts. During a 2-on-1 drill at the next practice, I made a back-diagonal pass to the other forward, and drove the net. Cross always yelled "go to the net," and that's what I did. We didn't wear masks then, and I somehow crashed face-first into the sharp edge at the top corner of the practice net. I instantly fell to the ice in a semiconscious state. Athletic Trainer Roger Bryant called for an ambulance, which took me to the UVM hospital. Teammates told me later they knew I was hurting when I didn't respond to Oakie skating along and making funny faces as EMTs carted me out.

I spent the night in the hospital with a concussion, numerous stitches, a displaced broken nose, and a fractured eye orbit bone. The hospital released me the next afternoon, but I had numerous medical appointments ahead, especially with the eye doctor. The injury occurred in early February, meaning my season was over. I had played in nineteen games and scored two goals and two assists. Those numbers represented my career total and prevented my No. 21 jersey from being retired. The journey had been long to make the lineup. Unfortunately, it ended with a mishap in a routine practice drill, but injuries are a part of athletics. So is adversity. Like many others, I had dealt with adversity throughout my hockey career and now I had to work through one again.

Our team finished the season on an 8–3 run to end up 15–16–1. As I recovered from my injury, my parents sent a letter to Coach Cross unbeknownst to me, thanking him for everything he'd done for me. I was initially upset they had written him, but got over it, since it wasn't about playing time. Fortunately, my father and mother were rational hockey parents; they didn't live vicariously through their children.

This is part of the letter Cross sent back to my parents:

> I know this year must have been an exciting one for Gary for after three years of hard work and waiting he finally got his chance to play for and help the University of Vermont hockey team. He has been a strong contributor to whatever success we have had. I mean that, not only for this year, but in the other years. It takes more than the players that are on the ice to make the team and Gary's contributions through the last three years could not be measured. I consider guys like Gary indispensable to our whole team philosophy.

A quote from Cross in a newspaper article a few years later reveals more about his philosophy:

> Team spirit is something you can't rev up for a certain game. You either have team spirit or you don't. It comes of having respect for each other, being unselfish and feeling happy. You can't have team spirit with selfish players. We like our players to be individuals—the more individual the better, as a matter of fact—until they step out into the ice. Then they should blend into an indistinguishable whole. They should be one.

Senior Night ceremonies took place at the last home game. Manager Mike "Tootie" O'Brien called me shortly before game time. He said Cross asked him to remind me about the intros. I told Tootie, I didn't know I had to be there, but would try to make it on time. Nothing had been said to me previously, probably because I wasn't around as much. Frankly, I felt silly going out on the ice in civilian clothes, as a borderline player. Better to leave that to Oakie and Yeates, my fellow seniors who were playing. So I didn't make it on time. I entered the locker room after the game and Randy Koch yelled out, "Hey, where were you during the senior introductions?"

"I was running late," I said, smiling. Other teammates also razzed me good-naturedly. I told Cross that I got the news late but still should have made a bigger effort to get there. He said he wished I had made it, but otherwise let it go.

I rode with the team to RPI for the last regular season game. There would be no playoff appearance for the first time in eight years. At the team banquet in the spring, Tim "Oakie" O'Connell accepted the MVP Award, and Tom McNamara was voted next year's captain. I received the Coach's Unsung Hero Award, selected by Cross. When he eventually retired, they fittingly renamed it the James M. Cross Coach's Award.

Oakie, Yeates, and I also received a coveted gift. George "Buzzy" Buzzell, an eighty-something super fan who came on the bus, continued his tradition of giving each senior a laminated team picture attached to a thin board. An individualized photo and various UVM stickers were pasted along the edges. It had the appearance of a child's arts and crafts project, but that made it all the more meaningful. Buzzy cared deeply about us, despite calling us "a bunch of shysters" during banter on the bus and elsewhere.

When Cross retired, his successor, Mike Gilligan, generously allowed Buzzy to stay connected with the team.

Another older man besides Buzzy played a small part in my hockey experience, though I never met him. I only read his letter. Then, despite my pack rat tendencies, I lost it. Playing hockey at UVM brings an element of notoriety, so even I got a piece of fan mail. The man told me that he was sorry to hear about my injury and went on to say how I appeared to exemplify the ideals one looks for in a young person. (Remember, he didn't know me.) He lived in Burlington and liked the fact that I was a Vermonter. His words were thoughtful. In retrospect, I wish I had met him.

I recovered from my injury enough by April to begin playing street hockey with the Sigma Nu boys. Jeff "Load" Deluca, one of our members, even organized a big tournament. (Jeff became an orthopedic surgeon and I asked him if he was ever called "Dr. Load." He said, "No, fortunately, I left that nickname behind.") One player, Scott "Corpse" Macomber, participated as a stay-at-home defenseman, a street hockey rarity. He stood at net-front and defended with his stick and size 12 sneakers, deftly maneuvering them like pinball flippers. We competed daily after dinner in the Waterman parking lot, using homemade nets for goals. The games were competitive and fun, and when we played, we scampered around the parking lot like little kids at recess.

Or should I say, college kids, which is what we were. One warm evening a group of us played street hockey as final exams neared. Jon Richmond, a Sigma Nu brother, walked by on his way to the library with a study buddy, as Tom McNamara remembers it, and said, "Mac, how the fuck do you guys figure you're going to graduate and get jobs after college?" And with a hint of huff and puff, he was gone, as his frat brothers continued chasing the orange ball across the pavement.

Despite Jon's concern, we all got through exams and graduated. Unlike some of my more talented teammates, a few of whom were drafted, I knew pro hockey wasn't realistic. Instead, I planned to continue part time at the Y, but my future involved no specific hockey plans, other than possibly coaching. The college phase of my life was ending, and it had been a fantastic four years. I loved UVM, the student body, my fraternity, Vermont hockey, and the education I received. It remained to be seen if playing hockey for UVM would play a part in my future.

Chapter 4

Hitting the Ice at Rice

The following fall, I gave my brother Donald a ride to campus to begin his sophomore year. As we drove by the athletic complex, we ran into Coach Cross, who asked if I had heard about the coaching vacancy at nearby Rice Memorial High School. I told him I hadn't, and he inquired if I had any interest in the position.

"I don't know," I said, "but it's something I'll consider."

"You won't have much time to consider, because they're down to four finalists and need to make a decision soon," Cross said. Apparently they had reservations about the finalists. He told me to think it over and give him a call. In the meantime, he would contact Rice and see if they'd be interested in interviewing a late candidate.

The next day Cross said that Rice wanted to speak with me, and I agreed to meet with them. Cross had considerable influence in the Burlington area, and a number of his former players coached high school hockey. A short time later, I met with the principal, Father Roland Rivard, assistant principal Bernie Cieplicki, and AD John Lemon. The interview appeared to go well and they asked me to submit my coaching philosophy. I wrote a two-page philosophy and dropped it off at the school.

While waiting to hear back from Rice, I traveled to Conway, New Hampshire, for a softball tournament. There I received sad news. Joey Oslin, a UVM teammate my senior year, had died in a car accident. A large group of us drove to the Boston area to attend his wake and funeral. Joey had just started his sophomore year at UVM, and the Bruins had recently drafted him. He was a very nice person. Joey and I weren't particularly close; we were a few years apart in grade and age and had different friends, but we were teammates. That bond is everlasting. Some forty years later, forty years that Joey never had, I still feel saddened by his untimely death.

I got the job, and the now-defunct *Vermont Sunday News* used this segment of my coaching philosophy, which they got from Rice, to announce the September hiring:

> I've been playing hockey ever since I can remember. I grew up on a prep school campus 100 yards from a rink, and my father was the hockey coach. It was only natural that I became a hockey player. Now I would like to coach.

> . . .

> My team will play a disciplined style of hockey, and act like gentlemen off the ice, but I will not infringe on their rights as individuals, unless detrimental to themselves or the team.

I was on my way to a coaches' meeting at Rice when a rusted fuel tank strap snapped, causing the tank to drag beneath my car. (Yes, you can't make this stuff up.) My parents had recently given me their old 1968 Ford station wagon, and road salt had taken its toll. I left a message with John Lemon to explain my absence. Bernie Cieplicki and I saw each other at the school a few days later. A no-nonsense disciplinarian, he was also Rice's renowned basketball coach. He said he'd heard that I missed the meeting because my car broke down and I told him I hated missing the meeting.

"What will you do if your car breaks down on the way to a game?" he asked.

A bit taken aback, I said, "Well, as the head coach, I'll have to find a way to get there—and I get your point." Coach Cieplicki nodded approvingly. At least he liked my answer.

In the weeks leading up to the season, I held an informational meeting at the school with all the hockey candidates, and I choose a friend, HD Pearl, to coach the Rice JV team. HD had played for the Sub-Cats at UVM. I also met briefly with Bill Dunn, the previous coach, who played for Cross. He would continue to teach English at Rice. Rice, a Catholic High School, played in the Division I Vermont High School Hockey league and had generally been a low middle-of-the-pack program. So I didn't feel much pressure as the season approached, except for the fact that I had never coached before and wasn't much older than my players.

Practice started in November at Leddy Park Arena in Burlington. Leddy served as the home rink for Rice and rival Burlington High School. Sam Simmons, another former UVM player, coached Burlington, and we saw each other regularly in the officials/coaches room. We practiced from 3:45 to 4:45 p.m., and Burlington followed at 5 p.m. After a tryout period, we sent a number of guys to the JVs. Cross's influence on me was evident, both in the structure of our sessions and the selected drills. Dan Morrisey, a former Rice player, served as my assistant that first season. As with any new coach, the players practiced with pizzazz and hustled through every drill. Their infectious enthusiasm helped get us off to a good start.

Face masks became mandatory soon after practice began. Youth hockey had worn masks for a while, but like in college, high school players didn't wear them. My players weren't happy about this and resisted attaching them until I instituted a deadline. On that day, everyone had one on except co-captain Terry Feloney. He came out to practice with a cooking pot on his head à la Johnny Appleseed. He smiled as I approached him and said he didn't need a mask because he wasn't wearing a helmet. I smiled back and told him the pot wouldn't do. A few moments later he reappeared on the ice sporting a helmet and face mask.

We opened the 1976–77 season with South Burlington on a Wednesday evening at Leddy. I was excited to be coaching my first game, yet apprehensive about our play and discipline. Considering I'd never changed lines or defensive pairs, I also worried about messing up the changes. Dan would be on the bench with me, but I planned to run both the forwards and defensemen, just as Coach Cross had done. We won the game 3–0, and SBHS coach Marcel St. Onge stopped by our locker room afterward to shake my hand. It was a nice gesture, and as a new coach, I hadn't even thought to shake hands with him when the game ended.

The changes went well, as did our discipline, but I had a small glitch late in the game. With a 3–0 lead, I told goaltender Munn Boardman, whose sister, Linda, dated my friend Herb Muther at UVM, to replace Jon Farnham, our other co-captain, at the next whistle. My misguided rationale was to get every player in the game and make it a total team win. When play stopped,

I saw Munn still fumbling around for a piece of his equipment. Play started again and I now had a feeling something was up, so I told Munn to hold off. After the game, he came to me and said, "Coach, I'm sorry, but I wanted Jon to get the shutout, although I would have gone out at the next whistle if you insisted." I told Munn he had a good point, but I didn't want guys thinking they could ignore my demands. As it turned out, that wasn't a problem with my players, and I never again tried to replace a healthy goalie who had a shutout going.

We beat North Country HS the following Saturday by the same 3–0 score as the SBHS game. Munn got the shutout against the defending regular season champions. Our second line of Tim McKenzie, Jeff Royer, and Bob Waterman showed promise, and Tim scored the first goal. Bob, a senior, later became a starting linebacker at Maine, and brought mentorship and maturity to his freshman linemates. Jeff possessed a good skillset and liked to showcase his self-proclaimed (and hard to explain) "dipsy-doodle" move. McKenzie's brother, Rob, captained the Rice basketball team. Seeing two brothers excel in different winter sports indicated the McKenzie parents encouraged their children to make their own athletic choices. I found that refreshing.

With only an hour for practice, we had to make good use of our ice time, so we met in the locker room at 3:30 p.m., fifteen minutes before practice started. The players had to be routinely dressed and ready every day at that time. After making a couple of announcements, I explained the practice plan and diagrammed drills when necessary. It saved considerable time at practice and allowed us to maximize players' ice time. I occasionally shortened the meeting to let them free skate when ice was available beforehand. Otherwise, just before 3:45 p.m., the whole team dashed out of the locker room and onto the fresh white ice.

We emphasized the old adage "As you practice, you will play." This meant a high compete level and game-like effort in every drill and every exercise. Back then, stops and starts sprints were more common in hockey than today as a conditioning method. We did them at the end of practice. Six to eight sets of these sprints represented the most severe version, and the more we did, the more guys cheered on their teammates to stride through the fatigue. Three years later, members of the 1980 Olympic Team named their rigorous starts and stops "Herbies," after their "Miracle on Ice" coach, Herb Brooks.

We split our next two games after the North Country win, before losing three in a row, but rebounded by winning a four-team holiday tournament during the Christmas break. In addition to getting strong play from our young forwards, our defensive corps, led by Terry Feloney and junior Bob Boucher, provided us with solid play. Farnham and Boardman rotated in net, although the rotation was conditional.

Bob Boucher logged loads of ice time. A two-sport athlete, he also excelled on the baseball team. He previously suffered a ruptured spleen in a summer hockey league, a potentially life-threatening injury that resulted in its removal. I also ended up hiring him as a summer counselor at the YMCA's Camp Greylock. Later, he played baseball at UVM, and served as an assistant at Western Carolina for Jack Leggett, his college coach. Bob became a member of the Rice Memorial Hall of Fame. Leggett, a two-sport (baseball and football) standout at Maine, is in four Halls of Fame.

Coaching high school players proved interesting. I could joke around with them and still keep the necessary separation to maintain authority. Of course, guys that age can be easily amused by teenage-type humor. One day, I entered the locker room for our pre-practice meeting and noticed out of the corner of my eye a picture from *Playboy* taped to the chalk board.

"Have we got everyone here?" I asked first, as I often did. No one said anything. Then, while still facing the team, I said, "Well, I know she's here." The room roared with laughter.

I let the incident go since the kids got a kick out of it and the picture wasn't too risqué, but also inferred that one time was enough. They got the message. I may have been close to them in age, and I felt confident enough to have some informal fun with them, but they were not my peers. I was their coach, not one of the boys.

But there is a lot to be said for being one of the boys. Our players probably didn't know it then, but the relationships they were forming as teammates would sustain them for the rest of their lives. When I corresponded with Tim McKenzie about this book, he and his former teammates were well into their fifties. "Outside of family, the Rice hockey team was the most important association I had at the time," Tim wrote, "and to this day my closest friends include teammates. Our team had a great bond, which I still feel when I see teammates that I haven't seen for many years."

I found out fast that coaching could be fun and even more consuming than playing. I didn't think it'd replace my love for playing, but it did. The team was on my mind all the time—in the car, at the bar, and when I lay awake in bed. Practice plans took time to construct and included UVM drills, as well as drills I had picked up. I designed other drills to prepare for opponents or to address our weaknesses. One time, our manager taped six temporary one foot high by six foot wide goals along the boards, so players could practice keeping their shots down in the stand-up, pre-butterfly goalie era. Lineup changes and combinations preoccupied me, and considerable thought went into our upcoming games. Coaching had become my calling.

Following the Christmas break, we switched Chris Furlani from the third line to the first and moved Kevin Kieny to the third line. (In later years, I referenced lines by the color of their practice jersey to suggest less of a line hierarchy.) The move proved pivotal. Chris complemented Mike Rozzi and Peter Trottier nicely and really made the line go. He could score and possessed notable playmaking and puck skills. The trio dominated down the stretch and became the top line in the state.

The changes made our team better, but I never looked at the move as a demotion for Kevin Kieny, although I initially got to see Chris on that line when Kevin got suspended for smoking a cigarette in the school bathroom. (How many times has that happened in the history of high schools?) Kevin was a valuable performer wherever he played. He stood about five foot five or so, but his size didn't matter. A fearless, hard-nosed competitor, he skated with a big motor and more will than skill. He brought enthusiasm and energy every time he stepped on the ice. The quintessential overachiever, he appeared to run on his skates. But he got around just fine. Loose pucks tended to come our way when Kevin played.

We got off to a 4–2 start in the new year as we approached a big game with Burlington at Leddy on February 9. Burlington stood in second place behind Bellows Free Academy–St. Albans, and we battled for the third spot. The BFA Bobwhites had beaten us twice and we lost to Burlington 3–1 in our first meeting. These two teams were perennial contenders, especially BFA, the four-time defending state champions. Sam Simmons coached the first two championship years before taking the Burlington job. Bill Beaney succeeded Simmons at BFA and directed the next two championships. Beaney was just getting started at winning titles. He ultimately won a record eight NCAA Division III national championships at nearby Middlebury College.

Rice held a pep rally at the school gym prior to the Burlington game. It included the entire student body. Our manager, David Dower, was anything but dour. Small in stature, big in personality, and a bit of a wisenheimer, he performed an important role in Rice hockey. His fellow students knew him well, so when our team attended the winter sports rally with the basketball teams, and I had to speak, I led off by saying, "This being my first pep rally, I asked my able manager, David Dower, if he had any thoughts as to what I might talk about. Needless to say, I doubt any of his suggestions would be appropriate for this type of gathering." The Rice students loved it. David was "can't miss" material.

A near-capacity crowd filled the Leddy stands for the Burlington tilt. Before we took the ice, I told the team that I knew playing BHS was special to them because we shared a rink, competed in the same league, and players from both teams grew up playing hockey together. "A rivalry based on mutual respect is healthy for both teams," I said. "It's about the competition, not animosity. We're a better team now and that makes this a true rivalry, so let's go out and show everyone how good we are."

We looked good and we won. Our players whooped it up after the game. Smiles and cheers abounded in the loud locker room. Mr. Boardman took film footage of our excited players and his son, Munn, the starter in net. Scott Mackay, a *Burlington Free Press* writer, stood at the locker room door and asked me some questions. The next day Mackay's article read, "Amidst cries of, 'we showed up the basketball team,' a beaming Gary Wright said, 'We beat a great team by playing consistent hockey. I'm ecstatic.'" I hadn't specifically heard some guys making the basketball comment after the game, but apparently Scott Mackay did, although I wished he hadn't quoted it. But Mackay, who wrote for the *Vermont Cynic* when we were students at UVM and went on to cover politics for the *Providence Journal* and NPR, wasn't one to miss using a boastful phrase like that. Basketball coach Bernie Cieplicki wasn't happy about it and said so to our players. I later apologized to him. I also told our guys the basketball team had been a dynasty through the years and that "we shouldn't be running our mouths after one big win."

My grandmother, the one who attended our UVM scrimmage in Rutland the year before, wrote me from Florida soon after the Burlington game. She spent winters there, and my father had sent her a copy of the article. She congratulated me on the win and said, "I'm surprised you used the word ecstatic. That's a 25-cent word." Apparently a 25-cent word is one that's used instead of another smaller word that everyone knows. At least she didn't weigh in on the basketball comment.

We concluded the regular season with a 10–6 league record. Winning six of our last eight games provided a strong finish and momentum leading into the playoffs. We ended up in third place in the nine-member Division I league and were slated to play Spaulding High School from Barre at Leddy in the quarterfinals.

The morning of the Spaulding game, the *Burlington Free Press* carried an article titled "Wright and Rice a Winning Pair." The writer, Mike McGee remarked:

> At the heart of Rice's success is the disciplined style of play which Wright demands. They have earned the reputation as a team which skates, passes and forechecks well, plays tight defense, stays out of the penalty box and emphasizes teamwork, an obsession with Wright.

In a picture accompanying the article, I'm wearing a flannel shirt with a short-sleeved Izod polo shirt underneath. The two-collared shirts look was somewhat fashionable then.

Spaulding played us tough, despite being the No. 6 seed. In a low-scoring game, predicated in part by a big game performance by Spaulding goaltender and future UVM player Gregg Thygesen, we won 2–1. Close games are often nerve-racking, but the tenseness is magnified in the playoffs, particularly for the higher seed. We had a lot to lose in that game considering our regular-season record, but we survived, and now the bye-rested Burlington Seahorses awaited us in the semifinals.

We successfully rotated two goaltenders throughout the regular season. Munn Boardman was due to play against Burlington, but I considered starting Jon Farnham instead, as I thought he was a slightly better goalie. His leadership as a captain and his performance in the Spaulding playoff win also figured in. But Munn had beaten Burlington recently. I labored over the decision for a couple of days and stayed with Munn. Like a manager choosing a starting pitcher for a pivotal playoff or World Series game, goaltender choices can challenge a coach. Faced with a similar playoff predicament a dozen years later as a college coach, I decided to break the rotation. That took more courage.

When Mike Rozzi stepped in to take the opening faceoff, we were a pumped and confident team. Our strong play down the stretch, and recent win over Burlington, provided that mindset. But beating Burlington again presented a bigger challenge. They still smarted from our recent contest and this was playoff hockey. When play continued after the puck-drop, BHS proved too much for us that night. The final score: 5–1. They went on to lose to BFA in the state championship game.

After the game, I spoke softly to our disappointed players and told them how proud I was of their efforts and how easy they made it for me as a first-year coach, and, of course, I recognized the seniors. Driving home that night, I thought about how most of our roster would return. Surely, we'd be among the favorites to win a state championship. The season had barely ended and already "wait till next year" thoughts preoccupied my mind. I guess I was starting to think more and more like a coach.

I continued working at the Burlington YMCA after the season, and during the summer I returned to my position as the program director of the Y's Camp Greylock. Mills & Greer, our softball team, won the Vermont Class A/Open state championship in late July. I thought the championship would be the first of many for our team and me as a softball player, but it never happened again. Those of us in athletics are often faced with the reality that our dreams and expectations won't be realized. Failing to win another state softball championship was disappointing, but I'm thankful for the one we won.

We entered the following season loaded with optimism. A plethora of players returned, including the Furlani-Rozzi-Trottier line. The *Free Press* ran a league prospectus under the heading "BFA Favored To Take Sixth Straight Crown." Willie MacKinnon, the former UVM All-American, replaced Bill Beaney as head coach at BFA. Bill left to coach at New England College. Interestingly, Willie and I were housemates on Lake Champlain in nearby Charlotte. We also played together on a team of mostly former college players from the Burlington area. I guess you could say we were housemates, teammates, and coaching adversaries. Friendly adversaries for sure: my team wanted to end the BFA streak.

We beat North Country 8–1 and Spaulding 10–5 to start the season. Our first line scored fourteen of those goals. Against Spaulding, we deviated from the disciplined play that had come to define our team. We took four penalties in the second period, along with a misconduct for unsportsmanlike conduct. The ref claimed he heard something said to him, but somehow couldn't identify who it was. Peter Trottier served the misconduct, but considering his first-line status, it wasn't my smartest move. After the period, I snapped in the room and, with a mix of sound and spit spouting from my mouth, threatened to throw the next guy who took a penalty off the bench.

The third period began with the game tied 3–3. We scored five goals and took no penalties in the fifteen-minute period but, still, I said this in the paper: "The second period was really disappointing. We refrained from our style of play—not just structurally but in loss of control of our emotions. We were talking to the referees and using alibis. That's not our game." My obsession with player conduct and penalties had already started, as evidenced by my angry words to the team and postgame comments to the press, despite winning by a big score. I coached for thirty-eight more years and that never changed.

The JV season was also underway. I had hired Peter "Crow" Brady, a former Vermont player, to be the coach. A "Bald is Beautiful" sign decorating his locker room stall at UVM indicated his sense of humor—and thinning hair. The JV squad served as a valuable feeder system to the varsity, as evidenced by the addition of six players from last year's team. It provided others a chance to benefit from a great sport like hockey even if they never made the varsity. This opportunity also allowed the kids to be part of an extracurricular activity at Rice, which helped them socially as well as athletically. Considering the JV program at UVM probably saved my career, I was a big advocate of the Rice JVs.

Former JV goaltender Tom Rocheleau became the starter and played well in our 4–0 start. (Tom said his "success on the ice gave me confidence in life.") Burlington, our next opponent, would be a good test for our team and Tom. He didn't disappoint. The Seahorses scored early in the third period of a scoreless game, and five minutes later Peter Trottier tallied the equalizer. The game ended in a 1–1 tie. Sam Simmons thought his team played one of their better games to date. I wasn't as pleased, since we were now the favored team.

Sam made an interesting observation to me one day about the public address announcements at Leddy Park high school games. The PA announcer opened each contest with a statement that went something like this: "Welcome to tonight's Vermont High School Hockey League game between (blank) High School and (blank) High School. Before we introduce the starting lineups, please be reminded that smoking is not allowed in Leddy Park Arena." While speaking, he usually held a lighted cigarette under the scorers table.

Much of our play was based on Cross's UVM system. Fred Shero had recently popularized the term "system" when coaching the Flyers to two Stanley Cups in the 1970s, and his sixteen-ruled "Flyers Bible" outlined his system. (Unfortunately, the Flyers game also included some violent tactics.) Our forecheck, defensive zone coverage, and specialty team play all stemmed from UVM, exposing our young players to more advanced systems. We even introduced the neutral zone play Cross adopted from the Russians, although, based on experience, I refrained from extensive weaving. That could result in collisions, which Cross called "head-on conclusions."

Our success continued deep into the season. Our guys practiced hard and competed relentlessly. Bob Boucher and Chris Furlani provided strong leadership as co-captains. Unlike in college and the pros, where recruiting and signings allow teams to select the individuals they want in their program or organization; in high school the player pool is already at the school. To an extent, your team is chosen for you. As a coach, that means you might lack enough good players—or players who are good people. I felt fortunate at Rice. I had good players and a roster filled with "character and chemistry guys."

Coaching a talented team didn't mean every game was like a public skate. One time, I lost it on the players in the locker room after a particularly bad period. After hollering myself hoarse, I kicked over their sticks that leaned against the wall and stormed out of the room. One stick remained standing, so my assistant Jon Farnham comically grabbed that stick and tossed it on the floor with the others. Jon subsequently reinforced my words with an abbreviated response: "What he said." Then he left the room and joined me on the bench.

When we bused to out-of-town games, "Dream Weaver," a popular song at the time, often played on a '70s-era boom box in the back of the bus. Guys would cheer or sing along with the song. My assistants had to explain to me that the commotion was about me and the singer sharing the same name: Gary Wright.

We finished second in league play to BFA with a 12–3–1 record. Two of those losses came to us by identical 4–3 scores. It was fun competing against BFA, especially with Willie as their coach, but losing to the Bobwhites was painful. We hoped for another chance in the playoffs, but both teams had to get to the championship game for that to happen. We had other business to take care of first. Since the top two teams received byes last season, we looked forward to a bye into the semifinals.

It didn't happen. The Vermont Headmasters took seven teams instead of six. It meant Champlain Valley Union (CVU) was playing us the next night in the quarterfinals. Not having the bye disappointed me, as did having to play Tuesday night when BFA was off. In the locker room before Monday's practice, I remained circumspect and told the team that it didn't matter whether we thought we deserved a bye or not. The Vermont Headmasters ran the tournament—and our job was to play in the tourney. I also said that good players love to compete and we now had a chance to play another playoff game.

We came to play in a game we didn't think we had to play by pumping in four first-period goals. After a sluggish second stanza, I reminded our players that we can't have off-periods in the playoffs if we want to go far. We got back on track with two goals in the third to bagel CVU 6–0 and preserve Rocheleau's shutout. North Country upset Spaulding and a semifinal showdown with them awaited us on Thursday.

The game took place at the Essex Junction Rink, a neutral site. It was an exciting barn burner in a state full of farms. North Country came back from a 4–2 deficit to tie things up 4–4 in the third period before captain Chris Furlani, always a clutch player for us, misfired on a breakaway with five minutes remaining. Fifteen seconds later, in true second-effort fashion, Chris scored the game winner off a rebound. Smiles permeated the postgame locker room, but the celebration was measured. As expected, BFA also won, and quickly our grins turned tight-lipped about the vast task ahead.

Other than rival Burlington, with whom we shared a rink, I felt most familiar with BFA, due to their league stature and because Willie MacKinnon and I talked a lot about the league. We didn't share everything, but we discussed coaching challenges and we talked about our players. Hearing about the person behind the uniform is always interesting. We also engaged in Xs and Os talk. For instance, Willie attributed much of his prolific goal scoring in college to "firing a hard pass into the net." His maxim was "on the ice is nice." He was referring to quick, well-placed "pass-shots" that were often taken in stride. Valery Kharlamov, the Russian great who would soon die in a car crash, said something similar: "It is important that a player does not go into a glide before shooting. The shot should be taken in your natural stride."

In a *Free Press* article headlined "Rice Challenges BFA's Reign," Mike McGee wrote:

> Both finalists should offer a striking similarity in the way they play the game, as each has built a reputation for strong skating and scoring prowess, and both use nearly the same type of system hockey.

Gutterson Fieldhouse hosted the championship game and the Division II contest played before us. Vermont Educational Television, later to be called Vermont PBS, broadcast the games. It's common for high school championships to be played in prominent venues that can accommodate big crowds. The games are also held in such a venue because it offers a quality athletic experience for the participants. Playing the championship at UVM was a big deal to our players. A few of them asked how going back to Gutterson felt to me as a former Vermont player. I told them it was special for me, and then joked that I'd be comfortable on the bench because I spent a lot of time there—and in the stands—as a player.

A crowd of two thousand watched the teams take the ice. Due to our slight underdog status, and BFA's experience winning titles at Gutterson, we stressed a fast start. It didn't quite go that way. Play went up and down, indicating our competitiveness, but the "down in our end" time grew longer. BFA was a little stronger, a little quicker, and a little deeper than us. They also kept our first line from scoring at their usual pace. It didn't help when Bob Boucher received a misconduct for absentmindedly tossing his broken stick over the glass.

But we battled throughout the game. Rocheleau played well under a barrage of shots, but he had to be lights-out for us to win, and that's a lot to ask of a young goalie. BFA prevailed 4–1 in a patented powerhouse performance. At game's end, Willie and I shook hands briefly. We would see each other later.

I met with our players after the game. They sat, still in uniform, their youthful faces awash in sweat and tears. I expressed my admiration for their impressive accomplishments, which included Rice's first ever appearance in the Division I championship game, and then said, "I know you're all as sad about the loss as I am, and you should be, because we didn't get it done tonight. But BFA is a great team and they had to be to beat us, because we're a great team, too."

Decades later, I visited with Paul Averill, Chris Furlani, and Tom Rocheleau at Tom's home on the shores of Lake Champlain. They shared their hockey memories and told me that the Vermont PBS station had archived the championship game. Chris had reconnected with linemate Mike Rozzi, and after he and Mike watched the game for the first time in forty years, Mike told Chris, "I can sleep now." All those years, he had thought he failed to pass the puck to Peter Trottier, whom he recalled being open in front of the net. Mike now felt a sweet sense of relief since what he saw on the film indicated that Peter was not wide open. Ironically, Mike was always more of a shooter than a passer.

The loss to BFA ended our quest to win the Division I state championship, but not our season. We participated in the New England Hockey Tournament, featuring the top two teams from Vermont, New Hampshire, Maine, and Rhode Island. Brown's Meehan Auditorium in Providence, Rhode Island, hosted the event. In an unusual move, we took a bus—with BFA. Although the choice was based on financial considerations, I liked the idea from a sportsmanship perspective. In a way, traveling together suggested the purity of interscholastic competition; despite being competitors, we shared much as league members, and together we represented our league and the state of Vermont. That didn't mean, however, that our two teams engaged in a "Kumbaya" sing-along on the bus.

Saint Dominic Academy, the Maine state champion, was our opening-round opponent. After arriving in Rhode Island and watching Mount St. Charles play like pros, Bob Boucher and Chris Furlani asked if I really thought we could beat St. Dom's. I reminded them that I hadn't seen them play, but I knew they must be good, so we'd have to play well to beat them. "And we wouldn't want it any other way, right?" I said. Bob and Chris both nodded. I'm quite sure they shared my response with the rest of the boys.

The next day, St. Dom's beat us in overtime. Their game winner came on a bad bounce goal during a net-front scramble, but in hockey as well as in life, what we all learn is that the bounces don't always go our way. I moved Kevin Kieny up to the second line in the third period with McKenzie and Royer to try and tap into Kevin's high-energy play. For the last ten minutes and overtime, we skated two lines to get our top guys on the ice more. The game ended with us battling furiously, exhibiting the "finish strong" mindset that we expected from our players.

BFA lost to Lewiston High School in Maine by a big score. Then the bus pulled out of the rink's parking lot with both teams aboard and headed up the highway. Willie and I spoke quietly about our respective games, mindful that both teams had lost and words can carry in the postgame quiet. As the bus drew farther from Providence, however, more voices and occasional laughter could be heard, indicating the resilience of youth. Later, we crossed into Vermont, the site of Rice's memorable season in the long-ago winter of '78.

I volunteered for the Special Olympics held on the UVM athletic grounds during the summer. Director Bob Noel, a college classmate, asked me to help out, and I invited Willie and a softball teammate, Dennis Dudley, to join me in the daylong competition. Each of us was assigned to one of the participants. We had a great time, and I've shared the Special Olympics motto with my teams through the years. It states: "Let me win. But if I cannot win, let me be brave in the attempt." I don't know who actually created that creed, but it's concise and powerful. It's as appropriate for hockey players as for Special Olympians.

We entered the next season having graduated our vaunted first line. Crow Brady returned to coach the JVs and Chris Furlani assisted him. I was joined by Bob Boucher and Jon Farnham. It meant three of the four captains from my first two years now coached at Rice. They all volunteered, an indication of how much their high school careers meant to them. Hiring good assistants is something I had success at for the duration of my coaching career; it all started with those guys and Crow.

Paul Averill and Tom Rocheleau were elected captains. Unlike the NHL, where goaltenders are rarely captains, Tom was our second captain at that position in three years. Paul anchored our defensive corps, and eventually became a dentist in his father's practice. His older brothers had played hockey for Rice and his younger brother, Howard, now skated on the JVs. Apparently, the Averill home had a mountainous pile of hockey equipment in their mudroom.

In a scheduling irony, we opened up with BFA at their home rink, Coote Field Arena, an austere building with metal walls and an exhaust-spewing tractor for a Zamboni. My teams were 0–5 against BFA coming into the game, and previous Rice teams hadn't fared much better, so it was surprising when we beat them 7–4. Dave Hauke, a sophomore who played JV as a freshman, scored four goals. Considering it was his first varsity season and the strength of the opponent, one would think Dave was a rising star in the league. That didn't happen, but he did develop into a good player.

The victory surprised us because we were young, and had failed to beat them the year before with a stronger team. It also thrilled us. A few people called the game a payback for the championship game loss; I would hear none of it. Regardless of how big the win, it didn't compare to winning a state title game. I don't know if a then nine-year-old St. Albans youth hockey player named John LeClair attended the contest, but he later skated for Red Gendron at BFA before moving on to UVM and a 406-goal career in the NHL. He certainly got to play locally. Gutterson Fieldhouse is just thirty minutes from his hometown, and the Montreal Forum, where he first skated for the Canadiens, is ninety minutes from St. Albans.

Sam Simmons left to teach and coach at South Kent School, and Ted "Boomer" Child replaced him at Burlington HS. His nickname stemmed from his booming slapshot as a UVM defenseman. Some even claimed his high-speed puck produced a sonic boom. He and Willie were good friends and started the Vermont Hockey School in Burlington along with Ted Castle, the assistant at the University of Maine. I worked at their hockey school. Willie tells the story of his handshake encounter with Boomer after his BFA team beat Burlington: "Boomer wasn't happy with the officiating, and he shook hands without looking at me, so he could turn and continue barking at the refs."

Tim "Oakie" O'Connell also began coaching in the league, following a stint in the World Hockey Association. Having so many young coaches from UVM enhanced the coaching experience. A group of us often went from the bench to the bar after games. Finbar's and Atwater Kent's were two of our favorite watering holes in Burlington's downtown bar scene. The agenda included lively high school hockey talk, a few beers, and belly laughs. Those were heady times.

Our power play (PP) included two defensemen at the point, a net-front player, and two forwards on the flanks. The flanks played on their off-side, which became popular at the time, as it improved the shooting angle. They often passed laterally flank to flank for a shot. In addition to point shots, we ran give-and-goes and backdoor plays. Considering the era and the age and skill level of our players, it was probably a suitable power play: not easy to run, but not too difficult either.

After a poor power play effort one night, I went off on the team between periods, telling them I was tired of watching frustrated players doing their own thing. I told them not to run our PP for the rest of the game; play it like 5-on-5 instead. My assistants later said our power-play players claimed I gave up on them. While admitting I may have overreacted some, I retorted, "Well, they gave up on our power play." I addressed the subject with the team, and we spent a whole practice on it. Strong words can help, but action straightened out our power play.

My young team played just under .500 hockey after the BFA win. Later in the season, we hosted South Burlington after losing four straight games. They came in with a 7–4 record under Oakie, my former teammate. The game remained scoreless until Kevin Kieny roofed a puck from in close to make it 1–0 early in the third period. Jeff Royer scored with two minutes left for the final margin of 2–0. The loud cheers from our bench reflected a shared sense of relief. Like many coaches, I remained stoic after Jeff's goal, but I was pleased, too.

"This is one game we'll have to savor," I told the *Free Press* afterward. "This gives us some momentum and hopefully will turn things around. Psychologically, we needed a win."

Oakie said, "Rice made the most of their opportunities and we didn't. I'm disappointed with the way we played." We obviously viewed the outcome differently. Oakie and I were coaches, not player-coaches, which was a good thing. He scored ninety-nine goals in his memorable UVM career; I may have goalies ahead of me on the all-time scoring list. However, I want to make it perfectly clear that they were mostly offensive-minded goalies!

I ran into defenseman Ed Hesford's father in the Leddy parking lot one evening. We exchanged pleasantries while facing each other in the dim light, and then the conversation shifted.

"You know, the team hasn't been as good since you changed the lines," he said. I had mixed up the lines a few times in an effort to turn things around, but he didn't specify what changes he didn't like and I didn't ask.

"If I change lines it's because I'm trying to make us better," I said with an edge. At that point, I told him that I had to get going. It was my first experience with an unhappy hockey parent. I drove home in a daze.

I never spoke much with Mr. Hesford again other than to say hi. The team had exceeded expectations in my first two years as coach, so everything was rosy until we started to lose more games that season. Even then, there weren't many problems. I suspected he was as concerned about Ed's ice time as he was about our record. And it seemed like he wasn't pleased with me and wanted to vent without getting his son involved. Regardless of his motives, his comments didn't affect my relationship with Ed.

There's a postscript to this story: Ed became an engineer like his father and took a job in Boston. He showed up unexpectedly at one of the Codfish Bowl Tournaments we participated in at UMass Boston during the 1990s. He'd read in the Boston papers that AIC was playing in the tourney. We had a good talk before I had to go. There was no mention of my brief encounter with his dad some fifteen years earlier, nor did I bring it up with him at the time. I did thank Ed for stopping by to see me.

We went 2–2 after beating South Burlington to finish 7–9 in the league. Winning three games down the stretch provided our players with renewed hope and vigor entering the playoffs. Seeded sixth, we met No. 3 seed Spaulding in the quarterfinals. They edged us 3–2 in a hard-fought game. Despite the loss, I felt pleased and proud of our effort. Further validation of our competitiveness came when Spaulding went on to win their semifinal game, before losing 5–4 to BFA in the Division I championship. It was BFA's mind-boggling seventh straight title.

A few months after the season ended, I took an assistant coach position at Maine. I sent the following letter to the Rice returnees in August of 1979:

Dear Team Member,_____:

You have undoubtedly heard that I've accepted a coaching job at the University of Maine starting this fall. Because I'll no longer be coaching at Rice, I want to explain my leaving to you directly. Therefore, I am writing this letter to you and your teammates who will be returning to Rice in September.

I have considered coaching at the college level, and when the Maine position opened up, I was fortunate to be chosen. In addition to my duties as an Assistant Hockey Coach, I will also be the rink manager of the Alfond Arena. The job should prove to be a tremendous and invaluable experience for me, and will greatly enhance my knowledge of the game of hockey. Needless to say, I'm excited about it.

Wherever I go in hockey, I will always remember my first coaching job at Rice. I often commented to people who followed our team that there was something special about the type of boy who played hockey for Rice. It would be difficult, if not impossible, for me to explain just how much I enjoyed being associated, not only with you players, but also with your parents, and other individuals close to the team. Although I am very excited about going to Maine, I am at the same time, sad about leaving Rice.

I wish you all well next season—I'll be down to see a game or two; and would like to emphasize that if there's anything I can ever do for you, don't hesitate to give me a call.

Sincerely,
Gary Wright

Chapter 5

Coaching Black Bears

I had begun to look at the University of Maine position ten weeks before writing the Rice players. It all began when Ted Castle returned to Vermont to serve as Cross's assistant after two years at Maine. Cross suggested to Jack Semler, Maine's head coach, who was one of Cross's former players at Vermont, that he consider me for the vacancy. At that point, applying for the position wasn't even on my radar screen. Castle also broached the subject, and I then met with Jack Semler informally when he visited Burlington. I appreciated the interest in me, but I wasn't sure if I wanted the job.

One day Cross came to the YMCA unexpectedly, looking for me. I had never seen him before at the Y, but I was impressed, and rather flattered, that he was actually visiting my workplace to encourage me to coach at Maine.

"I think you should give the position serious thought if you have any interest in coaching college hockey," he said. "Based on my dealings with you as a player and the job you've done at Rice, this could be a big break for you, and I'm confident you and Jack would work well together."

I said I was worried about areas like recruiting and whether I could identify the best players. He told me that I'd gain experience and knowledge simply by watching lots of games. Cross also stressed that talking to coaches at the game, observing a player's ice time, seeing if he plays on specialty teams, and how he's used late in a close game would all be helpful indicators. He was quite persuasive, both in words and because I held him in such high esteem, so I told him I would most likely apply.

The Cross-Semler friendship flourished when Jack started coaching. Jack and I were casual acquaintances, but I became the leading candidate based on Cross's recommendation. This created an unusual situation in that I was a relatively young and unknown high school coach from a league producing few college players, yet Maine pursued me over more experienced candidates. Moreover, I had doubts about making the move, as I had immersed myself in the Burlington community since graduating from UVM. I had a lot of friends in the area and enjoyed playing softball for Mills & Greer. My position at Rice and the YMCA were important to me. I knew if I took the Maine position, I'd still be coaching and playing softball, but leaving the Y's Camp Greylock would end my camping career. I had become the director and I loved the camp and the kids, a third of whom came from low-income families. Leaving Greylock would be hard.

I applied to Maine, despite the lure of Burlington, because in the end the chance to coach my favorite sport at the college level took precedence. In mid-June, I flew to Bangor, Maine, to interview with Jack Semler and members of the athletic department. There, I spent time at the rink with Jack and we toured the campus. I felt comfortable with him. I also met with Maine's longtime athletic director and former football coach, Harold "Westy" Westerman. During the interview, I mentioned to him that I'd been in rinks all my life, but I didn't have any rink manager experience.

"We are looking for the person, not the rink manager," Westy said. "The right person can learn to be our rink manager, but a rink manager who is not the right person won't work out for us."

Westy may have said that because hiring an assistant coach was the priority but, either way, his explanation always stuck with me. He was a man of exemplary character and he looked to hire people of character. In the years ahead, I increasingly made every effort to recruit the person as well as the player.

Despite my initial reservations about leaving Vermont, I ended up taking the Maine position and the announcement of my hiring came in late July. I told the *Burlington Free Press*, "It's a great opportunity for me and I'm really excited about it. I consider myself lucky to have a chance to work on this level and am looking forward to the challenge of a Division I program." The article also said I'd graduated from the Kent School. Maybe the writer, Andy Gardner, had me confused with Herb Muther and Ken Yeates, both Kent grads. I reminded Andy that I was a proud graduate of Proctor Academy!

Jack understood my obligation to finish the summer camp season at Greylock, so we agreed I'd start work shortly before classes started. Mike

Ryan, a current Rice player, worked at Camp Greylock, along with Bob Boucher, so two of my former Rice players were now on my staff. Just as Cross helped me with the Rice and Maine positions, I had an opportunity to hire Bob and Mike. Cross, of course, had done much more because he approached me about the two coaching positions, and his recommendation proved critical to both hires. He almost single-handedly started my coaching career, and I will forever be indebted to him for that.

Here's part of a letter that Jack sent to the Maine players about the upcoming season:

> The chemistry of a team that leads to each player putting himself on the line for his teammates, starts way before the first practice. It's an attitude that's always there but it builds up momentum as the season nears, and this season will be the most challenging since we've been at Maine. Let's pull together and start building that momentum, both physically and mentally.

When I started coaching at the University of Maine at Orono (UMO) in the fall of 1979, the hockey program was about to begin its third season, but its first as an ECAC Division I program (Hockey East formed in 1984–85). The team played at the Harold Alfond Arena, a campus facility constructed prior to the program's opening season. A nearly completed 775-seat balcony at one end of the arena increased the seating capacity to about 3,800. The additional seating was necessary. Large crowds had supported the Black Bears during their two successful Division II years, and with almost the entire team back to kick off the Division I era, greater Bangor buzzed with anticipation.

I moved into Coach Semler's house in nearby Hampden, turning the place into a three-man bachelor pad. John McCutcheon, the assistant athletic business manager, also lived there. McCutcheon would go on to a career in athletic administration, including a run as athletic director at UMass. Jack and I also had adjoining offices at the rink, and when I leaned back in my chair we could talk back and forth. It seemed I would never be too far from my boss. Both offices overlooked the rink. An actual taxidermist-preserved black bear towered on its hind legs above our office. Westy was fond of that bear and instructed the rink staff to regularly climb a ladder to dust off its nose.

One of my first rink manager duties involved assigning preseason practice times to youth hockey organizations. A representative from one of the groups stopped by my office. He said I had given ice times to the town of Old Town, but not the Old Town Indians. I told him my understanding was that I assigned slots to each town's organization and they divvied it up from there.

"No," he said, "the Penobscot Tribe is a separate organization and we get our own ice time."

"Well, let me look into this," I said.

"You better, because the tribe's not happy about it," he responded. I quickly rectified the situation after confirming I'd been mistaken. I didn't want the tribe after me.

We put the ice down in late September. Bob Laverdiere and his staff did much of the work, but it was ultimately my responsibility to make sure the ice and NCAA rink markings were laid down properly. A talented artist painted a snarling black bear head at center ice. Our players practiced on their own for a week, and during their first skate the stands and mezzanine area behind one of the goals got pelted with pucks. The rink staff had forgotten to put up the protective netting. It reminded me as a rink manager that when you're in a position of responsibility, you have to follow up.

Practice began the following week. Having come to Maine to coach, I was thrilled to finally be on the ice. My excitement also included an element of apprehension. I had coached for three years, but working with college players presented a new challenge. They were older and more skilled and I wondered how receptive they might be to my coaching. Much like a player, I needed to learn my role, which would be defined by the head coach. I hoped Jack would assign me plenty of responsibility, that he'd be receptive to my input. Ted Castle told me that Jack valued his insight. He said it was nice making suggestions to Jack between periods and then hearing him use the same words when he addressed the team. I ended up having a similar experience with him.

I couldn't wait for practice to start every day. Former UVM teammate Ken Yeates, now going to grad school at Maine, acted as our volunteer goalie coach, meaning he had to learn to coach a new position. I had some learning to do, too. We sometimes split the team at both ends during practice, with Jack at one end and me at the other. I'd work with the forwards or defensemen, or however we divided the team. We allowed about ten minutes for the practice splits, more if the players changed ends in the middle. At first, I planned accordingly, before noticing that Jack often went over the time allotment, leaving me to either let my drill run on indefinitely or ad-lib another exercise. Not a good place to be for a new college coach. I solved the problem by planning easily explained backup drills. Jack also helped by giving me a two-minute warning—which he sometimes forgot in the heat of the moment.

We opened up at Alfond with two non-NCAA games (later called exhibition games) against St. Mary's, a Canadian team from Halifax, Nova Scotia. St. Mary's won 4–3 on Friday night, and at the end of regulation on Saturday, the game was knotted up with a lacrosse-like score of 9–9. The officials skated to our bench to inquire about playing overtime in a non-NCAA game. Jack's initial response suggested some uncertainty, so I blurted out, "Jack, we should play overtime," loud enough for several players to hear. I instantly regretted speaking up. We ended up playing overtime, and St. Mary's scored to win 10–9.

I headed to the locker room after the loss as our players entered the handshake line. Jack burst through the door seconds later and yelled, "Don't ever do that again in front of the team. And you know what I'm talking about, right?"

"Yes, yes," I stammered, "I should have stayed out of the overtime discussion." At that moment, our players entered the room and we both shut up.

The phone rang later. It was Jack calling. He asked me why I didn't come to the Ground Round like we planned earlier, and I told him I just wanted to hang around the house.

"Sure," he said, "and you didn't come over because I got on you after the game?"

"Well, sort of," I said, "but it was stupid of me to speak up like that." He then explained that there was nothing wrong with a little "clanging armor" among us coaches once in a while, although it was best not to disagree in front of the team. He also told me he'd be at the Ground Round for another hour if I changed my mind. I decided to pass and grabbed a beer out of the refrigerator. There really wasn't much to celebrate, except that I didn't get sent back to Vermont.

We started league play at Boston University. Prior to the morning skate at Walter Brown Arena, Jack Parker belted out, "Where's Jimmy?" as Jack and I stood below while our players got dressed. When Parker turned away, I asked Jack if "Jimmy" referred to Jim Cross. He confirmed that Parker was referring to Cross, because he knew the two of them were close friends and he always saw them together at the coaches' convention. Parker was also a friend of Cross; they were both BU grads and they sailed together in the summer. When I last competed against BU, we upset them and Cross was my coach. There would be no win this night, though. We lost 5–3, but there were encouraging signs. In a later feature story in the *Maine Sunday Telegram*, our center Joe Crespi noted: "That was a very powerful team, right off the bat. Once we played them, we knew we could play in the league."

We hosted Northeastern before a near-capacity crowd in our next game, winning 6–3 behind Crespi's hat trick. From there, we went on to a 5–4–1 first semester record. Crespi and Gary Conn, the team's leading scorer in each of the two previous seasons, led us in scoring. Andre Aubut logged large minutes as our top defenseman. The highlight involved beating then nationally ranked Boston College on the road and UNH at home, both in the same week. Those victories further indicated that Maine belonged in Division I.

I missed some of those games when I went recruiting. My first trip was to Halifax, a seven-hour drive from Orono. Fortunately, I didn't have to take my newly purchased but secondhand Ford Pinto. The athletic department arranged recruiting cars with Village Subaru in Bangor, so I traveled in (semi) style. I stayed two days in Halifax and watched play wide-eyed from the stands. I didn't see many players of interest on my trip, but as a new recruiter, I wasn't particularly confident in my assessment. Still, the trip provided a chance to get my feet wet.

Jack never missed games to go recruiting, but he occasionally had me cover practice so he could recruit. I was pumped when I had my first opportunity. He gave me a few things to work on and otherwise left the content up to me. I carefully crafted a practice the night before and showed it to him the next morning before he headed out to a game. "Hey," he said, smiling, after glancing at the practice plan, "don't make it too good." The message was to run a good session but don't upstage the head coach.

Bill Demianiuk, our captain, stopped by my office before practice to ask if I needed help with anything. I didn't, but his gesture showed the awareness expected of a leader. Then I went over the practice with Yeates before heading onto the ice, where I felt a slight uptick in adrenaline as I glided round and round the rink, counterclockwise, along with our players, whirling by in their practice gear. Just before blowing the whistle to start practice, I heard goalie Jim Tortorella shout out, "Let's work hard out here, boys, no fooling around." (He spoke to the substitute teacher effect.) And there wasn't any fooling around. Our players worked hard, I introduced a couple of new drills, and we completed all of Jack's requests.

Back in the coaches' changing room, I asked Yeates how he thought the practice went and if there was anything we could have done better.

"Well," Yeates said after a short pause, "I think your shooting tips were good, but you went a little long when you started to repeat yourself." Having been classmates, teammates, and friends at Vermont, and close friends since, Yeates wasn't afraid to throw a little cordial criticism my way.

Jack Semler played hockey at Kent School, where his dad taught. He played hockey and soccer at UVM, and is in UVM's Sports Hall of Fame. He served in Vietnam as a second lieutenant in the Marines. His coaching career began as an assistant at Vermont, and he came to Maine after four years as the head coach at Princeton. He brilliantly recruited an entire team in just five months prior to Maine's inaugural 1977–78 season. Players from that class led the team to 15–16–1 and 23–11 Division I records in their junior and senior seasons. Jack was at once self-effacing and intensely competitive. He could explode in the locker room after a bad period or at a player for a selfish penalty. While once addressing the team during a big game, he grabbed tape and other objects off the floor. He then picked up something that started stretching from the floor to his fingers like bubblegum, only it wasn't tape, or even gum—it was a big glob of spit. David Ellis, a gritty defenseman from Prince Edward Island, observed this and said, "Coach, it looks like you've got yourself a PEI clam."

January began with a five-game losing streak against D-I opponents, but we rebounded with several big wins, including a wild 8–7 comeback victory at home against Boston University. When BU surged to a 6–1 lead, large numbers of students left for a fraternity party. Word soon spread that we were battling back. So back came the beer-guzzling partygoers, just in time to witness an astounding win. Buoyed by the victory, the students headed back for more frat house beer. There would be no beer for the boys from BU. Maine forward Brian Hughes, a Boston-area native, recalls that he'd "never seen Parker so mad."

I'm not sure if the fraternity partiers knew the words to the "Maine Stein Song," played by the pep band during games, but they would have related to the lyrics, which began with, "Oh, fill the steins to dear old Maine." A Maine student wrote the words and it was later popularized by heartthrob Rudy Vallee in 1930 to the point that it became the number one hit in the nation. Vallee grew up in Maine and attended UMO in the 1920s. Harvard coach Bill Cleary did a little jig near the band one time as they warmed up with the song before one of our games.

"I love this tune," he said to me. "And it's a drinking song." Ha ha ha.

We were bumped out of the playoffs on the last day of the season when Cornell beat BU to knock us from the eighth spot in the ECAC's seventeen-team league. But our players had proved they not only belonged in Division I, but they could win in Division I.

Jack got married after the season, with Jim Cross serving as best man. In a less official capacity, Oakie O'Connell pitched to a bunch of kids playing Wiffle ball at the wedding reception. I doubt they knew they had a former Division I All-American throwing to them, and if they did, it's unlikely they would've cared. Many of us former UVM hockey players attended, as well. John McCutcheon and I moved out of Jack's house just before the wedding and headed to the tiny town of Veazie, where we shared a house with Husson College baseball coach Jim Walsh. Jim and I tied up the phone most nights making recruiting calls.

Jack and I played a little Wiffle ball ourselves, along with other forms of competition like Ping-Pong, tennis, and games we made up on the spot. One day we went out on a softball field and staged a "home run derby." Considering I was a power hitter and played nearly seventy games every summer, it was the only competition I remember dominating. We didn't bet when we competed against each other, but Jack came up with a punishment far worse than losing a few bucks. The loser had to firmly shake the hand of the winner and say very sincerely, "You are the better player."

Larry Mahoney, a prolific writer with a slightly rumpled look and a Down East sense of humor, covered the hockey beat for the *Bangor Daily News*. He was just beginning a long career covering Maine hockey. He wrote an article during the summer announcing our incoming recruits and the new schedule, while Jack honeymooned in Ireland with his new wife, Sarah. Mahoney noted, "Maine opens its season against the University of New Brunswick at the Northern Maine Forum in Presque Isle on Oct. 31 and in St. Stephen, NB, the following night." Presque Isle is located in a potato-growing section of Maine, and Larry didn't mention in his article what he told me earlier: "You may want to warn your players about potato plants sprouting through the ice."

In addition to Mahoney's reporting, Gary Thorne, a lawyer and assistant district attorney, provided play-by-play as the voice of Maine hockey. His daughter Kelly attended the Maine Hockey School, which Jack and I ran in the summer. A native of nearby Old Town, Maine, and a graduate of the University of Maine, he went on to become the voice of the New York Mets and the Baltimore Orioles. He eventually enjoyed a national reputation broadcasting MLB, NHL, and college football games. I found it interesting that Gary and Tom Cheek, who called our Vermont games, both left college hockey for Major League Baseball. They certainly brought considerable professionalism and recognition to Maine and Vermont hockey, respectively, and their accomplishments thereafter were most impressive.

Gary wrote an article, "SR.," in the 1980–81 Hockey Press Guide about our large—and first—senior class. (SR, meaning senior, is the roster abbreviation for a player's class designation.) His article ended with:

> Now we share the SR. dreams, but will not speak them. One does not mention the no-hitter in progress. But just listen on a cold winter's night outside the Alfond Arena as that space between fallen snow and clear sky fills with sound as the red light at the other end ignites. That is the sound of a SR. dream four years in the making.

Two of our non-seniors left school soon after practice started. Freshmen Don Mattson from North Dakota and Dave Ottum, a Minnesotan, walked into Jack's office and told him they were going home. We considered them our top recruits. Ottum was selected All-State, a noteworthy achievement in hockey-rich Minnesota. I felt especially bad about him leaving, as he was one of my first recruits. Despite our efforts, we couldn't persuade them to stay. You often don't discover all the reasons kids leave school, but their departure certainly came under the broad definition of homesickness. As they were roommates, it's likely one influenced the other to leave, but we couldn't determine that. When I became head coach at AIC, however, I paid close attention to roommate selections.

The loss of those two guys didn't deter the determination of our team to start strong. We opened the season with a sweep over New Brunswick, and then flew to Marquette, Michigan, to play Northern Michigan University. Northern Michigan was the NCAA runner-up the year before, having lost to North Dakota in the NCAA Championship game. We certainly had a challenging series ahead of us against a formidable opponent.

We split with Northern Michigan, winning 8–7 on Friday and losing 7–3 the next night. In the third period of Friday night's game, a most unusual situation occurred. Gary Conn and John Tortorella, two senior linemates, found themselves together on what was essentially a 2-on-0 breakaway. John passed the puck to Gary and hung back just enough so Gary would be the shooter. John knew what he was doing. Gary Conn, who never seemed to miss, shot and scored.

John Tortorella is the toughest, most intense player I've ever been associated with. Years later, the intensity evident in him as an NHL coach and his insistence on "sustaining hardness on a puck" is the real deal. Unlike some coaches, who talk a tough game but weren't so rugged when they played, John walked the walk. He competed for every puck and blocked every shot. He battled like a cornered (black) bear. He played net-front on our power play, where no number of hacks, whacks, or speeding pucks could move him. John came to play every day; he came early, which included pregame naps in the locker room, and he stayed late. He could be penalty-prone, his only vice, but he did cut his minutes down as a senior. Dr. Archambault, our team doctor, respected John's toughness and spoke of the time he started stitching John's leg between periods and John threatened to pull the stitches out when he noticed they restricted his movement. The doctor put on a quick bandage and they agreed to restitch after the game.

We continued playing well after returning from Northern Michigan, beating Clarkson 5–4, when, as Larry Mahoney wrote in the *Bangor Daily News*, "Brian Hughes sent the home crowd of 4,006 into delirium with the overtime game winner." The team then exploded with twenty-seven goals in three straight wins against Ivy League opponents. We only lost twice during the rest of the semester.

We beat RPI, Holy Cross, and a Swedish team, Vasby, to win the RPI tournament, which wrapped up our schedule before the new year. Goaltender Jim Tortorella (John's brother) scored a rink-length goal against Vasby. The puck and his stick were sent to the U.S. Hockey Hall of Fame in Eveleth, Minnesota. During the on-ice awards ceremony following our last tourney game, Rob Zamejc, a first-line player for us, had a bag of ice on his bruised shoulder. Jack went up to him and quietly said, "Rob, why don't you put that ice on the bench until after the ceremony, so you don't show you're hurt." Rob complied. If he was perplexed by the request, he didn't show it. He just kept smiling the wide smile of a tournament champion.

Playing Vermont in January was a circle-the-calendar event for me. When we arrived the night before the game, I dropped off Dwight Montgomery's helmet with Reggie Snow at Mills & Greer. Dwight had broken his jaw earlier and his mouth was nearly wired shut. He had just been cleared for contact and play. Reggie attached a football face mask bar for further protection. Dwight had to sip his food through a straw and endure jaw-rattling contact that threatened the healing. Hockey has long been associated with such courage. In addition to seeing Reggie, I went downtown with friends after the game, including Sigma Nu's Peter Beekman and Dennis Keresey. Unfortunately, my parents were traveling in Europe at the time and couldn't attend. I missed not having them at the game.

I hadn't been to Gutterson since my Rice team lost in the state finals. Walking into the rink brought back memories that, along with playing my alma mater, coached by Cross and Castle, helped make it a special night. The game turned into a doozie. Future major league pitcher Kirk McCaskill, an NHL and MLB draft pick, scored a hat trick for the Cats, while crisp-shooting Joe Crespi piloted us with a pair. We led 5–3 with a minute to go when Vermont scored to make it 5–4. Then they tallied again to tie it, and the large crowd erupted into thunderous, fist-pumping, rip-roaring cheers. It was one of those memorable moments that added to Gutterson lore. But unlike some teams, our guys had heard such noise before—at Alfond. An overtime goal by Bill Deminiauk quieted Gutterson down, save for a bunch of Black Bears bear-hugging to the side of the UVM net.

Dartmouth visited Alfond three days later. Robert LaFleur scored four goals in an 8–4 win. A new-to-the-game woman, Leigh McCarthy, attended and wrote a wonderful piece about her experience, titled "Maine 8 Dartmouth

4," which appeared in the *Bangor Daily News*. Our Hockey Guide included the article the next year. Here's a snippet:

> I didn't want to go. It was cold. I had never seen a hockey game and it wouldn't put a dent in my life if I never saw one. The tickets had been bought. The babysitter had been hired. Reason weighed against me. We went. The game started. The players were wild electrified kachina dolls, gods of fire and wind, gods of ice. They skated backwards, they skated sideways, they hopped and jumped and threw themselves down with abandon. Their replacements came up over the boards with the intensity of doughboys rising out of the trenches in the Ardennes. They slammed their bodies at each other, they bashed into the boards with the force of elephants and skated away without noticing that all their bones should have been shattered in the crunch. The goalkeeper stood in ultimate defense of his territory with a stick wrapped in shining tape and a first baseman's glove. I never saw the puck. He always saw it, knocked it away, impounded it. I couldn't see, but I could feel the invisible village within the net the goalie guarded. Some atavistic fury drove him, drove the defensemen, to the savagery with which they protected their village from the Dartmouth Huns. It was over. Maine's blue knights had won their hockey game. I loved it. I was amazed. It was fast, it was exciting, it was fun. I wonder if we can get tickets to the Yale game.

We continued to win and Gary Conn continued to light the lamp. He scored thirty goals his senior year on his way to being named a Division I All-American. Here was a player initially contacted by baseball coach John Winkin and still around when Jack got the Maine job with only a few months to recruit a team. BU assistant Toot Cahoon encouraged him to consider prep school, but other D-I colleges showed scarce interest. He played at Marblehead HS, known for producing college players, so exposure wasn't an issue. One knock on him concerned his skating. Larry Mahoney lightheartedly referred to him as a "snowshoe skater" in one of his articles. Larry had a point—to a point. Gary was not a classic skater, and he wasn't particularly quick or fast. But his work ethic, physical strength, playmaking, clutch goal scoring, and high-compete level more than compensated. He also knew how to think the game. I'll let Jack's quote in Gary's bio serve as the last word here: "He's the best forward I've ever coached."

When I contacted Gary about this book, all these years later, he said, "You gave me one of my best calls ever when you phoned me at home in Marblehead (Massachusetts) to tell me I was an All-American." It's nice that he recalls my call. He credits playing "chicken" before practice with his teammates as an exercise that helped toughen them up with the puck. It was a rough keep-away game that allowed the other participants to take runs at the puck carrier. And he usually didn't leave the ice after practice until he shot ten straight pucks into the upper corner. Gary was inducted into Maine's Sports Hall of Fame in 1989.

The regular season ended with us in fourth place in the overall standings, percentage points ahead of Cornell, but we received the No. 5 seed, because the league was split into East, West, and Ivy Regions, and those three first-place teams were awarded home ice. Cornell won the Ivies, so we had to go there for the first round of the eight-team quarterfinals. We had beaten them handily, 7–2, at Alfond during the regular season, but it would be a different story at historic Lynah Rink. We lost 7–4, despite Gary Conn's two goals. The nine-hour bus ride home was silent and sorrowful.

Still, we finished 23–11, and our seniors completed their Maine careers with a cumulative record of 78–47–2. Those individuals had not only played four years of college hockey, but they started the program for which they played. Jack Semler received the New England Division I Coach of the Year award. It was the same award his mentor, Jim Cross, received in 1975. However, unlike Cross, Jack passed on attending the banquet in a tuxedo and sneakers.

The next season began with a very different team. Thirteen seniors had departed, including Jeff Nord, who shared the goaltending position with Jim Tortorella in previous years. Jeff took a redshirt year after sustaining an injury early in his junior season, so we expected him back. Then he signed with the NHL's St. Louis Blues over the summer. Ironically, one of our three incoming goalies, Pete Smith, was drafted by the Blues. The roster included fifteen freshmen as we neared the season opener.

Bill Bryan dealt with most of our freshmen in the Admissions Office. A tall, folksy individual, he wore both tweed and an L.L.Bean red-and-black woodsman's hat. He once coached the freshman hockey team at Colby. He was a farmer, an ice fisherman, and a scout for the Pittsburgh Pirates. His brother, Bob, and Marshall Dodge met at Yale and formed the famous Bert & I duo, telling humorous Down East Maine stories. I already had two of their albums and told versions of them at Camp Greylock campfires. Bill was a principled man and said when he interviewed prospective students, "an important consideration is whether I want to be in a foxhole with them."

We opened with New Brunswick again in Presque Isle. There was no potato interference, but we handled the puck like a hot potato in a 6–5 loss. We then lost some league games before rebounding to beat BU and Vermont. We went mostly with Duffy Loney early and then switched to Pete Smith with better results at first. With almost our entire defensive corps back from the previous year, and knowing we needed help up front, we moved Dwight Montgomery to forward with mixed results. It was almost like exchanging a top defenseman for an average forward. Dwight battled his weight at times, which affected him more as a forward, although that's not the sole reason the experiment didn't work as we'd hoped. Switching positions is not easy under any circumstance.

We had several French Canadians from Quebec when I played at UVM, because that province borders Vermont, and Montreal isn't far from Burlington. Jack's familiarity with Cross and the Vermont program was a factor in recruiting Quebec players. Many coaches didn't go there because of the language barrier. Robert LaFleur told Jack early on that, "I don't come to Maine just for funny." Now, we might have been even more successful in Quebec if I had paid more attention in mother's French class.

Two of our Quebeckers, Andre Aubut and Robert LaFleur, were now seniors. A Division I All-American his sophomore year, Andre Aubut (pronounced *oh-boo*) was a multifaceted defenseman and fan favorite. Three thousand or more yelled "Boo" when he rushed the puck or scored—and they weren't booing him. Robert was strong and stocky with large thighs that propelled him to high speeds on a hockey rink. He scored twenty-seven goals as a senior and led the team with fifty points. He had seventy-two career goals, and could have had more. During his sophomore year he missed some speedy breakaways, so Jack asked me to work with him. Because he had a good shot but average hands, I suggested he keep things simple on breakaways and consider the following: "Don't over-stickhandle in close. Stick to one move when you can. If in doubt, shoot." The last point comes from Eddie Jeremiah, the distinguished Dartmouth coach.

We struggled throughout the season. David Ellis, a bear-strong physical defenseman, once told me during a net-front coverage drill: "If you don't have a guy's stick, you don't have anything." Speaking of sticks, his bone-crunching checks on opponents entering our zone often sent them flying in one direction and their sticks and gloves in another. Gary Conn and Brian Hughes told me, "Some of the BU players said they were afraid of Ellis." David was also a first-class captain who had everyone's respect. Maine fans were accustomed to winning, and a small group behind our bench began directing criticism toward us. Mostly it could be ignored, except one night the heckling escalated and David surprised our bench by turning and addressing them. I don't recall his exact words, but he called them out for being bandwagon jumpers and acting like tough guys from the relative safety of the stands. He said we were competing hard on the ice, and if they didn't like it, they could support us or leave.

Mainly season-ticketholders sat in that section and I could see their collective gasps when David started in. The hecklers said nothing, and they were rarely heard from again. All of us in athletics learn not to respond to caustic comments and catcalls in the arena of sport—and life. But Jack and I were OK with David's response. He only did it once: he rebuked the individuals in a professional manner and he spoke on behalf of our team. He was the captain.

The following year proved to be our worst, resulting in a disappointing 5–24 record. After graduating the big and successful 1981 class and another good group the past year, we became a team of mostly freshman and sophomores. And we got even younger when Ken Fargnoli, our captain, hurt us by becoming academically ineligible. Now, a young team can often lead to a promising future, but being young doesn't necessarily guarantee success down the road. In fact, when coaches repeatedly proclaim that their team is young, it can become an excuse for poor play, so we tried not to overplay that card. Our hope and belief at the time was that we would be much improved in 1983–84, provided we added a strong recruiting class.

I scoured the U.S. and Canada looking for players that season. My long recruiting trips often left Jack on the bench by himself. I usually phoned from the rinks where I was recruiting to get updates from the Maine press box and those of our opponents. Sports Information Directors (SID) and their assistants answered by shouting something along the lines of, "Maine 3, Providence 3, five minutes left in the third." Then they hung up. I called back when the score was close. If not, I returned to my recruiting spot, either happy or sad. That season the news was mostly bad.

Recruiting on the road involved meeting with coaches and players, as well as spending additional time with college coaches. Ted Castle and I got together some, and I often sat with Dartmouth assistant Phil Grady at games in Minnesota. He always exuded enthusiasm. Most coaches evaluated the players who could help their programs. Phil, however, ranked everybody, which amounted to some forty players per game. It allowed him to check his notes when non-recruited players applied to Dartmouth. When I met with defenseman Roger Grillo at Apple Valley High School, he said he wanted to be a high school social studies teacher and a hockey coach. I liked the detail of his future plans. Roger went on to become an assistant at Vermont and later head coach at Brown, before working for USA hockey. But that was close enough.

Head coaches have fewer opportunities to go on the road, but Jack and I occasionally recruited together. One time we got caught in a raging blizzard on the way back from the Maritimes, forcing us to stay at a lonely place that looked scarier than the Bates Motel. We survived the night and then skidded our way to the Maine border in Calais. From there, we planned to take Maine's rugged Route 9, nicknamed "The Airline." Only it was closed. The blizzard had blanketed the roller-coaster-like road, and the highway department shut it down. We learned that emergency vehicles and people living along the road could chance it in an emergency. I suggested we go ahead with caution. Jack said no, but after a short discussion, he relented. I drove and Jack sat in the back seat, bracing himself at every turn. It took twice as long, but we made it home safely. And I had delivered the "goods," that being my boss.

Cheryl Reynolds, our hockey and arena secretary, hosted an end-of-season staff party on the day the refrigeration system was shut off. Cheryl did a nice job running our office, but her skating abilities were suspect. She fell backward while teetering on a pair of rental skates and banged her head on the ice, sustaining a concussion. With our host hurt, the party ended, but not with the kind of "bang" we were looking for.

Over the summer, I played softball with a team that included eventual University of Maine Sports Hall of Famers in baseball, Dennis Libbey and Dick Devarney (Dick excelled in football, too). We played in a Bangor league and entered several out-of-state tournaments. We finished as state runner-up after losing in the Class A championship game. Softball was king back then and losing that game hurt. It was the closest I'd come to a state title since winning the Vermont championship with Mills & Greer.

On the hockey side, I watched Hockey Night in Boston games, which included top prospects from the East Coast, and again co-directed the Maine Hockey School. Bob Boucher, Red Gendron, and Phil Lanoue, the Milton High School coach, all came over from Vermont to join our staff. (They stayed in my spartan apartment, and one sweltering night Red fell asleep in my beanbag chair after a night on the town. He woke up with his head stuck to it.) Tom LeBlond, a former Maine player, also worked with us.

That summer, I read Ken Dryden's new book, *The Game*. It's a beautifully written and insightful book that everyone should read. When I was young, my mother read Dr. Seuss books to me over and over, often at my request. As an adult, I've read *The Game* almost as much.

We entered the 1983–84 season believing we were better. Most of our team returned, including fifteen-goal scorers Ray Jacques and Ron Hellen. Our recruiting class featured characteristics necessary for us to win: character, skill, and grit. Amongst other positional deficiencies, our goaltenders the previous year combined for a low .831 save percentage, so we had high hopes for our two new netminders. In another move, Stu Haskell had become athletic director when Westy retired the year before, thus letting me out of my rink manager duties. I could now focus more on coaching and recruiting.

Jeff "Macko" MacLaughlin joined our staff as a part-time assistant. Some of his friends affectionately called him Macko-wacko, a nod to his free-spirited nature. He played at Vermont with Jack. Adding Macko improved our player-coach ratio and provided bench help when I went recruiting. I wanted Macko to assist with recruiting, but he showed little interest, and Jack didn't feel we should force a part-time coach to go on the road. I disagreed with that and argued my case because I felt we needed another recruiter, but then let it go. There's a point at which an assistant must take no for an answer, otherwise it can erode the important relationship between a head coach and his assistant.

We lost our opener to Lowell in Lewiston, Maine, swept Concordia at Alfond, and then defeated Northeastern at home. A season-ending injury to tri-captain Ron Hellen stole some of the luster from our three straight wins. We picked up more steam in December with a sweep over Colgate, followed by successive overtime losses to BC and BU and a win over Harvard to end the semester. The second Colgate win was an afternoon game, and I headed out recruiting right after. I planned to stop halfway, but I felt so wired about the wins, I turned up the tunes and motored straight to Toronto.

I liked learning the playing styles of opposing coaches. Most systems are somewhat similar, but sometimes you see something different. George Crowe made it to the NCAA Final Four in 1979 and 1980 utilizing the Dartmouth Forecheck, an aggressive, all-in, balls-to-the-wall forecheck. Two forwards jumped the two defensemen, and the third forward was positioned higher in the zone, ready to cover for a green-light crashing defenseman, or engage in the offense. Colby coach Mickey Goulet used the Sinker against us. He lined up three forwards and a defenseman on the blue line, and one D (the sinker) stayed deep in the zone to retrieve a dumped puck. We usually beat them because we had stronger teams, but Mickey and his players made it difficult.

Bowdoin coach Terry Meagher, another interesting tactician, and I were watching a prep game at the Bowdoin rink in January when he received a phone call. He came back and said, "Gary, that was [beat writer] Larry Mahoney and he said Jack resigned today, effective at the end of the season. He's working on a story and wants to talk to you now." I told Larry that I had no information and didn't feel comfortable commenting yet. As I prepared to leave, Terry asked if there was anything he could do for me. "Thanks," I said, "I'm blindsided by this, but I'm fine." I didn't tell Terry my mind was racing with all sorts of questions and concerns. One of them being, what am I going to do now?

Jack seemed relieved when we spoke that night. He didn't give any one reason for resigning, but generally said he wanted to do other things and spend more time with his family. He said he had just made his decision, so he told Stu Haskell and then met with our players. He'd consulted only with his wife and Jim Cross as far as I know. Cross announced his retirement prior to the season, and I think that played a part in Jack's thought process. Now they'd both be done at season's end. Coincidentally, Maine and Vermont were playing at Alfond in their last regular-season game. Gary Thorne wrote an article in that night's game program titled "A Reflection." This opening speaks to Jack's decision:

> This is not a requiem for Jack Semler. None is necessary. For those who know him, and as time goes by, for those who don't, the reality will set in that when he said he was retiring because he had had enough and it was time to move on to something else, that constitutes the simple statement of exactly how he feels. As with all that he's done in his career in hockey, what he says is what he means and vice versa.

Our second semester highlights included wins over Dartmouth, Brown, UNH, BC, and Jack's former team, Princeton. The lowlight was a tough two-loss trip to play Clarkson and St. Lawrence, which included listening to the nauseating noise of the Clarkson Hockey Bell eleven times. We finished 14–20, with five of those losses in overtime. It was a big improvement over the previous season, but still not good enough.

Jack's announcement surprised our players, but they continued to compete. Hockey players play and they rebound—maybe not completely, but quickly—in this case from the news of Jack leaving. Before the last practice, I skated around talking with Rene Comeault, a talented defenseman (and strong student), and one of our tri-captains. He missed a dozen games with a knee injury, but had since returned to the lineup. Suddenly, Rene said, "Look at this," as he pointed to the door where players and coaches enter the ice. Jack stepped onto the ice and started slipping and sliding before clinging to the boards. The team had doctored up his skate blades. Everyone tapped their sticks repeatedly while skating toward him. It was a nice touch.

We played Vermont the next night. Larry Mahoney wrote about Jack's seven years at Maine. The game program also included a nice piece on Jim Cross by Dick Whittier, the longtime Vermont SID. It was always great to see the Vermont staff, which now included Chuck Ross, a former teammate at UVM, but all of us were distracted by mixed emotions that night. Ted Castle, of course, had worked for both coaches and also played for Cross. A victory would end our season with four straight wins, a modest achievement, but finishing strong is always important. Win, lose, or draw, though, I felt sadness and nostalgia about this being the last game of both my former college coach and present boss.

We led 5–4 with minutes left when Vermont pulled their goalie for a 6-on-5 attack. The Cats pressed us hard and we shot at the empty net from our end. We missed, the refs called icing, and the faceoff came back in our zone. Several seconds later, Vermont tied the game. Then they scored in overtime and celebrated. Our bench sat silent. Jack and I and Macko headed to the Vermont bench and met their staff halfway. Here we were, Jim Cross and five of his former UVM players, meeting up and shaking hands warmly. And then we all walked slowly off the ice, as the Maine fans, initially silenced by the loss, applauded Jack and our players in season-ending appreciation.

Jack turned reflective about that final game when he wrote, "It was pretty fitting when UVM won the game. I remember feeling like it was sort of right for Jim's team to beat the team coached by his protégés."

On the one hand, that's not something you'd expect to hear from someone as competitive as Jack Semler. But hockey is about more than winning and losing; the human relationships play an integral part, and the respect that he had for his mentor, Jim Cross, was as much about admiration and compassion as competition.

Chapter 6

Arriving at AIC

On a brisk Sunday afternoon in early March, the team gathered for a banquet at the Oronoka Restaurant in Orono. The Friends of UMO Hockey sponsored the event. Ron Hellen and Rene Comeault were named co-captains for the upcoming year, and senior Todd Bjorkstrand received two awards. Gary Thorne served as emcee. Several speakers spoke about Jack, and Macko, in the words of Larry Mahoney, provided "superb comic relief." Jack received a Maine rocking chair with an attached plaque from the Friends group, and an engraved gold watch from our players.

"It's unbelievable to be leaving on such a happy note," he said in the *Bangor Daily* the next day. He deserved it. Jack Semler was a very classy coach.

Stu Haskell had met with me earlier to say that after the season, I would direct the program "until we hire a new head coach." He told me the college would conduct a national search for a head coach and I was welcome to apply, but the intent was to hire someone from the outside. That made sense to me. We had two strong seasons during my time at Maine, but we didn't win enough overall for me to be a serious candidate.

Stu made it clear the new head coach would choose his own assistant. He said he'd tell the finalists that, if hired, he hoped they would consider me, but ultimately the new coach had to make his own decision. This also seemed reasonable, as I'd been around long enough to know that when a head coach leaves, schools seldom retain assistants. I got to know Stu well when he previously served as the athletic business manager and his wife, Gloria, ran the cash register at our public skating sessions. I liked and respected him. His professionalism and honesty in dealing with me during that uncertain time was appreciated.

I continued recruiting and overseeing some of the necessary administrative tasks. I also remained available for any players who might need help. Things felt surreal with Jack gone and my coaching future in limbo. I ran into Toot Cahoon at the Harvard Rink, while watching what I seem to remember was a prep school all-star game, and Toot said, "I guess there's a lot going on up there, huh, Gary." He was an assistant at Lowell then, and he spoke to both the head coach search and my precarious position at Maine.

I had previously hired Julie Sutphin-Worgull as director of Maine's figure skating program, where she also taught some power skating to our players, produced an annual ice show, and directed a drill team that performed between periods. She understood some of my employment worries, and one afternoon gave me an impromptu pep talk in the office: "You must make sure," she said, "that you continue working hard to impress Stu Haskell and the new coach coming in. Don't flaunt your work ethic, but purposefully go about your business every day. They'll notice. Proceed with confidence and the understanding that you're a good coach with a bright future, who will not succumb to any self-doubt or pity because of your situation. You should also protect yourself by at least starting to research potential openings at other schools. And, finally, whatever happens, make sure you finish strong, just like you tell your players to do."

I can't say that I've recalled Julie's talk word-for-word, but I do remember the gist of her sage advice. It was helpful at the time and obviously still resonates with me. Sometimes coaches need a little coaching themselves.

The search committee chose four finalists: Mike Addesa, the RPI head coach; Dave Conte, an NHL scout; Dave O'Connor, a UNH hockey (and football) assistant; and Shawn Walsh, an assistant at Michigan State. Each came to campus for interviews. I knew Addesa and O'Connor, but had not met Conte or Walsh. All three college coaches came from strong programs. Conte played at Colgate. Stu arranged to have me meet with each candidate during the visits, to answer their questions and generally talk about Maine Hockey. I hadn't expected to meet with them, but I appreciated being included in the process, considering the tenuousness of my position at Maine.

I didn't ask any of the candidates if they'd keep me on their staff, but Dave Conte and Dave O'Connor both broached the subject, indicating they would likely retain me as an assistant. Mike and I didn't discuss the matter. Shawn Walsh said he'd consider me but preferred to bring in his own guy.

I respected his straightforwardness. Although I felt like a lame-duck coach, the meetings did provide hope that I might be able to stay. And they gave those guys a chance to learn more about the hockey program and what it would be like to work at Maine.

After his interview, Mike Addesa decided to stay at RPI. It seemed he made the right decision, because the very next season RPI won the NCAA Division I national championship. Some people consider his 1984–85 team to be the best in college hockey history. Mike was a good coach and recruiter, but he was unpopular with some coaches. During a previous game at Alfond, with RPI leading by several goals, he walked onto the ice to start a new period. One of his beefy hands slid along the top of the boards for balance, and the other grasped a hot cup of coffee. I guess you could say he appeared to be on a coffee break. Jack wasn't happy about it, and started referring to him that night as "Cup of Coffee Mike."

I kept in touch with Jack after he left and visited him at his new place near the Maine shore. He ran a small business selling lobsters from a roadside stand for a short time. Some coaches might feel uncomfortable to be spotted in such a setting, but Jack is an unpretentious and unassuming individual. No job seemed beneath him. And that humbleness was part of his charm. It also happens to be a desirable characteristic for hockey players. "Some kids are just not as coachable," said former Michigan coach Red Berenson, "and usually those kids don't get better. But humble kids do get better." It's a credit to our sport that hockey players are considered among the most approachable of all professional athletes.

Shawn Walsh was named the new hockey coach in mid-April. A few days later the phone rang about 6 p.m. in my Veazie apartment: "Gary, this is Shawn Walsh. I just arrived on campus and the rink is locked. Campus police let me in, but can you unlock the office for me?"

"Yes," I said, and raced to the rink to let Sean into his new office. He let me know he was upset about being locked out. I hadn't dealt with him except for our meeting during his interview, and no one mentioned anything to me about arranging for his arrival, but I apologized for the mix-up. It certainly didn't look good that the new head coach of the most visible sports team in the state of Maine, who would lead the program to a national championship in just seven years, couldn't get into his office on his first day at work.

The plan was for me to keep going until Shawn hired a new assistant. He came in like a whirlwind and worked long hours, often until 10 p.m. or later. I stayed most days until about 7 p.m. or so, unless he needed me around. I wanted to indicate I would work late, but I didn't want to come off as trying too hard to impress him, partly because he again made it clear he'd likely bring in someone else. Shawn's intense focus as a coach became evident to me right away, and he would underscore his singular purpose outlook by holding up curled fingers to represent a puck and saying, "I'm married to a little black thing like this."

Shawn left me a daily to-do list. I didn't save any of them, but here is a sample of the types of assignments I recall him giving me.

- Line up a recruiting car for Wednesday–Sunday

- See me about calling high school and Junior Coaches

- Run off 50 copies of yesterday's Maine Hockey article in the *Bangor Daily News.*

- Put together 25 recruiting packets (Admissions View Book/ Application, Press Guide, Hockey Questionnaire, Schedule, Newspaper Articles, Head Coach letter)

- Pick up more pens and notepads

- See me about setting up Thursday's on-campus recruit visit (All rink lights on during visits)

- Write a good letter to selected recruits and include your thoughts on my hiring

- Keep mailing first-time recruiting packets from Orono post office if campus mail has gone out

I told Shawn about a prospect from Bridgewater HS named Terry Chipman. We decided to make a home visit to meet Terry and his parents in Massachusetts. I knew Bill Crane, his coach, so we arranged to have him stop by during the visit. Shawn drove like a bat out of hell. He seemed like the fast-lane type anyway, as opposed to Jack and me, but this was fast in a literal sense. I think we averaged close to eighty miles per hour during the trip. It felt like NASCAR. Shawn had one of those fuzz-buster contraptions on the dashboard that could detect police radar. We made the round trip in race-car time—without a speeding ticket.

We met with Terry and his parents, and Coach Crane stopped by. At one point, Shawn started talking about his forechecking theories. He used a set of salt and pepper shakers and a couple of glasses to demonstrate a particular forecheck system. I'm not sure if Terry's parents knew what was going on, but it was a good show. On the way back, I asked Shawn about the salt and pepper forecheck depiction. He said he liked to share systems stuff with recruits and their families because it gave them an indication of his hockey knowledge and added to an overall professional presentation.

Shawn told me later that he planned to hire Jay Leach, a Merrimack College assistant, as his new assistant coach. One of Jay's brothers, Jon, played for us at Maine during the first four years of the program. I had already started applying for coaching openings and accelerated the process when I learned about Jay. Shawn stressed that I could use him as a reference for any coaching positions I applied for. He also said he was impressed by the way I handled myself during the six weeks we worked together. "You're better than what I expected," he said. I didn't ask him exactly what that meant, as I thought it best to appreciate his compliments and leave it at that.

Soon after I resigned, Stu Haskell said Bob Burke, the associate athletic director at American International College (AIC), had called to inquire about me, since I had applied there. He said Mr. Burke asked a lot of questions, and Stu felt their talk went well. "I told him I thought you would be a great hire for them," Stu said. I thanked him and told him how much I appreciated everything he'd done for me.

Bob Burke phoned and introduced himself in a rather gruff-sounding voice. He said it was a part-time coaching position, although they hoped to combine it with another job on campus to make it essentially a full-time position. He asked if I'd still be interested in coming down for an interview. I told him I definitely had an interest, and we arranged a date for my visit.

I arrived in Springfield, Massachusetts, the night before the interview and, after checking into a hotel, drove to the campus to familiarize myself with the route. I didn't want to get lost the next day and end up late for the interview. After finding the Butova Gymnasium, which housed Mr. Burke's office, I drove around looking for the rest of the campus, but couldn't seem to find it. I gave up as darkness descended on the city. The next day I learned why: The main campus and the athletic complex, which also included two dorms, were a quarter mile apart. I had heard AIC was located in a rather rough urban environment, and I saw subtle indications of it that night, but it didn't concern me. I needed a job coaching college hockey.

My interview started on a Monday morning in June. Bob Burke's secretary greeted me warmly and identified herself as Mrs. C. (The C stood for Ciosek, not her hometown, Chicopee, she joked.) She said Coach Burke would see me shortly. I met with him for over an hour in his office. He was in his mid-forties, balding, and had a linebacker build. His demeanor matched the gruffness I heard on the phone, but he appeared friendly enough. Bob told me about the history of the hockey program and he emphasized that, although his background was in football, he liked hockey. He seemed focused on hiring a disciplinarian. "I'm tired of hearing complaints from our opponents and officials about our bad conduct," he said. He indicated that a more full-time coach would be better equipped to maintain discipline on and off the ice. He said he and the dean of students had talked about combining the coaching position with the housing director vacancy. The housing position included a stipend and an on-campus apartment.

We toured the campus, and I liked the consistency of architecture with brick buildings adorned by white pillars. The grounds were well groomed. We had lunch in the faculty dining room, followed by a meeting with Blaine Stevens, the dean of students. Stevens said he'd consider a coach as his housing director if it was the right person. (That reminded me of what Westy, the Maine AD, told me with respect to being the rink manager.) Still, I tried to sound like I knew something about housing without telling him my room at Sigma Nu had been a mess.

We concluded the day back in Bob's office. He reiterated his support for the hockey program and said he thought Dean Stevens would work with him on hiring a coach. He spent more time selling me on the merits of the program than asking questions, which appeared to indicate an interest in me. Before leaving, I thanked him for the interview opportunity and added: "I love coaching college hockey, and I'm confident you'll never regret your decision if I'm hired here."

I thought a lot about the position while waiting to hear from AIC. I wanted to be a head coach, but there weren't many openings at the Division II/III level. I wasn't a big name in hockey, so my choices were limited. I felt my best shot was at a place like AIC, where there's less competition, because the job was low-paying and had been posted as part time. The urban environment, along with not having a rink on campus, would also deter some coaches.

Four days after my interview, Larry Mahoney wrote an article in the *Bangor Daily News*, under the heading, "Former UM aide Gary Wright finalist for AIC Hockey post." In the article I said:

> If I'm fortunate enough to be chosen, I think it would be a great opportunity at AIC. I certainly regret that I have to leave, but I understand Shawn's situation and I can't say I wouldn't have done the same thing myself. Any new coach wants to pick his own assistant. I appreciate Stu Haskell's support and the fact that Shawn was willing to give me a look. I'm naturally disappointed the team hasn't done as well lately and, in many ways, I'm responsible for that. But, otherwise, it's been a very positive experience for me.

Bob Burke called and offered me the position. I accepted. There was no salary negotiation, moving fees, or other perks. After all, I was talking to AIC, a small Division II school, not one of the big schools. Besides, I felt a great sense of excitement and relief at my good fortune. I probably would have taken the job for nothing. I called my parents to tell them the exciting news. My mother had been looking for high school openings in case I didn't land a college position. Now she and my father could celebrate my appointment as a college hockey head coach. I know I did. I went out for a few beers with the boys at the Bounty Tavern, a popular singles and dance bar in Bangor. Then we decided to go somewhere else, but I was so happy I didn't care where.

I drove to Springfield a few days later, pulling a rented Ryder trailer that contained all my possessions. (I didn't need moving fees, anyway.) I moved into the head resident apartment in Magna Hall, a four-floor coed dormitory. The housing office would be my base and was located on the Student Affairs floor of the Campus Center building. I also had a hole-in-the-wall office in the Butova Gymnasium, which I shared with the baseball coach. I worked out of both places at first, before finding it practical to do everything out of the housing office. In effect, it became the Housing and Hockey Office. My priorities weren't necessarily in that order.

AIC, my new workplace, opened in 1885 in Lowell, Massachusetts, and a few years later the college moved to its present location in Springfield, an American Hockey League-size city located in Western Massachusetts. The school was founded to provide educational opportunities for the influx of French Canadian immigrants entering the U.S. at the time, thus the "International" in American International College. The college had an undergraduate enrollment of about 1,600 students when I arrived in the summer of 1984, along with graduate programs. Commuters represented about 45 percent of the undergrads. Business was the most popular major then, followed by criminal justice. That would change over time.

The college's athletic program, nicknamed the Yellow Jackets, participated in the Northeast-10, an NCAA Division II conference with basketball as its feature sport. The NE-10 didn't sponsor ice hockey, so we played in the sixteen-team ECAC East, a league consisting of NCAA Division I, II, and III colleges, who basically competed at the same level. It was a marriage of convenience. For my first few years that group was generally referred to as Division II.

Hockey started at AIC in 1948 and the program had a fairly rich history. The team won the ECAC championship in 1969, and the mid-'70s featured some strong squads. The years leading up to my arrival had not been as successful, but still representative. Dave Forbes, who played on the 1969 team and graduated in 1971, was the program's most notable player. His NHL career included four seasons with the Boston Bruins and two with the Washington Capitals.

Bernie Cieplicki sent me a card in a red envelope shortly after my arrival. I hadn't communicated with him since my years at Rice. The heading on the card said, "Good luck In Your New Venture," and inside it read, "May the future hold the fulfillment of your greatest hopes and dreams." Bernie wrote underneath, "Gary, though this is not an entirely new venture, it is a little different from your first coaching responsibility at Rice. Best of luck, Bernie Cieplicki."

As I mentioned, Bernie was the no-nonsense assistant principal and basketball coach who said, "What would you do if you had a game?" after I missed a meeting due to a car problem. I didn't deal with him much at Rice, which made hearing from him a surprise. His question had stuck with me ever since, however. I often responded similarly when players gave me excuses about missing or being late to required functions. So perhaps it was fitting he referred to my position at Rice as a "coaching responsibility." After all, "responsibility" seemed to be the crux of his question. He implied I had to make every effort to attend the meeting and, by extension, needed to demand the same degree of responsibility and commitment from my players.

Bernie's thoughtfulness was appreciated. Unfortunately, I didn't return favor and write back to acknowledge his kind words and perhaps tell him how his question still resonated with me. The card did not have a return address, so when I received it, I was busy with my new job and hardly made an effort to respond. Then I forgot about it until discovering the card recently in a box of old letters when researching this book. I wish I had sent him a note back. But it's too late now. He died in 1999. His basketball legacy lives on through his sons, who are college coaches, and his grandchildren. He even touched a hockey coach along the way.

Lincoln Flagg preceded me at AIC, and I wanted to respect his coaching efforts. Newly hired coaches often arrive like they're the new sheriff in town, which is OK, but sometimes their boastfulness undermines the previous coach. Statements such as, "I'm going to instill real discipline in this program," and "We're changing the culture around here," can be implied to criticize the former coach and, at the same time, boost the ego of the new hire. It sets the new coach up to be sort of a savior, to receive full credit for rescuing a program. The irony is that when those coaches eventually move on, the next coach often comes in and implies the same thing about them. Self-confidence and ambition are fine qualities, but they should be tempered to respect the other person. When I got to AIC, I tried to subscribe to the expression "Don't come to town to be a big deal, but to do big things."

I often met with Bob Burke at the beginning. We went over budgets, scheduling, scholarships, myriad Division II rules, and such. The program had eight athletic scholarships, which were divided up between fifteen players on the twenty-five-man roster. I had two and a half scholarships to work with for the upcoming season. My job going forward was to divvy them up as I preferred, though the returning players were grandfathered. Managing the scholarship funds to ensure the best players had the bigger scholarships, and making sure we didn't make recruiting mistakes that resulted in scholarship offers to unworthy players, would be paramount.

Bob told me a top returning player had written asking for more scholarship money. He said he'd take care of it since the kid contacted him before I was hired. "Maybe you should tell him no since he's already here and we need the money to get more players," I said. Bob waggled his index finger in the air and said, "A bird in hand is worth two in the bush." Seeing my puzzled look, he told me it meant we should make sure to keep a good player, because there's no guarantee we can go out and get a better player. It was the first of many truisms he uttered during the twenty years I worked for him.

Only one recruit had committed, Paul Ventre, a defenseman from Saugus, Massachusetts, who later referred to himself as my "first inherited recruit." With barely ten weeks until school started, I had to find players in a hurry. I made recruiting calls during the day, while also doing housing work, and made more calls at night. I also phoned high school, prep, and junior coaches looking for leads. I called mostly from my office in those landline-only days, so I had to dial the archaic AIC switchboard every time I made a long-distance call. The operator didn't always answer right away, and other times no one showed up to work. Plus, the switchboard closed at 9 p.m.

I did have a favorite operator, though. Her name was Brenda Cremonti. We only met a few times, but we certainly got to know the sound of each other's voices, and she often called at 8:55 p.m. to give me a convenient "last call" warning. I suppose you could say she was our version of Sarah, the telephone operator on the iconic *Andy Griffin Show* in the 1960s. Andy and his bumbling deputy sheriff, Barney Fife, often referred to Sarah when they used the phone, but she was never seen. Brenda worked the switchboard alone at night, and she didn't know much about hockey, yet for several years we partnered up to make hundreds of recruiting calls. It takes a lot of fine people behind the scenes to run a college hockey team.

My calls included some of the returnees, such as Mark Peloquin, a defenseman, who played for Gary Dineen in the Springfield Junior Pics program. We talked initially about how his summer was going, and I inquired about local players that might be candidates for AIC. Then, rather pointedly, I said, "Mark, I noticed on the stat sheet that you led the team in penalties."

"Uh, yes, that could have been," he said. "Well, you'll have to get those minutes down," I said. He told me he'd work on it. Then I switched to a lighter subject. I didn't want my first call to be too confrontational, but it might have been a little late for that.

I also sent a letter to the returning team members. Here is the slightly edited version:

July 2, 1984

Dear Team Member,

Now that you've been notified of my selection as your new hockey coach, I am contacting you to formally introduce myself. Let me begin by saying I'm extremely excited about being appointed to the position. I feel we have the potential to have an outstanding hockey program at AIC, and I'm committed to making us the best team we can possibly be. Obviously, the same level of commitment is expected from each of you.

In the following paragraphs, I have outlined some areas that should provide insight into how the program will be conducted. We will discuss this further next fall, but for now you'll get an indication of what to expect during the upcoming season.

Academics: How you do in school is a big concern of mine. Your objective as a student-athlete is to excel both academically and athletically, and success in each of these areas can only be accomplished through discipline and hard work. Team members in academic difficulty will be required to attend an evening study hall along with the freshmen.

Penalties: I've been informed that last year's team took far too many penalties, and after reviewing the stats, I am inclined to agree with that assessment. This coming season our penalty minutes must be half of what they were last year. Enough said.

Practices: Our practices will include both team play and individual skill development. The sessions will be challenging and diversified. We'll perform traditional drills, as well as drills that will be new to you. Practices will be conducted in an organized manner, and everyone must give their best effort at all times.

System of Play: We plan to stress a disciplined, team-oriented system with an emphasis on defense. We will be a hard-nosed, tight-checking team that forechecks aggressively and backchecks hard. Our offense will incorporate some of the European concepts, with a focus on moving the puck quickly and attacking the opponent's net aggressively. Considerable time will be spent working on the power play and penalty kill.

Some Expectations: We want players who have strong character. You'll be expected to represent our team admirably, both on and off the ice. Trouble in the dorms, cutting classes, "chippiness" on the ice, and abuse of others in any manner won't be tolerated. We want a team the athletic department and college can be proud of, and we hope to feel a sense of pride in ourselves.

I'll send out an off-ice conditioning program soon. In the meantime, each of you should be working out regularly. Your workouts should include weight training. If you aren't committed in this area, you are hurting your potential as a player, and you are hurting the team, so please start working out immediately.

Again, I am excited to be the new hockey coach at AIC. Next season is going to be an awful lot of fun, and if we can all pull together and work hard, we'll have a good shot at a successful season. Surely the playoffs are within reach. It all depends on how bad we want it.

Sincerely yours,
Gary Wright

I sent a questionnaire along with the letter, asking our players about their summer conditioning, suggestions for improving the program, their personal and team goals, and what they liked most about AIC hockey. Their responses indicated that team discipline, better equipment, and having a locker room at the rink were chief concerns. I heard that my correspondence caught their attention. Matt Schimenti, who owns a highly successful construction

company in the New York City area and is a trustee at AIC, was one of the
players who received my letter. Years later, in a speech to AIC students, he
referred to it as "The Letter."

Off-ice conditioning wasn't my area of expertise, but at Maine our team
was involved in a strength and conditioning program with Dr. Joe Pechinski,
the director of the university's Human Performance Center, and I had
learned from that. Plus, more and more information had been coming out
on hockey fitness. Interestingly, the letter accompanying the off-ice program
Herb Brooks sent out to his 1980 team included this quote: "Many have the
will to win, but few have the will to prepare themselves to win."

My parents gave me a book, *Lloyd Percival's Total Conditioning for Hockey*,
which was co-published by Paul Eriksson, a friend of theirs in Vermont.
Joe Taylor, a colleague of Percival, completed the book after his death.
Percival also included conditioning information in *The Hockey Handbook*.
Unfortunately, he wasn't taken seriously by many NHL coaches and other
North American hockey experts in the years before the 1972 Summit Series.
That began to change when the Russians proved their worth against the
NHL's elite. The Russians and their famous coach, Anatoly Tarasov, had long
considered *The Hockey Handbook* as their hockey bible.

I read and reread my father's copy of *The Hockey Handbook* as a kid. The
book was full of fascinating information on the game, including a short
poem that I memorized:

> *When I was young and in my prime*
> *I used to backcheck all the time*
> *But now that I am old and gray*
> *I only backcheck once per day.*

I pointed to my graying hair when reciting those lines to my AIC teams
in later years, telling them that none of them were old and gray like me and,
therefore, they had no excuse but to get their butts back on the backcheck.

The off-ice conditioning program was sent to our players in July. It ended
up being nearly fifty pages long. I may have gotten a little carried away
constructing such a lengthy program, but I was so pumped up about my new
job, I might just as well have paraded around campus every day while holding
a hockey stick skyward.

I left to spend a few days at our camp on Lake Dunmore, along with a week at the Vermont Hockey School (VHS). It was my eighth straight summer instructing there and I loved working with the staff. Ted Castle, one of the directors, spent eight years as a college coach and once at the VHS he, Wendall "Wendy" Forbes, the veteran head coach at Middlebury College, and I sat in the coach's locker room when Ted asked Wendy about his incoming recruits.

"We've got a great class," Wendy said.

"Who are some of the guys you've got," Ted asked.

"Well," Wendy said, "I can't remember their names right now, but we've landed some good ones."

Jim Cross and Jack Semler also worked at the VHS. We were each assigned about fifteen kids, who received an evaluation form from us that included comments about their skating, passing, shooting, and other fundamentals. Our comments were mostly positive and pleasantly constructive. But writing them felt like a homework assignment. Cross secretly slipped half of his unwritten forms in with Semler's assigned evaluations one time. Jack shook his head afterward, surprised that he had to fill out more evaluations than usual.

Coach Cross stood still against the boards during a session, his back to the stands. He held his arms and hands tight to his torso and his upper body pressed up against the glass. "I've found the perfect spot on the ice," he said. "No parent can see me."

I returned from Vermont shortly before school started. Frank Zanetti had another year as the graduate assistant coach, but when I explained the level of commitment expected of him, which far exceeded his responsibilities from the previous year, he decided to resign from the position. I appreciated his frankness (pun intended). He played for AIC, as did his uncle, Fred Zanetti, who skated for the college's first team. Frank, like his uncle, was very loyal to his alma mater, and I don't think he wanted to commit to something he couldn't follow through on.

Mrs. C posted an assistant coach opening after Frank left, and the quality of respondents wasn't great. The lateness of the posting and relative obscurity of the program likely contributed to the lack of interest. I interviewed a couple of applicants among the twenty or so who applied, and none of them appeared to be the right fit. In the end, I decided not to hire anyone and wait until the next year, as opposed to being stuck with the wrong person. In the big picture it turned out to be the right decision, but going it alone in my first season as a college head coach would prove to be a challenge.

Four recruits committed to AIC, but I wanted five or six. The team needed an infusion of talent on the ice, and with ten seniors on the current roster, a bigger recruiting class would have helped to even off the classes. It also meant I had to replace the seniors by myself, since I had no assistant.

The recruits committed to AIC were Paul Ventre, who played for former AIC grad and three-sport athlete Chris Serino at Saugus HS, near Boston; Bill Gutenberg, a forward from Michigan; John Byberg, a defenseman from Ontario; and Pat Forte, a forward from Minnesota.

I watched Byberg play when I was at Maine. I ran into Mike Addesa at Hockey Night in Boston, and he recommended Gutenberg. Bill Kangas, a fellow UVM alum and a new assistant there, put me on to Pat Forte. They were both from Eveleth, Minnesota, where Pat led the Iron Range in scoring as a junior, before his degenerative knee problems caused Division I schools to back off.

I learned to multitask at Maine with my dual roles as hockey assistant and rink manager. That experience helped get me through the first summer at AIC, with an even bigger learning curve as a head coach and housing director. In a few days, though, school would start, with resident assistants coming back for RA training, new students beginning orientation, old students moving back into the dorms, and the team returning, including new recruits. The first practice would be October 15 at midnight, but with everything I had going on, it seemed a long way away.

Chapter 7

Sprouting at Smead

My office phone jangled shortly before school opening events began. It was Mark Fitzpatrick calling to say he couldn't make our introductory team meeting the following week. I had been tipped off that Mark, a fast-talking senior, generally missed the first week of school, so his request didn't blindside me.

"Mark," I said, "everyone was told three weeks ago about the meeting, and with classes starting, you are expected to be on campus anyway.

"Coach, I just can't see how I can make it," he pleaded. "You'll be at the meeting if you want to play hockey," I said. And our brief conservation ended.

When I conducted residence assistant training, RA Cheryl Wortman told me I should check out her little brother Kevin; eventually I did, and lo and behold he became the best player I ever recruited.

During the RA workshops, I leaned on my coaching, rink managing, and camp directing experiences. Those are all leadership positions requiring strong organizational skills and the ability to work with people, attributes necessary to being an effective RA. One of my messages to them was that like a team captain, they'd be dealing with their peers, which requires courage and a mature approach. I stressed that the RA title is universally recognized as a position of responsibility, so it's a nice thing to list on a résumé. That is, if the person does a good job. Employers can always make reference checks.

The new students arrived soon afterward for orientation, and then the returning students moved into the dorms. The housing office got hectic during those long days, and the late-night noises of loud college students penetrated my Magna apartment.

I opened our first team meeting by saying it was nice to finally talk some hockey. All the recruits and returnees came to the meeting. Even Mark Fitzpatrick showed up. I stood up front, facing unfamiliar faces, while glancing at notes. The players stared back from desk chairs as I talked. Surely they were sizing up the new coach. My mouth was desert dry from first-meeting nerves, but I was prepared and soon I spoke forcefully about the upcoming season. I reiterated parts of my initial letter, announced that off-ice training started soon, and discussed study-hall schedules. Near the end, I emphasized Mr. Burke's success in eliminating the position's part-time status, which meant they'd get a full-time effort from me. After pausing, I said, "I can't wait for the season to start, and you should all feel the same way."

We hit the ice October 15, 1984. Players were split into two teams, and 4-on-4 scrimmages lasted for two days. A whistle blew every forty seconds and they changed on the fly. Fewer players on the ice allowed for more puck "touches" per person, which helped my evaluation from the stands. After all, I had seen none of the returnees play and only a couple of the recruits. This was essentially a tryout period, though there weren't many walk-on candidates.

Twenty-five players made the team. Two walk-ons, one of them a goalie, were added to the roster, and I cut two veteran players. I limited my criteria for cutting returning players to individuals with attitude or discipline problems. Otherwise, I wanted to honor the commitment AIC had made to recruited players and vice versa. I believed we were in the graduation business, and if I or someone else made a mistake concerning a player's ability, that wasn't the kid's fault. I realized that not all coaches felt the same way, but I held true to that philosophy throughout my career at AIC.

There was only one problem. I didn't have a lot of information on those two players, and I may have been too eager to send a message that I'd run a tight ship. A person close to the team had misgivings about Barry Smith, one of the two individuals, so that was a factor. Barry's high penalty minutes also concerned me, but they weren't a deal breaker. In the years ahead, I learned more about him, which led to doubts about my decision, but at the time I was comfortable with it.

I met with the team in the locker room before the start of our first practice at Smead Arena, a state-owned public rink, located a half mile from the Butova Gymnasium. Our players dressed in the gym and put their skates on at the rink. The arrangement didn't feel much like college hockey. The meeting covered, among other things, that each player would receive one roll of tape per week, that the garter belts and cups still hadn't come in (late-arriving cups isn't good), and that slamming sticks or firing pucks in anger wouldn't be tolerated. I announced that due to class conflicts on Tuesday and Thursday afternoons, "we're moving those practices to 5:30 a.m., which is a little early, but the good news is we'll have everyone there." I could hear a few muted moans, but it didn't bother me. Winning hockey is never easy.

The practice kicked off with a Marc Nelson power skating exercise I learned at the VHS. The session included a partner passing sequence, 2-on-0s utilizing one, then two pucks, alternating 3-on-1s, and a Ted Castle pass-and-replace drill at both ends, where the final receiver navigates three cones before shooting. Two flow drills and a conditioning skate wrapped up the practice. I know this is what we did because I've saved almost 2,500 practices in five large notebooks. The simplicity of that session is a reflection of it being our opening practice, which emphasized the fundamentals. It is also a product of a time when drills weren't as advanced as they are now.

Coaching without an assistant was hard. I did all the recruiting myself, and changed the forwards and defense during games. I had a little help at practice. Forward Steve Hunter and defenseman Joe Nicholson served as co-captains, and whenever we did F/D splits, one of them ran the other end. When I worked with the defensemen, Steve oversaw the forwards and also participated in their drills. It was the other way around when I took the forwards. We'd meet prior to practice to discuss their assignments. The situation wasn't ideal, but we made it work.

Joe became a Vermont state trooper after graduation. (Thankfully, he never pulled me over for speeding.) Prior to his hiring, one of their representatives called and asked a lot of questions about Joe.

"If a referee calls a penalty on him, does he argue the call or go straight to the penalty box?" he asked at one point.

I told him that Joe's never mouthy. "He goes right to the box," I said, "because he respects the ref's authority and he's a team player who knows we don't allow conduct like that."

It was a great question and I assume the caller thought that if Joe lost his cool when receiving a penalty, he might also overreact to the complaints of a ticketed motorist.

I found the proverb "It's lonely at the top" certainly applied to coaching alone. The biggest thing was not having someone to bounce ideas off. I made lineup changes, made recruiting decisions, and dealt with player issues without input from assistants. Assistants can also act as a sounding board for team members, and they can lend support to coaching policies that players disagree with. During games there wasn't another pair of eyes to point out guys who were playing poorly, or to make suggestions to counter an opponent's tactics. I was always by myself—on the bench, on the blades, on the bus. Moreover, I didn't have a staff to commiserate with after a bad loss, or to celebrate with after a big win.

We finished the season with a 16–15 record. A few victories against lower North/South Division teams padded our record before I started strengthening our future schedule. Still, we had nice wins against Salem State, New England College, and Middlebury. I appreciated coach Wendy Forbes's graciousness when he stopped by our locker room after the game. In addition to the VHS, I knew him from my Middlebury connection, and he and my father were friends.

Among the sparse crowds at our home games were a dozen AIC cheerleaders, replete with uniforms and pom-poms. One time I complained to my father that college hockey doesn't really involve cheerleaders.

"I don't see a lot of people at your games," he said, "and now you want to remove a group of enthusiastic students making lots of noise?" The cheerleaders stayed.

We lost in overtime to Westfield State, our crosstown rival, whose top player was future NHL coach Peter Laviolette. The 9–8 loss to Westfield stung. Pucks poured into both nets—but one more into ours. Don Moorhouse was our backup goalie and Larry O'Donnell played a similar role for Westfield. Both of them joined my staff following graduation. When I asked Larry years after if he played in the game, he said, "Giving up eight goals sounds like me." Then he remembered he spent the night on the bench. So did Don. Maybe it's just as well they didn't play; otherwise the score might have been even higher!

New coaches often talk about recruiting their own players. This refers to bringing in better and more dedicated players who can fit into the coach's particular style of play. I inherited the team, but they felt like my own; they behaved themselves on campus and on the ice. I was the seniors' third coach at AIC and yet they still bought in to the program. Jeff Long and Lee Gross were successive student government presidents, which was impressive. (Lee came from Los Angeles and fancied himself "recruited" after receiving a hockey form letter.) My upcoming teams would be more talented and include greater numbers of dedicated players, but I have fond memories of my first team.

During the summer, I worked another session at VHS. I stayed with Donald in his home near the downtown area; he had remained in Burlington after graduating from UVM. I often walked to the bars at night to meet up with VHS staff members or other old friends. That summer I was out drinking—and drinking a lot—for most of my ten nights in Burlington. I did sober up by spending an in-between weekend at Lake Dunmore. But it hardly made up for the beers I practically chug-a-lugged on the other nights.

I woke up with a hazy hangover during the second week. Squinting at the clock, I shouted "No!" and frantically got dressed. I ran into Leddy Park Arena soon after and saw thirty kids and three instructors on the ice. One instructor was missing—me. Not good.

"Hi Gary," Neddie Grant, a former UVM player, said (a little loud) from the ice.

"Sorry about this," I said back, as I ducked into the coaches' room. The other instructors gave me a ribbing when I slithered onto the ice in my unzipped sweat top and half-tied skates. I was twenty minutes tardy and still feeling a touch tipsy.

Driving back to Springfield, I reflected more on my drinking habits and how they impacted my life. I didn't tolerate tardiness from my players, so the embarrassment of arriving late to the VHS practice hit home, especially since it involved alcohol. I didn't consider myself an alcoholic, but I was a big social drinker and had been suspended once for drinking in prep school. I drank a lot during my Sigma Nu days and after playing softball. I loved going out after hockey games. Mostly I celebrated with a few beers after wins, but I wasn't averse to the "win or lose, hit the booze" philosophy. When the party ended or the bars closed, I'd lead the charge to continue imbibing elsewhere. "Let's have one more" seemed to be my mantra.

I often got up after a night of heavy drinking and told myself I needed to stop. That time I did. The two-week session at the VHS in Burlington was the last straw. I quit without help, and it wasn't as hard as I'd thought, though I know many people need support with their drinking habits and alcoholism. We are all different and I wasn't an every-day drinker or collapsed on skid row, but I did drink a lot, and I occasionally experienced blackouts. So maybe I was some kind of alcoholic.

I haven't had a drink since that summer. (In *Leave No Doubt*, by NHL coach Mike Babcock, he wrote that in his younger days his mother said, "You know, Michael, at some point your beer-commercial lifestyle is going to have to come to an end.") When I'm in a drinking setting, I'll go with non-alcoholic O'Doul's. I do miss sharing alcoholic beverages with others, but O'Doul's is a tolerable substitute. If I'm having a really good time, I'll consume several of them, often at the same rate I used to drink alcohol. I may have to pee more, but I don't have to deal with hangovers, health issues. or the bad behavior that can accompany heavy drinking. And I'm never late on the ice.

We improved over the next two seasons, although our sub-.500 records didn't indicate it. For one thing, we upgraded the schedule by adding Colby, Hamilton, Union, and RIT, the defending national champions. The RIT game took place at Smead Arena on Super Bowl Sunday. It was a matinee game and started twenty minutes late. Bruce Delventhal, their coach, wasn't happy about it. RIT had a rink on campus and opposing coaches with their own facility didn't always realize the challenges faced by those of us without rinks. RIT won 15–3. (Note: "15" isn't a typo.) The next day, the mortifying score appeared in the sports section of the *Boston Globe*, my favorite newspaper. The final tally underscored the vast divide between us and the national champions. And to think I was initially thrilled to schedule RIT.

Union came to Springfield on a Tuesday night, and I benched Jeff Arnold and Brian Salamon, two of our top forwards. They each received double minors for an altercation they initiated in front of our net, as a result of a Union player slashing goaltender Doug Salamon. The Union player deserved a minor penalty, but I felt our guys overreacted and hurt us with their infractions, so they sat for the rest of the game. Doug Salamon argued between periods that his brother Brian and Jeff shouldn't be benched, thus he suffered a similar fate. Following the game, Jeff's mother complained that she only got to watch her son play part of the contest after driving all the way from Philadelphia.

I left the rink and drove straight home. I now lived in a small campus house, reserved for the housing director. I collapsed on the couch, staring at things I did not see, my mind fixed on the game's nightmarish events: benching two first liners, sitting my starting goalie, brushing by angry parents. The 7–0 blowout loss seemed like an afterthought. I worried about how those events would affect us going forward, and what to do about Doug. At the game, I dispensed tough discipline, but I felt alone and vulnerable when I got home. I didn't know it at the time, but my worries weren't over.

Doug skipped our next practice. That, combined with the incident in the locker room, was too much for me to take, and I dismissed him from the team. The *Springfield Union-News* ran an article by Fran Sypek, headlined, "Tiff with Coach Costs AIC Goalie His Job." The opening sentence read, "Doug Salamon spoke up for what he thought was right and that's why he's no longer on the AIC hockey team." He claimed that he didn't show up to our next practice because "I was mad over what happened. I didn't think Brian and Jeff deserved to be benched for helping me."

The article contained a few quotes from me including the following: "He challenged my authority. The locker room was not a place for it. That is something that should take place behind closed doors." Sypek wrote that I "grudgingly believed afterward" that I was left with no choice but to dismiss Doug from the team. That's exactly how I felt. I also believed Doug's priorities were with baseball, where he served as captain. Jeff and Brian both remained with our team and graduated as members of the coveted 100 Point Club.

The fallout from the Union game fiasco persisted when Bob Burke met with me about the *Union-News* article. He said that AIC President Harry Courniotes wasn't happy about the article because it reflected unfavorably on the college and the hockey program. Apparently he thought the tenor of the article had a tabloid-like feel to it, which it probably did. Bob didn't seem overly concerned about it himself, but he agreed with the president that saying "less is best," as opposed to vigorously defending my actions. I don't recollect too much else from our discussion, but I surely didn't want the president mad at me.

We brought in a goaltender named Bryon Lewis at the start of the second semester to replace Salamon. He had played for DG Weaver at Milton High School in Vermont. DG spent a year as a third goalie at UVM, and I had known him since college. Bryon played well in nine games for us, and as a BMX rider who also performed bike tricks, he developed a following of neighborhood kids.

Things didn't work out as well for Pat Forte. He started his freshman season out of the lineup due to his rare knee disorder, and then got cleared to play. His knees worsened after that and he dressed for five games at the start of his sophomore season, before doctors deemed his career over. He had several surgeries in the upcoming years and never played again. Pat was a tremendous person and teammate, so we were all sad when he left school at the end of the semester. He also had good parents. He experienced some homesickness during his freshman year and his mother, Marjorie, advised him to stay and "sprout where you are planted."

I hired Jon Straffon as my first assistant and Larry O'Donnell came aboard the following season. Jon played at Kent State before they dropped hockey and was hired as my graduate assistant (GA), the only available compensated position. There was no stipend, but he received room and board, tuition and fees, and books. The living arrangement for GAs amounted to a meal ticket at the college's dining commons and a single room in an undergraduate dormitory. The GAs coached in the hockey program during the two years it took to complete a master's degree.

I appointed Larry as the head resident of Hines Hall, where he lived in an apartment. He was paid a stipend out of the housing budget, which allowed us to hire a second coach, meaning he worked for me in housing and hockey. Before playing at Westfield State, he attended Mount St. Charles Academy in Rhode Island. The powerful Mounties once won twenty-six consecutive state titles. John Dunham, the Trinity hockey coach, and Herb Hammond, the bench boss at Brown, both recommended Larry to me. They knew him from hockey schools. Larry showed up for his interview wearing a pair of gaudy red pants. "Do you think you can work with me?" he asked at the end of our meeting. I gave him a vague answer, as I wasn't sure if I could.

In addition to adding two assistants and fortifying the schedule, we made other improvements. Nancy Heavey, an AIC student, led our team in an innovative aerobics program. Some players initially complained about aerobics being a "sissy" activity, but their tunes changed when Nancy ran the sessions with perpetual pep—as they whined and wilted. We met the same sort of moderate resistance later when we started doing yoga and working with sports psychologists. The sport of hockey has evolved, and players need to be accepting of new ideas and strategies to enhance the game and improve player performance.

We also upgraded our hockey equipment. I was surprised when I saw the condition of our gear. It was mostly old or of poor quality, and the game jerseys were unsightly. The Old English-styled "AIC" ran vertically on the left front of the jersey, leaving the right side blank. When Shawn Navin transferred in during the second semester of my first season, we had no hockey pants to give him, so he wore a mismatched pair during his red-shirt year. By the next season, we had black pants for everyone, and a year later Reggie Snow, from Mills & Greer, designed us a classy game jersey. The pants and other equipment were ordered through Gateway Hardware, a one-of-a-kind store in Springfield that carries mostly hockey equipment, but shoppers can also purchase lottery tickets, stamps, and rat poison. Owner Tom McCarthy and his staff know hockey equipment like few others.

After wearing our equipment in and out of Smead like a pack of peewees, we finally got our own locker room. The rink manager and the higher-ups of the state-owned facility allowed us to convert an old incinerator room into a locker room. I believe the incinerator serviced the entire Blunt Park complex, which included Smead Arena, back in the 1960s and early '70s before that form of burning was banned. The apparatus weighed over ten tons and AIC—which meant me—had to have it removed. First I made countless calls to determine if the incinerator contained asbestos. It was like trying to find out if there are maple trees on Mars, but it turned out to be asbestos free, and the incinerator was removed by a local concrete-cutting company, curiously called Witch Enterprises.

The Alumni Varsity Club and others donated to the locker room. Matt Schimenti's father owned Schimenti Construction and provided the ceiling. Matt, who worked for his dad, installed it with his teammates. The narrow room was newly painted and carpeted in school colors and it gave us a much needed home in Smead Arena. There were a couple of drawbacks in that there was no toilet or shower close by. Some guys showered in the locker rooms at the other end of the building, but most waited until they got home. Also, our players peed in a bottle during games rather than walk through the main lobby to get to the nearest bathroom. However, those inconveniences no longer mattered: we had our own locker room. It raised the stature of our program and we even held our heads a little higher.

Two-time captain Mark Peloquin helped Matt construct the locker room. However, after Mark and I originally spoke on the phone, he started acting up again, so I suspended him for a week. I told him to let me know next

Monday "if you're ready to play the AIC way." Mark was waiting when I entered the rink a week later. He told me that he'd thought things over and would cut down on penalties, so I said I'd see him on the ice. Mark held himself accountable for his suspension. He didn't bitch or mope. Later, he provided strong leadership as a captain. Soon after moving into the new locker room his senior year, we played our home opener against Salem State. Mark, who wasn't a scorer, had the winner in overtime, and the Yellow Jackets swarmed onto the ice to embrace their elated captain.

Jeff Arnold, a married man, continued his impressive point production as a senior. A high-heel kick slowed his stride, but he still got around OK and, besides, he could score from anywhere. He, Edgar Alejandro, and Tom Mullen, whose brothers Joe and Brian were former NHL players, are the only AIC players to complete their careers with over two hundred points. We occasionally practiced at night, and one time as midnight approached, Larry lumbered over to me and said, "Jeff just told me he needs to leave because his babysitter has to be home soon." We let Jeff go, and ended practice soon after. I thought he had a pretty good excuse.

Bob Burke told me that he was pleased with the program's progress. He also said he thought it would take a couple more years before we started to win consistently. He may have made that statement to take some pressure off me. I appreciated his support, but I couldn't imagine waiting that long to start winning.

Neither Bob nor our staff knew how good our incoming recruits would become, but with three of us, we started to recruit better. I sent Jon and Larry out on the road constantly, and we pounded the phones at night. Jon had a nicer car, but Larry and I owned a couple of beaters. If we didn't have a Wednesday or Saturday game, we often drove ninety miles to the Boston area to watch parts of two or three games each. For instance, I'd go to a high school game at 2 p.m., and then head to a prep contest at four o'clock, followed by a Catholic Conference tilt in the evening. Larry or Jon sometimes joined me to focus on a particular recruit. It made for a long day on the road and in the rinks. We survived on snack-bar fare between periods and games. The unheated rinks led to a case of what Ted Castle called "recruiter's chill."

We entered my fourth season with heightened hopes. We had some good returnees and our freshmen projected to be AIC's best recruiting class ever. In a press release titled "10 Recruits Join Ice Squad," I said:

Our objective was to sign impact players who possess the necessary mental and physical toughness to make an immediate contribution to AIC Hockey. We believe we have done that. These individuals will play a major role in whatever success we're able to achieve.

And then we lost our first four games. It wasn't what we needed coming off two losing seasons. There's an expression, "You can't win if you don't win," which speaks to how winning instills confidence in a team, and you often hear coaches talk about "learning how to win." Well, one way to learn how to win is to win—and we hadn't done much of that at AIC. I felt a dash of doubt myself, but I also knew it was early, so we took Sunday off, practiced briskly on Monday, and beat a good UMass Boston team on Tuesday. We were a relieved bunch of coaches and players on the bus ride home. The box lunches never tasted better.

Six weeks later, Jerry Radding, a sportswriter at the *Springfield Union-News*, and an AIC alumnus, wrote an article headlined: "AIC Skaters Recover Quite Nicely from 0-4 Ice Start." It explained how we went on an 8–2 run once we got on the "winning side with victories over UMass Boston (10–5) and Quinnipiac (8–2)." (After the second period, Quinnipiac coach Jim Armstrong asked about playing running time in the third. He looked distraught, so I agreed to it, as did the refs. I never saw anything like it again, though there were times I would've liked to ask for running time myself.) In the article I said, "We expected to do well this year, but I can't say we had total confidence because of the past." That past, as the article discussed, amounted to "ten years since a hockey team from AIC has made the playoffs."

The write-up also mentioned the play of Vezio Sacratini, a freshman from LaSalle, Quebec, who centered our first line. Vezio already had thirty-five points at the semester break. His grandmother, Clementina Sacratini, got off the boat from Italy and never learned another language, so when I called and asked for Vezio during the recruiting process, she would shout something in Italian if he wasn't home, and then hang up the phone.

I ran into Brian Durocher, a former Boston University goalie, at a prep school Christmas Tournament. He had read the article while spending the night with his parents in nearby Longmeadow. It would have been interesting reading to Brian, who started as a part-time assistant at AIC. Like many young coaches hoping for a career in college coaching, he worked long hours for poor pay. He also worked at a lot of places. After AIC, he assisted his old coach, Jack Parker, as a part-timer at BU, and then made full-time stops at Colgate and Brown prior to returning to BU as a full-time assistant and associate head coach. That led to his appointment as head coach of the BU women's hockey program. Brian has an easygoing personality, which has benefited him on both the men's and women's side, unlike his great-uncle, Leo Durocher, a baseball Hall of Famer, whose volcanic temperament earned him the nickname "Leo the Lip."

Even though we were making progress on the ice, I worried about player retention. Numerous recruits came and left in my first few seasons. There were different reasons, such as our location, a lack of modern athletic facilities, and the condition of some of the dorms. But I found the main culprit was my recruiting practices. In short, we brought in some marginal students and others who weren't committed hockey players. We needed to stock our roster with guys who loved the game, players who wanted to play college hockey badly. Anatoly Tarasov once said, "You must love the game to be a good hockey player." We needed more guys like that.

So we recruited the person as well as the player, student-athletes who'd strive to excel in the classroom and on the ice. And if someone wasn't a great student, he had to at least be a serious student, or focused on getting a degree. Along with Larry O'Donnell and our new assistants Rory McAdam and former goalie Don Moorhouse, we started conducting more thorough background checks. Instead of just talking to the recruit's coach, we also checked with one of his previous coaches. I took fewer risks on kids with attitude or academic issues. And we consulted with our players after they hosted recruits. If they weren't comfortable with the visiting recruit, we didn't take him. Those strategies and others started to pay off. All but two of the large freshman class that began my fourth season ended up graduating from AIC.

We didn't worry about Mike Bieniek's academics. He was a dean's list computer science major and a prolific scorer. In a *Union-News* article titled "Jackets' Bieniek On Line," a nod to his prowess as a forward and a computer major, he allowed: "Yeah, I'm probably faster on the computer than I am on ice. They used to call me the computer jockey." He skated for Jeff Jackson on the St. Claire Shore's Falcons, a junior team near Detroit, before Jeff started a notable career at Lake Superior State and Notre Dame. He sent me a detailed letter describing Mike and two of his teammates we were recruiting. I was a lowly first-year Division II/III coach from out East, and we'd only met once when Jeff sent the letter. Maybe that's why he's been so successful.

Our second semester began with a 2–1 home win over Hamilton. The game featured great goaltending from our guy, Mark Buckley, and the Continentals' Guy Hebert, who played eleven seasons in the NHL. Our newfound success was attracting more fans. It helped that Hub Burton and Scott Coen from Channel 40, a local TV station, started covering us with game highlights and live interviews. Mrs. C even got into the act. She organized hospitality rooms for the period breaks and sent out campus flyers announcing our games. In one of them, she wrote:

> We'd like to see you at the rink to support our very exciting team. I caught the hockey fever—I know you will too (extremely contagious). I guarantee you this Saturday night won't be the loneliest night of the week.

We finished the regular season 21–9, and 16–8 in league play, placing us sixth in the ECAC East. We bused to Brunswick, Maine to play No. 3 seed Bowdoin in the quarterfinals of the single-elimination tourney. The game was played in front of 2,200 fans at venerable Dayton Arena. Two goals by freshman Ken Maffia and another by defenseman Darryl Frenette gave us a 3–1 lead late in the third. With under two minutes left, Bowdoin coach Terry Meagher put together a line of three seniors who hadn't played as a unit all season. It was a last-ditch effort that worked, as Bowdoin responded with two tallies to send the game into sudden-death overtime, and they won it off a scrum in our crease when a near-frozen puck finally got poked in. Coach Meagher called it "one of the most exciting comebacks I've ever witnessed," in Brunswick's *Times Record*. I had a different take. To this day, I consider it one of the most gut-wrenching losses I've ever experienced.

The loss, however, didn't diminish the impressive achievements of our players. We proved we belonged among the league's elite, both by our record and our performance at Bowdoin. In time, the hurt healed and with most of our roster returning, we entered the next season with high expectations. An 8–2 start that included a win over the previous year's 1988 Division III national champions, Wisconsin River Falls, got us off and running. Gord Hahn, one of their players, had left AIC, partly because he didn't care for my coaching, so that amplified the win. One of our early defeats was to the Merrimack Warriors, the defending league champions, but we'd get another crack at them later.

Kevin "Worto" Wortman gave us strong play in the early going. A nineteen-year-old sophomore, he was six feet, 200 pounds; his remarkable foot speed and skating stride, combined with a heavy shot and pro-like skillset, attracted numerous NHL scouts. The trench-coat-attired scouts stood out in the less-than-comfortable confines of Smead Arena, where the lights hummed and the collapsible wooden bleachers wobbled underfoot. But Worto made it worth their trip, especially the efforts of former Cornell head coach and scout Lou Raycroft. Lou worked for the Calgary Flames, who ultimately drafted Kevin in the eighth round. It was a proud moment for Kevin and our hockey program. He eventually played five NHL games with the Flames.

Most of our players didn't skate like Kevin, so Julie Sutphin-Worgull came from Maine to work with us. She's the friend and figure skating instructor who gave me the pep talk when Jack left Maine. Laura Stamm became popular in the 1970s and '80s when she taught power skating to NHL players, and Julie and others followed suit. Julie worked with our whole team together and some guys individually. Rob Dow had some pronation in his stride, so I had her work with him. Rob appreciated Julie's instruction, as opposed to some pros, who Laura Stamm once told me had "too big an ego to work with me."

We hosted Merrimack on a Monday night in mid-February. They went undefeated in the league the year before on their way to becoming ECAC East champions. In an unusual move, Merrimack was awarded an at-large berth in the NCAA Division I tournament, where they won a series with Northeastern and lost a close one to eventual national champion Lake Superior State. (As a D-II school with scholarships, they didn't qualify for the D-III NCAAs.) Merrimack came to Smead with only one league loss, six NHL draft choices, and a commitment to play in Hockey East the next season. As *Springfield Union-News* sports writer Steve Kelly wrote: "There wasn't any room on the marquee for American International College."

But there was room by the end of the game. The *Union-News* headline the next morning read "AIC, Buckley Steal the Show." Buck brick-walled the Warriors with thirty-eight saves, many of them spectacular, and not only gave us a chance to win, which is what every team asks of its goalie, but led us to the 5–2 upset. Kelly mentioned how our students chanted "Warm Up the Bus," and wrapped up his article by writing: "It wouldn't be a comfortable ride back home for Merrimack. But the AIC skaters probably felt like skating down Roosevelt Avenue in a merry romp back to their campus. In a season of many wins, they had just earned the biggest."

The Merrimack victory was part of a 12–1 streak down the stretch to finish the regular season at 23–6. Momentum never assures anything but, combined with our lofty record, it sent us into the post season chock-full of confidence. It also left me with a goaltending dilemma. Mark "Buck" Buckley and Bryon Lewis alternated throughout the season, meaning Bryon was due to start our quarterfinal game with Salem State. Bryon was a good goalie, but I thought Buck gave us a slightly better chance to win. I consulted with Larry, who doubled as our goaltending coach, and decided to go with Buck in the playoffs.

I met with Bryon in my office to explain my decision straightforwardly. These are my main points as best I remember them:

- I want to go with one guy in the playoffs, and after careful thought, I've decided on Buck.

- You and Buck both had strong seasons, so while keeping the rotation may be fairer, this is the playoffs, and Larry and I have Buck slightly ahead of you.

- Buck's recent win against Merrimack and two wins versus Babson are factors.

- It was a difficult decision because not much separates you and Buck. And because I know how hard you work.

- I don't expect you to like the decision. In fact, I don't want you to like it, because I need high-compete guys in net.

- It's important that you support Buck. It's important that you accept my decision.

- You must be ready if we call on you.

Bryon took it like a trouper. Leaders tend to take bad news calmly, and Bryon did just that. He asked good questions and despite being disappointed, showed himself to be one of those guys that gets it. I respected his response. Going forward it became clear that I needn't be concerned about the last two points.

The Salem State game was a classic college hockey contest, with one thousand fans filling Smead Arena to witness the action. Salem started to shadow Vezio Sacratini. It was more pronounced than anything we had experienced before and Vezio became flustered, so I made an off-the-cuff decision and had him and our second-line center, Martin Labonte, switch between the two lines at will. For instance, Vezio could change in the middle of his shift and be replaced by Martin, and then they might switch with each other again halfway through the second line's shift. Basically, when our first two lines were on the ice, they could be skating with either center at any time. The strategy worked, and our two centers were quite creative with their cunning changes.

But the game wasn't going so well. We entered the third period down 3–1, but Buck, despite the Salem players saying, "You'll be getting out the golf clubs after the game," made a bundle of big game saves. With the crowd continuously chanting "A-I-C, A-I-C," we scored twice to tie the game 3–3 and force overtime. Marc Lussier, who had the extra frame winner to beat Babson earlier, did it again when he scored on a breakaway 2:46 into OT to send us to the semifinals. Our fans went hog wild in the stands and several stormed the slippery ice to pig-pile with our players.

Don Moorhouse wrote about the win in *Slapshot*, the "Yellow Jacket Hockey Newsletter," and as an alum he marveled at the boisterous "A-I-C" chants emanating from our student fans. He would eventually broadcast UMass Hockey games and become a music writer for the *Springfield Republican*, previously called the *Union-News*. The last part of his article reads: "I remember the years as a player when the team was struggling. AIC became an acronym for all sorts of derogatory sayings. I would like to set the record straight: AIC stands for American International College, a small liberal arts college with one of the best teams in Division II."

The leaky Smead Arena flat roof dripped water down on our practice shortly before we traveled to Bowdoin for the semifinals. The arena staff positioned buckets around the ice surface to collect the water so it wouldn't freeze into large lumps. I semi-seriously told our players the buckets were also drill enhancers to help keep our heads up in preparation for Bowdoin. "Drill enhancers" are cones, boards, tennis balls, sticks, etc., lying around to further challenge players in a drill. Only this time, the "enhancers" weren't voluntarily placed and they never left the bumpy ice. We had a fairly focused practice considering the obstacles; that was important because hockey players need to keep making strides, even on rough ice.

Bowdoin was the No. 2 seed, and as the No. 3 seed, we had to travel. Larry Mahoney, the Maine Hockey writer, covered the game for the *Bangor Daily News*. Seeing him again was one of the few positives that night. We lost 7–4 to end our season. Our players slumped with blank stares following the game. After a few minutes, I recognized our two seniors and everyone clapped respectfully.

"I'll have more to say later, as I realize this sucks now," I said, "but I want to add one more thing: We made it to the quarterfinals last year, the semis this season, and next year it's the finals or bust, so let's get there and win a championship."

The bus ride back can be among the happiest feelings in hockey—if you win. When you lose, especially if that loss ends your season, the feelings are flipped. Thus, collective disappointment enveloped our bus that night, as it cruised through the moonlit countryside. The loss to Bowdoin wasn't the last-minute shocker we experienced with them the previous year. But it still stung. I kept replaying the game in my mind as I sat up front. Mostly I pondered mistakes we made: Missing open nets. Odd-man rushes against. My bench management miscues. Difficulties dealing with Bowdoin's team speed. Turnovers we made in the neutral zone. An empty-netter that drove up the score.

Despite all this, I couldn't help but think how we'd graduate just two players. Everyone else returned. Merrimack was joining Hockey East. Bowdoin graduated some key seniors. We had gotten better than Babson. As the long night wore on, these positive thoughts pushed aside painful recollections of the game, showing that when you're a coach, even the dismal hours that follow a playoff loss can foster the feeling that hope springs eternal.

Photo courtesy Proctor Academy Archives

A game at Proctor Academy in the 1960s.

Photo courtesy Proctor Academy Archives

*My first year on varsity. I'm second from left (#15) in the back row.
Coach Spencer Wright, my father, is seated up front.*

Photo courtesy Proctor Academy Archives

*With Dad and Donald at the alumni game the year after graduating.
Dad is coaching the alumni team and Donald skated for the varsity.*

*The 1976 UVM team picture. Coach Jim Cross is on the far right of the back row. I'm the first
player on the left in the second row. Fellow seniors Tim O'Connell (left) and Ken Yeates (right)
flank goaltender Tom McNamara in front.*

My first season on the bench at Rice High School.

Photo courtesy AIC Athletics

Celebrating the 1990 ECAC East Championship at Middlebury.

Left to right: Eric Lang and Trevor Large with me and our 2008 seniors at the Olympia. Lang and Large would later coach together at Army West Point before becoming head coaches at AIC and Canisius respectively. Mike Field (fourth from left) later served as my assistant at AIC and went on to become the associate head coach at Arizona State.

Adam Pleskach hustling at the Olympia.

With my parents after a game at Dartmouth.

Photo courtesy AIC Athletics

AIC's Seth Dussault (left) in the booth with Erik Douglas.

Captain Steven Hoshaw representing us in the pregame ceremonial puck drop with his counterpart, Michigan's Andrew Copp, at Yost Arena.

With eight of my former assistant coaches at the American Hockey Coaches Association (AHCA) convention in Naples, Florida, after receiving the John "Snooks" Kelley Founders Award.
(Left to Right) Glenn Stewart, Bobby Ferraris, Joe Exter, Eric Lang, me, Steve Wiedler, Larry O'Donnell, Trevor Large, Mike Towns

Hobey dock-diving for a loose puck (ball) at our camp on Lake Dunmore.

Chapter 8

Chasing a Championship

On August 3, 1989, I finished a letter to our team, made about thirty copies, and mailed it to my players and staff. Here are some excerpts from the letter:

> I have enclosed a copy of our 1989–90 schedule. As you can see, it's a super schedule. We are playing three of the eight Division I Hockey East teams. Merrimack, Lowell and Providence will all be visited by the Yellow Jackets. You gotta love it. . . . In addition to the aforementioned teams we have a great schedule in general. Besides the trip to Alabama-Huntsville, we play our usual rigorous ECAC East slate. It all adds up to what should be one heck of a year.

The letter also mentioned the birth of a child to senior-to-be Brian Walsh and his wife, Charlene. It included an attempt at inside humor:

> It's a pleasure to announce that Brian Walsh has a new son, Brian Jr. We can only assume that "Little Walshie Jr." will be a hockey player and that he'll skate headfirst into the net, just like his old man.

Fortunately for us, when Brian crashed into the net, the puck often went in with him. His roommate-teammate, Mark Cappadona, moved down the hall so his wife and son could visit him. He then added an unusual piece of dorm furniture to the room: a crib.

I'd previously met with Brian concerning his academics. His grades were often on the bubble and he had to take summer classes to stay eligible. During our meeting, he proudly pointed out that his recent grades were mostly Cs, with only a couple of Ds.

"That's good," I said, "but you need to get a few more Bs to offset those Ds."

He paused for several seconds, his pale Irish face twisted in thought, before responding: "Coach, the only 'B' I ever saw stung me."

Scheduling three Hockey East teams was a big deal. Through the years, less and less crossover competition existed between Division I and Division II/III teams, so we felt fortunate to schedule those games. Lowell would be an exhibition game, but the Merrimack and Providence matchups were regular non-conference games. Playing Merrimack worked because we'd been in a league with them for years. Mike McShane, the Providence Friars coach, called about playing and I jumped at the opportunity.

NCAA Division II schools could officially start practice on October 15, which came on a Sunday. We staged our own version of Midnight Madness and hit the ice at 12:01 a.m. to make it legit. Things worked out nicely, because the first practice was essentially held on a Saturday night. The late-night opening lent an air of festiveness to the occasion. That, combined with the usual anticipation associated with a first practice, and the knowledge that we returned a very strong team, made it an exciting time to be a Yellow Jacket. You could say our team buzzed, not from booze, but from the excitement generated by a determined bunch hungry for hockey.

We played our exhibition game at Lowell a week later. Down 7–6 late in the third period, we had ample scoring chances, including Darryl Frenette's point-blanker from the slot. Lowell added an empty-netter soon after to make it 8–6. The early returns were encouraging, though. We made a good account of ourselves against a Hockey East team. During the 1981–82 season when Lowell was a Division II power, they beat AIC by an astounding football-like score of 22–0. I suppose by that measure, our program had come a very long way.

Our next games were scheduled at Alabama-Huntsville (UAH) in two weeks. We only had six practices before playing Lowell, so the extra time to prepare helped. I always wrote up practice plans at home in the evening and went over them the next day with Larry, Don, and our new GA, Alex Smith. Each coach received a shrunk copy of the practice plan that could be taped to a glove. I often gave a heads up the day before the next practice if I needed my assistants to create a new drill to address a team weakness, or if I planned a F/D split. Back on Monday, October 16, at our practice following the Midnight Madness skate, we divided into three stations, hockey-school style, where players rotated every seven minutes. I had guys retrieve a rimmed puck from both corners, roll, and shoot at my end, and Larry ran a quick-hands rapid-fire drill at his. Alex did a body-checking exercise with football dummies in the neutral zone.

Our practice jerseys featured lines of a different color, while the defensemen and goaltenders collectively wore black. Our first line always wore green, and at the start of the season featured Vezio Sacratini centering for Ken Maffia and Peter Morris. I picked green simply because it had remained my favorite color. As I mentioned, it originated when I was a young kid idolizing the green-clad Proctor athletes, particularly the guys wearing skates. Ironically, my first three teams—Proctor, UVM, Rice—all wore green and white. (Catamount colors include gold.) I liked Maine's black and two blues, and the AIC yellow and black, but adding a touch of green at practice felt right.

Alex Smith was once a sports reporter for the Gannett Newspapers in White Plains, New York. I tried to take advantage of my assistant's strengths, so I arranged to have him write a guest column for the student newspaper, the *Yellow Jacket*. An article he wrote about our upcoming trip titled "Hockey in Alabama?" opened with these lines:

> The birds do it, older couples and retired people do it, professional baseball teams do it and now the AIC Yellow Jackets hockey team will do it. What is it you ask? Well, it's a trip south.

And ended with this:

> So move over birds and make room in the old folk homes, and start up spring training because the Yellow Jackets get their season in full swing over the weekend—Southern style.

Alabama-Huntsville is the only NCAA college that sponsors hockey in the south, and they offered a guarantee that paid for our flights and other amenities. Otherwise we couldn't have afforded the trip. They gave guarantees to entice schools to fly down and play them because as an independent they didn't have a stable conference schedule. I sat near the back of the plane with freshman Eric Forselius. He wasn't a big fan of flying (neither was Wayne Gretzky), and he shuddered at takeoffs, landings, and turbulence to the point that his flying fears started to make me jumpy. As the head coach, I tried not to show it.

We tied UAH 6–6 and lost 7–4 in the second contest. A crowd of 2,500 Alabamians watched our Friday night game, and 1,500 fans showed up on Saturday night. During the college football season their Saturday crowds were smaller. Alex wrote that "two of the biggest cheers the second night came when a ref fell down and when they announced that Auburn beat Florida 10–7." (I assume our Friday tie wasn't announced at that game.) The contests took place at the Von Braun Civic Center, named after the famous aerospace engineer. Our team toured Huntsville's U.S. Space & Rocket Center museum on Saturday.

Larry and I engaged in a little "clanging armor" at Friday's game. The refs called a number of penalties and at one point we had a defenseman in the box and another one injured. Moments later, we needed someone to serve a penalty and I, steamed about the penalties, choose one of the Ds.

"No, don't do that, I'm about out of defenseman," Larry said rather loudly, or so I thought.

"Larry, shut the fuck up," I yelled back, as some of our players almost spit out their mouth guards trying not to laugh at my outburst.

The period ended and our staff gathered outside the locker room. Larry and I were still amped up.

"You've really crossed the line," he said, his voice strained. "Don't just think everything is going to be all right after this." I told him I didn't need him telling me what to do in front of the team. He felt I had overreacted and disrespected him in a public sense, and that my F-bomb was "uncalled for."

The next day, we worked things out and I acknowledged that although both of us were wrong, my behavior had been worse.

Co-captains Darryl Frenette and Peter Morris provided first-rate leadership. Darryl hailed from Verdun, Quebec, and Vermont coach Mike

Gilligan had recommended him to me. Having played with Quebeckers at Vermont and coached them at Maine, it was only natural that we targeted Quebec as a prime recruiting area. Darryl committed to AIC a week after visiting our mostly vacant campus on a hot August afternoon. A Division I caliber defenseman, he was chosen ECAC East Player of the Year at the end of the season. Ron Anderson told me he would have recruited him at Merrimack "if he was a left shot." We couldn't afford to be that picky.

Peter attended Admiral Farragut HS where he played quarterback for AIC grad Stan Slabey. That helped us recruit him. A dean's list student, he was coming off a twenty-seven-point season. Peter's passion for the game was noted by coaches and teammates alike. His teammates joked that even in the off-season you couldn't get him away from a hockey discussion for more than a minute. Looking back, defenseman Bill Teggart said, "Peter was always a natural leader. He was an old soul. It's no surprise to me he became a school superintendent."

We won three straight league games after returning from Alabama. On November 7, we traveled to Salem, Massachusetts, home of the Salem Witch Trials, and beat Salem State 7–4. Peter Morris scored twice and Mark Buckley had twenty-nine saves as we bewitched the Vikings. Soon after, we won our home opener over Holy Cross 8–1. Dan Bouchard made a mere nine saves to get the win. He transferred from Babson the previous year and was now game eligible. A subsequent 7–2 win over UMass-Boston kept us moving forward.

A week later, we played a non-conference tilt with Framingham State. Ten goals, only one penalty and a shutout by Bryon Lewis led us to a 10–0 rout. Tim Friday, a defenseman on RPI's 1985 NCAA championship team and Framingham's head coach, commented in Larry Silber's article in the *Springfield Union-News*: "It's obvious that AIC has a tremendous amount of talent; they can come close to the Division I teams on their schedule." Perhaps spurred by Friday's comments, Silber then swung by our locker room and, curiously, asked, "Do you think you can win your first ECAC title in two decades?" He ended the article with my appropriately evasive answer: "We still have a lot of games to go."

The thirty-two goals we scored in our last four games represented big-time production, even in an era of higher scoring averages. Our offensive output could be attributed to the large number of skilled players on the roster. I believe Jack Parker is the coach who said, "The team that gets off the bus with the best players, wins." We had equal or better talent than most of our opponents, and we subscribed to a style of play that allowed our players to flourish offensively. Our defensemen also generated offense. Frenette and Wortman totaled fifty-five and thirty-five points respectively that season and fellow blueliner Tony Sericolo, who kicked field goals for the football team, provided excellent depth and physicality.

We encouraged our players to perform with imagination. The concept of "offensive support" had become prevalent in the game of hockey, some of it from soccer, and I embraced it with our team. I felt fortunate that Cross had stressed the importance of supporting the puck carrier, though I don't recall him using the term "support." We gave our D the green light to join the rush, and incorporate into the attack. We started using modern terms like "timing," "delays," "cycling," and "stretch passes," among others. And we emphasized quick transition. We became a possession-first team and dumped the puck only when necessary.

We utilized a unique strategy we called "super changes" to maintain possession during changes by passing back to the defensemen as our forwards bolted to the bench. The Ds then passed up to our fresh forwards and changed. The conditions had to be right, but we executed eight to ten super changes a game. And it forced our opponents to overstay their shifts. We also passed to our goaltenders during the super changes. Lacrosse and soccer goalies are utilized similarly, although not necessarily during changes. At least one defenseman stayed out to support the goalie and our first forward off the bench beelined back to add another outlet. Mark Buckley was best at this, as he passed and handled the puck with aplomb.

Dave Reese, a former UVM and Springfield Indians goalie, coached Mark Buckley at Trinity Pawling and insisted he develop his passing and puck handling skills. Those skills augmented our super changes. He also told Buck to consider AIC, "because the Student Prince is a great restaurant in Springfield, and because Gary Wright has to be a good guy if he went to Vermont." Blind loyalty, maybe? An All-American for the Cats, Reese later played for the Boston Bruins until he gave up six goals one night to Darryl Sittler.

Buck came from a hockey family. His brother, David, skated for Boston College and his dad, Paul Buckley, played at Kimball Union and Norwich

University. Paul was later inducted into the Norwich Hall of Fame for hockey and football. When he saw Buck's rather low grade point average one semester at AIC, he said, "I was hoping that was your goals against average."

We continued our winning ways by beating Williams 5–3. Bill Kangas, the former UVMer who recommended Pat Forte to me, was coaching his first home game at Williams. Two nights later we returned to the Williams neighborhood and defeated North Adams State 5–1. Vezio Sacratini then had four points to help us defeat St Anselm's 6–3. That made for three road wins in one week. It was also our seventh straight victory and put our record at 7–1–1 overall and 6–0 in league play. We were on our way, or so it seemed.

Our player notebooks contained write-ups on various aspects of our system. We covered them at team meetings. I also wrote up a one-page "AIC toughness" sheet that was included with the other areas of our play, and got posted on our locker room bulletin board. Here are eighteen of the twenty-five "Toughness in AIC Hockey" categories:

- Toughness in hockey is mental as well as physical.
- Toughness is preparing yourself to play every day.
- Toughness is competing as hard on the road as at home.
- Toughness is making a big play after a bad play.
- Toughness is accepting a coach's criticism without excuse.
- Toughness is a good attitude when unhappy with your ice time.
- Toughness is moving your feet when your legs feel like lead.
- Toughness is hustling on the backcheck when behind the play.
- Toughness is rooting for the power play when you're not on it.
- Toughness is always being true to the rules of the game.
- Toughness is scoring a clutch goal when it really counts.
- Toughness is consistently winning 1-on-1 battles.
- Toughness is taking the check to make the play.
- Toughness is not retaliating to a cheap shot.
- Toughness is being a big-game performer.
- Toughness is first in the corners.

- Toughness is playing physical.

- Toughness is blocking shots.

I tweaked the sheet over the years, sometimes at a player or assistant's suggestion. When we went over it early in the season, each toughness category was supported with examples from hockey and other sports. For instance, I cited Stan Musial, former St Louis Cardinals Hall of Famer, who had 1,815 career hits at home and 1,815 on the road, when discussing our emphasis on consistency and "competing as hard on the road as at home." When stressing the importance of maintaining a "good attitude when unhappy with your ice time," I used bad body language on the bench as an example of subtly disruptive behavior. It takes courage to stay strong and support your teammates when things aren't going well for you, personally. And I often used life analogies when talking to the team about this. While both physical and mental toughness are necessary in hockey, when a player's career ends, mental toughness will rule the day, and help you cope with the adversity that life inevitability offers.

Vezio Sacratini wasn't very physical, yet he checked off many of the toughness boxes. A five-foot-seven, 160-pound center, he was voted ECAC East Rookie of the Year, and Player of the Year as a sophomore. Dave King, a coach for both NHL and Canadian Olympic teams, called me to inquire about him for one of their national teams. He didn't get chosen, but it indicated his prowess as a player. Vezio spoke three languages (English, French, Italian), he excelled on the golf team, and Larry O'Donnell said his outgoing personality "fills the stands with Vezio fans." Those fans were often new to hockey and included students, professors, maintenance workers, and campus police. Vezio could be high-strung, but he was a great player who performed with verve and thrived in our system. "A magician with the puck, Vezio's peripheral vision and on-ice intelligence is remarkable," was my quote in his press guide bio.

Having three assistants made my job easier and provided for a better coach-player ratio. Another new hire outside of hockey aided my ability to coach the team. Blaine Stevens, the dean of students, approved a new assistant housing director position, which gave me needed help in the housing office. I hired Bruce Johnson to fill the position. Bruce graduated from UMass and played baseball at Melrose High School for former Dartmouth hockey great

Henry Hughes. He attended many of our games and became a loyal fan, despite the fact I overloaded him with piles of housing paperwork so I could spend more time in rinks.

Dean Stevens didn't know much about hockey, or any other sport for that matter. An omnivorous reader, he complained that he once went to a Red Sox game and "couldn't get any reading done with all the noise." The season before, as I stood on the bench during a game, I heard his voice speaking to me from above the glass.

"This is a pretty good game so far," he said, "and the boys are skating well."

I couldn't believe he was talking to me during the game, so I inched away without glancing back or responding. The next day, he asked why I ignored him.

"I can't be interrupted when I'm trying to coach the team," I said.

"Well, sometimes you come into my office and interrupt me," he said. He sort of had a point.

New England College came to town soon after Union ended our seven-game winning streak. An early goal put the Pilgrims up, until David Bates fired off his patented big windup, high-sailing slapper to tie things up at mid-period. (David's slapshot tended to wander, much like his focus. He once asked Larry what it cost to go to Williams during a game at their rink.) Brian Walsh powered us to the 7–3 win with two goals. Our next game was a non-conference contest with one of the top Division I teams in the country. Providence loomed ahead.

With ten days to prepare for Providence and for semester-ending exams, we mixed in days off for studying with practice. Winning put a little extra spring in our step and skating strides. Anticipating a game with the Friars soared our spirits even higher. And then we got bad news. Vezio Sacratini decided to forego his eligibility and commit to playing in the Italian Professional League. He based his untimely departure on "my interest in playing on Italy's 1992 Olympic team." His grandparents were born in Italy, so he qualified as an "Italo" player, and would be eligible to play for Italy in the Olympics if he played parts of three seasons there.

Vezio's departure appeared to be a blow to our team. He was our offensive catalyst and led the league in scoring. (He remained the leader long after he left.) We were a legitimate contender in the chase for a championship. Now our hopes were in danger of being dashed. I had my own concerns and

I wasn't happy about him leaving our team during the season. To me, his decision seemed selfish and left us in a fix, although my feelings softened over time. I also worried about the psyche of our team, to whom I spoke after Vezio chose to leave:

"Vezio is obviously a loss, but good teams can lose good players to departures or injuries and still win championships. It will make things harder for us, but "hard" is a part of hockey, and we're up to the challenge—right? We have a strong team, as evidenced by our record. Our outlook is bright. We just need everyone to step up their game. And I know you guys will do that."

We moved our second-line center, Martin Labonte, up on the first (green) line to play with Peter Morris and Ken Maffia; our third line center, Derek Decosta, up to take Labonte's place on the second line with Mark Cappadona and Marc Lussier, and so forth. Labonte and Lussier were Quebeckers who excelled together in prep school and continued meshing at AIC, so our staff agonized over breaking them up. Moreover, Lussier had four goals in our two previous games. Still, I felt strongly about front-loading our green line. They had been critical to our success, so we moved Labonte up and hoped for the best.

Providence was ranked fourth in the country with a 10–2–1 record. An article by Dave Phillips in the *Providence Journal-Bulletin* on game day mentioned Vezio's departure and also that three of the Friars' top players were away with the U.S. Junior National team, preparing for the world championships in Helsinki, Finland. After writing about Vezio and the missing Providence players, Phillips joked, "At least the Friars will get their players back."

We set out for Providence, Rhode Island, to fight the Friars. We brought along three guests: Bruce Johnson from housing; John Debonville, AIC's alumni director, who was hosting an alumni event; and future NHLer Jim Dowd, a Lake Superior State player and friend of Peter Morris. Dowd was on Christmas break and came up from New Jersey to visit Peter, so I allowed him to ride with us. Vezio Sacratini also came along to watch. Bruce and John sat up front near us coaches and talked a lot. John graduated from Providence and was downright giddy about our playing his alma mater. I stayed mostly to myself, my mind preoccupied with the events of the last few days and thoughts of the game.

The puck dropped at Schneider Arena at 7 p.m. A crowd of just over a thousand paid the $6 ticket price, unless they had season tickets. The game remained scoreless until Springfield native Rick Bennett walked in alone and deked Buck Buckley to put Providence up 1–0 late in the period. Bennett was considered a Hobey Baker candidate. Minutes later, Ken Maffia scored to tie the game. The period ended 1–1, thanks to what John "Jocko" Connolly of the *Boston Herald* described as a "litany of saves—18 in all—by AIC netminder Mark Buckley."

Martin Labonte's power play goal put us up 2–1 early in the second period. Rick Bennett netted another near the nine-minute mark to knot things up. We had planned to split the game between Buck and Dan Bouchard, so they switched a minute later. I wanted them both to experience playing Providence and told them, "I need thirty minutes of focused play from each of you, and let's see if we can beat those guys." I thought Dan's free-spiritedness made him a better candidate to come in cold. It wouldn't faze him to miss his normal warm-up routine. Interestingly, Providence changed goalies at the same time. The Friars scored soon after and maintained their 3–2 lead for the rest of the period.

Providence kept their territorial edge in the third, but we competed hard: blocking shots, battling in the dirty areas, and playing high-energy hockey. We didn't back down to our favored opponent. The period saw no goals until they tallied sixteen minutes in to take a two-goal lead. But Labonte stepped up in his new role and scored thirty seconds later to make it 4–3. That's how it ended, despite our desperate attempts in the waning minutes. Coach McShane and I shook hands at game's end, and I thanked him again for the opportunity to play his team.

Our players and staff headed home for the holidays after the Providence game, except for Don Moorhouse and our three Springfield area players— Dan Bouchard, Mike Hall, and Eric Nielsen—who were home already. I spent a week at my parents' house in Cornwall. We played neighborhood hockey games on the pond down behind our house. The participants included my siblings, Lesley, Donald, and Catharine, plus in-laws and old friends. December of 1989 featured record cold temperatures in Vermont, making the ice firm and fast. The bitter cold froze our toes and turned our noses Rudolph red, but our hearts were warmed, and the games reminded me of the carefree days of my youth, when I skated on the pond at Proctor.

After Christmas, our staff scattered around New England and Ontario to recruit. Practice resumed on Tuesday, January 2. It would be an all-hockey holiday until classes started in three weeks. Our first practices included drills such as BFA Counters (from Red Gendron), Swedish Stretch Pass (stolen from Tim Taylor, who claimed all coaches are "drill pirates"), and a Continuous 3-on-2 with Regroup drill. We also did a Mike Bieniek shooting exercise, named after our former captain and leading goal scorer. It emphasized a slight shift in puck placement before shooting.

Double sessions were conducted on Wednesday and Thursday. The first morning, we split the team in half and worked with each group separately. The smaller numbers allowed for more coaching during the walk-through part of our neutral ice drills, one of which came from Joe Marsh at St. Lawrence. The next morning featured the power play. Regular practices were held both afternoons. We also lifted weights. I referred to the first few days back as "Hockey Boot Camp." On Friday, we returned to single daily practices as our game schedule approached.

We started out 1–3–1. Not the way to stage a playoff push. A 4–0 home loss to Hamilton hurt. Our team watched the game tape the next day. While critiquing the film, I suddenly said, "Rewind that." Yes, I'd seen something concerning. Peter Morris had purposely tripped Hamilton's goalie after the whistle.

"Peter, are you kidding me," I said, as he sank in his chair. "You stay here after." I then told him he'd sit out the first period of the next game. Later, I heard that Peter's teammates kept laughing and saying "Rewind that" to him as they walked to dinner.

We did have a 6–4 win over the league-leading Babson Beavers, who came to Smead unbeaten in their last eleven games. The Babson win was beautiful, but a tie with Merrimack defined the stretch. We were trailing 6–3 with sixty-four seconds left when Darryl Frenette's goal made it 6–4. Martin Labonte narrowed the gap to 6–5 a half minute later. Marc Lussier, who came on when we pulled Mark Buckley, then scored an apparent buzzer-beater. The refs conferred briefly before signaling the game-tying goal. Our players on the ice jumped for joy, and our bench went bonkers, as guys cheered and banged their sticks against the boards. No one scored in the ensuing overtime. Considering Merrimack was a Hockey East team, we were playing on the road, and the magnitude of our comeback, the tie felt like a win.

After the game, the Merrimack players remained in their equipment so they could return to the ice for punishing stops & starts. Our guys loved it. Apparently Ron Anderson didn't love his team's performance. He skated them when we left. Coach Anderson used a similar tactic after beating Colby in a previous game. The problem was, Ron, a former NHLer, not only skated his team on Colby ice, but Merrimack won the game. Colby coach Mickey Goulet felt insulted by the move, and Ron later apologized. The NCAA outlawed postgame punitive skates a few years later.

Our inconsistent win-one, lose-one hockey continued. We had built a championship-caliber team, and our season seemed to be unraveling. Three games epitomized our plight. North Adams State beat us 7–6 at their place with just nineteen shots. We lost 10–7 at UConn and 5–2 at home to Fitchburg, an ECAC Northeast team. The *Union-News* described us as "struggling to earn an ECAC East playoff berth" in the Fitchburg game article. How quickly we seemed to have fallen. Dean Fuller's Fitchburg team had also upset us the year before, and my AD, Bob Burke, told me President Courniotes asked him, "Why the hell do we keep scheduling Fitchburg if they keep beating us?" I hoped Bob didn't tell him I scheduled the games.

The loss to the Connecticut Huskies felt like a bad dog bite. We played on a raw, rainy night in late January. One of the last colleges to play outdoors, their rink had a boat-shaped roof that sloped to several feet above the ground. The open ends allowed more outside air to come in. Teams dressed in an old-fashioned warming hut. I told Coach Bruce Marshall that I loved coming to UConn each season, because it reminded me of my youth and the wholesomeness of playing outdoors. "You wouldn't feel that way if you had to play here every day like we do," he said.

The setting didn't seem so wholesome that night. Our captains, Darryl Frenette and Peter Morris, argued during warm-ups over something silly. Considering our recent woes, it was the last thing we needed. Then Mark Buckley let in some soft goals and I replaced him with Dan Bouchard. We took too many penalties. We played poor defense. We continued our downward spiral and gave up an embarrassing ten goals to the Huskies, who, like their canine namesake, were unbothered by the elements. And unchallenged by the Yellow Jackets.

I went for a lonely walk after the game, trudging down a side road in a V-neck sweater and sports jacket. The rain fell through the foggy air, but my brain was so fogged with frustration that I ignored the drenching. A while later, I arrived back to a waiting bus. My shoes squished rainwater as I climbed the steps and dropped into my seat. I didn't eat the postgame box lunch and I didn't talk to anyone, other than to tell Larry to announce to the team that we were taking tomorrow off and practicing on Wednesday.

The next day, I called Bruce Johnson to say I wouldn't be coming to the office. I also told Larry to run the upcoming practice. "I'm bullshit about this," I said, "and I hope my absence indicates how disappointed I am." I then drove up to Northampton and walked around the trendy town. There was no rain, and my thoughts were clearer as I contemplated the state of our team and the worrisome challenges ahead.

I met briefly with our captains on Wednesday morning. None of us sat down. Among other things, I admonished Darryl and Peter for their warm-up spat, and I reminded them that their teammates elected them for their leadership, especially during the difficult times. "Never is it needed more than now," I said.

Bruce Marshall called our sports information director (SID) Frank Polera during this time. Frank had come from UConn and they knew each other well. Bruce said several people had spotted me after the game "walking in the rain with no coat on" and wanted to get the scoop. Frank confirmed the report. The two of them laughed about my wet walk for years to come.

We loaded the bus on Thursday to play New England College. I got on last. Apparently, our guys debated over whether I'd even show up. We beat New England by a big score at the Concord Arena, a rink from my Proctor past. We were better, but still not good in our next few games, and after an ugly 11–8 win over St Anselm, where I had to pull Buckley again, I decided to go with Dan Bouchard as our starter the rest of the way. Buck had been a league all-star as a junior, but he was struggling with his confidence and his play, so the move had to be made.

We won our remaining three games with Dan in net to finish the regular season on a four-game winning streak. Included in those games was a 10–2 pasting of UConn at home, and a 7–5 win at Middlebury with my family in the stands. The Middlebury Panthers had emerged as a league power under Bill Beaney. They scored four second-period goals to take a 5–4 lead, before back-to-back power play goals put us ahead for good in the third.

The late-season surge secured home ice for us in the first round of the eight-team tournament. Norwich was our quarterfinal opponent. The momentum of our recent success provided a renewed sense of optimism. Dan stabilized our goaltending, yet we still had dependable depth with Bryon and Buck. Our power play clicked at 35 percent, we weren't giving up many shots, and our fire-wagon attack was lighting a lot of lamps. Norwich coach Tony Mariano told this to the *Burlington Free Press*: "We've got to play well defensively. They're good one-on-one, they're clever, and they do a lot of things with the puck."

Bill Avery scored for the Norwich Cadets on their first shot of the game. Not a good omen. But a power play goal by Peter Morris and Martin Labonte's marker with six seconds left made it 2–2 after the first period. Two more Norwich goals and one by AIC sent us into the final frame down 4–3. Morris, Marc Lussier, and Eric Forselius all tallied before Avery notched his second for the Cadets. They pulled their goalie at the end, but Dan Bouchard stuffed their attempts and we secured the 6–5 win. We were excited and relieved to be moving on to the semifinals.

In a *Springfield Union-News* article titled "Jackets Pull It Out in The End," Peter Morris talked about Forselius's game-winner:

> "It was great to see a freshman score in a game like that and to set him up is a great feeling."

Well said. College rosters are cyclical and every year you need to bring in new players to replace the graduating seniors. If you're going to be good, then some of those freshmen have to provide instant help. Peter's comment also spoke to the connectivity needed between all the classes. His best buddies may have been upperclassmen, but he captained the entire team.

The ECAC East had changed to a final four format at a central location. Babson finished first in the regular season and received the only quarterfinal bye. However, the committee deemed Middlebury College to have the better venue for hosting the event. The semis featured No. 1 seed Babson vs. No. 4 AIC, and No. 2 Middlebury vs. No. 3 Bowdoin. Our game with Babson was scheduled for Friday, March 2, at 4:30 p.m., followed by the other semifinal. The championship would be Saturday night.

Larry hosted a party at his apartment after the Norwich win. AIC admissions director Peter Miller attended, and he liked the idea of us being associated with the other three finalists. He believed that participating with those elite colleges further raised our academic profile. Peter walked around saying, "Babson-Bowdoin-Middlebury-AIC, isn't this great." As he drank more beers, listing the four teams became a bit of a tongue twister for him, and for our bespectacled SID, Frank Polera, who parroted Peter by hollering, "Babson-Bowdoin-Middlebury-AIC." Ha ha ha.

We were slight underdogs entering the game, but we had split with Babson in the regular season and given them their only league loss. Coach Steve Stirling, who eventually became head coach of the NHL's New York Islanders, had the busy Beavers playing stingy defense. (NBC hockey analyst Pierre McGuire previously assisted Stirling.) Their starting goalies combined for an impressive 2.2 goals against average (GAA). In a game preview, I stressed, "The thing that stands out most about Babson is they play great team defense. They backcheck as well as any team we play and they have good goaltending."

Our bus left for Middlebury, Vermont, early on a frosty Friday morning. Babson and Bowdoin arrived the night before, but we left the day of the Babson game, despite the nearly four-hour drive. Bob Burke preferred that we travel on the day of the game due to budget constraints, though he left the decision up to me. I decided not to go the day before, partly out of respect for Bob's concerns, and also because we had a rugged bunch of guys who were conditioned to our no-frills infrastructure. I assumed (and hoped) they would be undeterred by the long drive. However, I didn't anticipate a cold bus. The heating system wasn't working right and the bus driver couldn't find the cause. There was some heat, but not enough to stave off the winter weather outside. That only added to my concerns.

So we shivered up I-91, turned onto Route 103 and drove through such Vermont towns as Chester, site of the Chat & Chew Restaurant, and Ludlow, where skiers zigzagged down Okemo Mountain. We eventually reached Route 7 and stopped at the Palms in Rutland, a classy place where we routinely ate a pregame meal. The food had already been ordered and ownership knew the deal: A pasta dinner with meat balls or chicken, salad, bread and butter and water. I didn't include dessert to keep the price down and the food healthy, but I relented when owner John Sabataso asked if the boys could have "just a little bit of ice cream on the house." A short while later we were on the road. The town of Middlebury and the college were fifty minutes away. Game time was drawing closer.

I usually hung out in the adjoining basketball court before games at Middlebury. Sitting in the stands, I witnessed a most unusual occurrence. Larry O'Donnell and Paul Donato, the Babson assistant, were playing HORSE. I smiled, despite my nerves. Here they were, two friends and friendly rivals, about to play a huge playoff game that would send the winner into the ECAC East Championship game, and they were out there missing layups and trying trick shots like a couple of loosey-goosey teenagers at the park. I doubt any of the big-time NCAA basketball assistants were horsing around before their Final Four contest.

We came out strong in the first period, with no sign of "bus legs." Dan Bouchard wasn't facing many shots, but looked sharp against his former team. Ken Maffia, a guaranteed goal-scoring machine in playoff games, scored off a faceoff to put us up 1–0. That's how the period ended. Babson had power play goals from Mark Allen and Dan Hunter in the second period. Eric Forselius sandwiched a goal in between the two Babson man-up tallies. We went to intermission with the contest knotted 2–2. Our season was on the line.

The third period had been our time to shine. We did it again with a pair of lamplighters early in the frame. Sophomore Derek Decosta used his cheetah-like speed to get behind the Beaver defense, caught a stretch pass from Kevin Wortman, and scored on the breakaway. A minute later, goalie Mark Kuryak deflected a Peter Morris shot to the end boards, but Peter grabbed the loose puck and stuffed it in the far side. For the rest of the game, we urged our players to compete hard and keep the shifts short. An empty-netter at the end made it 5–2. We were on to the championship game.

Ted Ryan covered the tournament for the *Burlington Free Press*. He had been writing about UVM hockey since I played there. (He would cover the Cats for decades to come.) Steve Stirling didn't mince words in the game story: "They played really well, it's as simple as that. They came out flying in the third and we didn't. They didn't have too many lulls. They ate us up one-on-one." I shared Stirling's comments with our team the next day, as they reinforced the way we needed to play in the championship game.

We stayed and watched the first period of the Bowdoin-Middlebury game because I wanted our players to continue soaking in the tournament atmosphere. I sat with my family of fifteen, including in-laws. My father, as he often did, told me our faceoff play made him nervous. I reminded him that our first goal was off a draw. Back then faceoffs weren't emphasized as much, so maybe he was slightly ahead of his time. After the period, we boarded the bus and happily headed to the Sheraton Hotel in Burlington.

That night, our staff and SID Frank Polera went downtown to celebrate the win. Larry told Alex Smith, "We're heading into Gary's World," a reference to my Burlington years. We visited the Daily Planet, where I hoped to run into Moon, one of the bartenders. He wasn't there and Frank yelled, "Where's M-O-O-N," ha ha ha, for the rest of the night. We drank a few beers (O'Doul's for me) listening to the rock band Phish at Nectar's bar. Phish started as UVM students and became one of the top bands in America. Coach Moorhouse, a real rock-and-roller himself, managed a Springfield band called Breakdown, so he was in his element.

Senior Jim Agan's parents hosted a pregame meal at their house the next day. I was deep in thought during the drive back to Middlebury. Marc Lussier had separated his shoulder against Babson, putting us down a key forward against the Middlebury Panthers, who beat Bowdoin 5–2. We needed someone to take his spot with Decosta and Cappadona. We were lean at forward, so we moved defenseman Bill Teggart onto that line. I hoped Bill's experience as a big-body defenseman would translate into a power forward performance. I didn't expect too much considering he was playing a different position in a big game. Besides the roster concerns, I had plenty of worries about Middlebury. Bill Beaney was a creative coach, and he had recruited an excellent team. The championship game seemed a far cry from when we coached Vermont high school hockey against each other.

Playing Middlebury felt special to me. My grandparents met at the college as students, and my grandfather served as director of admissions. They're buried across from the rink. Their three sons, including my father, are all alums. My mother got her masters there. My two sisters are Middlebury grads, and Catharine teaches at the college. In the years ahead four of my nieces and nephews, along with other relatives, would also attend Middlebury. The tourney took place at the Duke Nelson Arena. Duke coached football and hockey at the college and was athletic director. Dad played football for him and they became lifelong friends. When Mr. Nelson visited, his coach voice boomed through our house.

We arrived at the rink to find a long line stretched around the building. Tickets were going on sale two hours before the 7:30 p.m. game. Mark

Buckley wondered why his father stood in line, because he always left him comp tickets. He soon found out that he was purchasing tickets for some friends. I liked that. His son wasn't starting, but Paul Buckley still came in force. Bill Conniff rode up from Springfield. An eccentric yet loyal AIC alum, he had been badly wounded in World War II. He sponsored one of the hockey awards. Apparently, the game had sold out by the time Bill got to the ticket booth. He started rapping his cane on the window. A few minutes later he sat comfortably in the stands, munching on a hot dog.

At 7:20 p.m., I entered a hushed locker room to give the pregame talk. I told our team that we needed to commit to our 1–2–2 neutral zone defense, and not chase the Middlebury forwards too far laterally. And that our forwards needed to come back hard and smart, and cover their second wave, because their Ds would be active. I also reminded our guys that, like us, they were terrific in transition, so we had to be quick from offense to defense— and defense to offense. Then I ended like this:

> "Our playing styles are similar, so in a way, we need to beat
> them at their own game, by playing our game. Three weeks
> ago, we were struggling, wondering what went wrong.
> Now we've won six straight. The turnaround is a credit to
> you guys; you persevered and gave us this chance to win a
> championship tonight. Now let's go get it."

Fans packed the rink and a mass of Middlebury students filled one end. As the American and Canadian national anthems ended, the nearby Zamboni door opened and more students surged in. The apparent gatecrashers ran by (and through) our bench. Soon, Pierre Belanger, the mustachioed referee, dropped the first puck. I took a deep breath. The championship game was underway.

Two minutes in, Peter Morris scored off a tic-tac-toe passing exchange with linemates Martin Labonte and Ken Maffia. A pair of Middlebury scores followed to put them up 2–1. We answered with two goals to regain the lead, and then Bill Teggart validated his position change by thwacking a puck that nicked the cross bar on the way in. The period ended 4–2. The second stanza started with a flurry of Middlebury shots deftly stopped by Dan Bouchard. The Panthers continued to press, but Kevin Wortman scored two spectacular goals, one of them shorthanded, to put us up 6–2. Tim Craig then tallied for Middlebury and the period ended 6–3. We had a nice lead, but our opponent was too good for us to feel safe.

Bill Teggart had more in store between periods. His dad had told him about Winston Churchill's speech at the Harrow School during World War II, a few months after the Nazis repeatedly bombed London and other English cities. Churchill likely said "never give in" in the speech but Bill, as others have, used "up" in place of "in." I wasn't in the locker room when Bill, who would one day become a courtroom lawyer, rose and addressed his surprised teammates:

> "Boys, during World War II, the Nazis bombed England. Winston Churchill, the prime minister, faced what many were predicting was imminent destruction. Despite the grave predictions, the British survived the bombings and the allies eventually won the war. Soon after the attacks, Churchill returned to speak at the boys' military school he once attended. He told them what he felt was the secret to outlasting the Nazis, and an important quality to have in life. 'Never give up,' Churchill said. 'Never, never, never give up.' Boys, we have come too far and been together too long to let Middlebury back in the game. Now let's get out there and win this championship."

As Bill talked, he noticed a "Bill is losing it" look on Mark Cappadona's face. Moments later, he said, "Wally, you probably remember this."

"I was there," Wally said from within the room.

Our five-foot-four legendary trainer Wally Barlow once worked for Eddie Shore's Springfield Indians. He was tough like Shore and often called our guys "big babies" when they complained about injuries. Wally came from England, but no one is sure whether he meant he was at the speech or in one of the bombed cities.

We took the ice after Bill's speech. Middlebury pressed hard in the third, and Brent Truchon's saves kept them in the game. They made it 6–4 near the seven-minute mark, before Labonte's backhander regained our three-goal lead. But the Panthers weren't done. Craig, just a freshman, scored his third and fourth goals of the night as the Middlebury fans cheered wildly, the student section stands shook from stomping feet, and an earsplitting song played on the loudspeaker. Suddenly, the score was 7–6 with forty-two seconds left. We sent out our green line, along with Frenette and Wortman, and Maffia netted an empty-netter with seconds left on the clock. We were ECAC East champions!

Our bench erupted and emptied at once, as our players rushed to mob Bouchard—and each other. Watching my players celebrate was the best part. Their joy was my joy. Our staff then shook hands with Bill Beaney and his assistants. Bill was gracious in defeat, and I felt happy but humble. Having experienced back-to-back playoff losses to Bowdoin made me appreciate his position and mine.

Clayton Chapman, ECAC commissioner, presented the championship trophy to co-captains Darryl Frenette and Peter Morris. Kevin Wortman, who Ted Ryan described as "doling out big hits, making key defensive plays and providing two critical goals" in his *Free Press* story the next day, received the MVP trophy from Middlebury AD Tom Lawson. At the end of the ceremony our entire team, coaches and support staff, posed for a group photo with the trophy. The photographer didn't have to tell us to smile. We were already smiling. And the nicest thing of all is that the smiles were shared.

The celebration continued in the locker room. I often jumped over barrels and did somersaults in the room after big wins, which the players enjoyed, and this time Larry took my place and dived into a trash barrel. But mostly the moment belonged to our players. They celebrated in a more public forum during the awards presentations and now they exalted in the privacy of the room. Then I walked out into the hallway to see Bob Burke, who had driven up with his wife, Andrea. He hired me and provided great support as my athletic director, so I wanted to spend a minute with him.

I also visited with my family. They joked about how my mother kept saying "Oh no, oh no" during tense moments in the game. Jim Ellefson, my future brother-in-law, asked what Bill Beaney said to me as we walked off the ice after the first period. I told him Bill said I could use the Middlebury entrance to get off the ice quicker, and I thanked him, but I was fine using ours. I explained to Jim that I didn't want to walk by their locker room out of respect for their privacy if I didn't have to. Donald gushed about Wortman's "Orr-like" performance. Everyone kept congratulating me. I felt like I had reached the heights of hockey happiness. When it was time to go, we all walked out of the rink together and stopped just short of the bus, where we said our cheerful goodbyes in the chilly air.

Peter and Darryl asked about picking up some beer to bring back to campus, "since we just won the championship and bars and stores will be closed when we get home." I said we'd stop and they could purchase several cases and put them under the bus. We went to a store in town and then started south on 7. Mark Cappadona came to the front of the bus and kept saying, "I can't believe we just won," and, "We shocked the world." Well, maybe not quite the world, but it didn't matter. In our world, we had gone as far as we could go, and it felt wonderful.

We didn't know it yet, but the college would include a special section in the Alumni News about our accomplishment, there would be a banquet in the spring, and our team members received championship rings. In April, our coaches and captains went down to Springfield City Hall to accept a proclamation from the city council, commending our team for winning the championship. Jerry Radding would write a story in the *Union-News* titled "MVP Wortman Calls AIC Title Team Affair." Kevin got it. He was a great player who subscribed to the "Big Team, Little Me" concept. His buy-in made us even better.

I eventually settled into my seat and I continued to hear excited chatter and loud laughs further back. The boys were having the ride of their lives. Some of the overhead lights got turned off up front where our coaches sat, but they shone like spotlights on our players. It didn't sound like many of them were staying in their seats. Or falling asleep. Surely they would party long after the bus got home. They were young and very happy, after all, and they were champions.

Chapter 9

A Good Cry

T he 1990–91 school year followed an eventful summer. I hired Paul
Cannata to replace Alex Smith as our new GA. Alex had decided
to forgo the second year of his assistantship to return to teaching
and coaching in high school. When I told Bruce Johnson, my assistant in
housing, that Alex was leaving, he said he wasn't surprised, "considering that
you gave him a list of three hundred things to do every day." Paul went to
Roxbury Latin and then played for Phil Grady at Hamilton College. He had
an engaging personality and a quick wit, and both Grady and his previous
coaches spoke glowingly about him. I felt good about the hire.

I also applied for the University of Lowell (later called UMass-Lowell)
head coach position. I became one of three finalists, along with BC assistant
Joe Mallen and former Boston Bruin Bruce Crowder, a Maine assistant.
After buying a new sports jacket and gray flannel pants, I drove to Lowell for
the daylong interview. (Since I wasn't known as a snazzy dresser, Bob Burke,
Bruce Johnson, and Dean Stevens joked about how each of them would loan
me an article of clothing for the interview, as if I was being outfitted like Mr.
Potato Head.) I toured the campus and the Tully Forum, where they played
as a member of Hockey East. I spent time with AD Wayne Edwards and
also interviewed with the search committee. Just before leaving, I met alone
with Dr. Edwards. Near the end of our talk, he leaned forward in his chair
and with a slight Southern drawl said, "One of the most important things to
me is to hire someone I can trust."

I didn't get the job. They hired Bruce Crowder, and I heard that the people
at Lowell felt his playing days at UNH, along with his NHL career and
coaching position at Maine, gave him "big time" experience, making him a

more attractive candidate. I understand that thinking, but there are successful college coaches who come from lesser-known programs and backgrounds. Two prior examples were Mike Addessa, who played football at Holy Cross yet won a national championship in 1985, and George Crowe, who took Dartmouth to Final Fours in 1979 and 1980. Crowe graduated from close by Springfield College, the birthplace of basketball, which didn't sponsor an NCAA hockey team. Ironically, James Naismith, the professor who invented the sport, was Canadian.

Soon after, Bob Burke told me President Courniotes agreed to make me a full-time hockey coach. Winning the ECAC championship and being a finalist at Lowell were both factors in the decision, although Coach Burke had long lobbied to eliminate the position's part-time pay status. Bob and I visited the smoke-filled office of the chain-smoking president, and he told me that, starting with the 1991–92 school year, I would be full time. The thought that I had just one more year in housing put me on cloud nine.

We got off to a 7–3 start. Included in that stretch were two overtime wins; one over nemesis Bowdoin and the other on the road at Holy Cross. Martin Labonte had the dramatic game winner against the Polar Bears, and Jeff Paolini's slapper sank Holy Cross. We played Middlebury during this time and lost 6–5. Kevin Wortman blasted two goals late in the third, but Middlebury countered with two of their own to win the wild affair. It was small consolation, but we kept Tim Craig from scoring that time.

Jeff Paolini was one of three Saugus players on our roster. The others were Kevin Wortman, who was fast becoming a household name in college hockey, and fourth-liner Don Maccini. They all played for AIC grad Chris Serino at Saugus High School, before Chris became the head coach at Merrimack. When Wortman was a freshman at AIC, the defense corps included fellow Saugus native Paul Ventre. Larry O'Donnell ran the defensemen, and sometimes late in tight games, Paul motioned Larry over and said, "We need to get Frenette and Worto out there more, so I'll just watch." I've always loved that line. It speaks to the unselfishness that's essential in a team sport.

Paul's requests to Larry weren't always altruistic. On occasion, he informed Larry that his aging grandmother was in the stands and she looked forward to watching him play. It didn't buy him any extra ice time, but Paul's sense of humor added a little levity to the seriousness of the competition.

When Coach Serino brought Wortman and Don Maccini to visit our campus, he told me that Don had a rather strange sense of humor. I found that out soon enough. A professor approached me on campus one day and said he was having "punctuality problems" with Maccini. "He's walked in late several times," he said, "and he always gives me a ridiculous excuse in front of the class. The other day he announced that his roommate's dog threw up on his homework and he was late because he had to clean it up." One day at practice, Maccini, a friendly wiseass, asked if he could be on the green line. His teammates giggled and looked at me. "Don, you're just lucky to have a uniform," I said.

We played the Colby Mules in the afternoon semifinal and Middlebury and Potsdam State met in the second game of the Middlebury Holiday Classic. It was no surprise that Bill didn't have our squads face each other in the semifinals. We were the strongest teams, and putting us in different brackets set us up for a possible meeting in the finals. If so, it would be a lesser version of the ECAC East Championship game.

Charlie Corey coached at Colby after his successful tenure at Lawrence Academy. He was a character. One time at Colby, Charlie stopped outside our locker room between periods.

"Hey, we've got a good game going here," he said, while sipping on a drink.

I kind of liked the coaching camaraderie implicit in his surprise visit, as opposed to a cutthroat approach. We talked for a short time, and then I said, "Well, we've got a game to coach here."

"Ah, we'll be fine," he replied, as we both laughed and parted ways.

The game started without seniors Ken Maffia and Kevin Wortman. They sat out the first period for coming back an hour late after the break. It hurt, but punctuality has always been a basic tenet of our program.

Charlie's team played a version of the Colby Sinker that Mickey Goulet used against us at Maine. Unlike the NZ trap once employed by the New Jersey Devils, Colby conceded much of the neutral zone by lining up at their blue line, with one D deep in the zone. Not big on dumps, we tried to penetrate the blue with possession, but it resulted in numerous turnovers. Between periods we instructed our players to attack at least three abreast, allowing the puck carrier to slide lateral passes to speeding teammates when fronted by their semi-stationary defenders. Another adjustment featured "near-side chips," where we directed pucks behind the defenders, so they could be retrieved as a continuation of the rush.

Coach Corey's team were underdogs, so he chose to shrink the rink with a more defensive approach. With Maffia and Wortman back for the second period, his tactic would surely be put to the test. They helped, but it wasn't enough. Colby's Mark Lombard logged the game winner at 7:22 of the second period, and the Mules added an empty net goal to win 2–0. Beaney told me his players were disappointed because they wanted to face us in the championship game. Our guys felt the same way.

Lateness wasn't the norm for Ken Maffia, an otherwise dependable player. He'd skated for Bill Belisle at Mount Saint Charles, who referred to him as "the other center," ostensibly because Dave Capuano, who went on to Maine and the NHL, was the first-line center. But Ken became an outstanding player himself. A league all-star and big game goal scorer at AIC, he was an overlooked D-I–caliber player. He could be refreshingly straightforward at times, and one time he had a hat trick after being benched for the first period. He told me later that he liked feeling like a rebel as he scored those goals while his classmates went bananas.

Maffia probably wouldn't have come to AIC if it hadn't been for Larry O'Donnell. We drove down to Rhode Island one night in Larry's dented-up Datsun to watch him play for Mount Saint Charles, and while watching the Mounties warm up, I turned to my loquacious assistant holding court behind me and said, "Larry, he can't crossover."

Larry had coached him in youth hockey and appeared unfazed by my assessment. "You'll like him when the game starts," he said confidently. He was right.

Middlebury defeated Colby to win their tournament, and we soundly beat Potsdam in the consolation contest. We continued from there to go 5–2 through the rest of the month. We still had a good squad, although we weren't as strong as our previous teams. Our championship team featured large (and talented) junior and senior classes, and now we lacked some of that experience and depth.

But we had tremendous players leading us. Captains Marc Lussier, Tony Sericolo, and Kevin Wortman, along with our other seniors provided mentorship to our younger players. Their impressive careers and accolades as ECAC East Champions hadn't diminished their humility. Kevin Daly, one of the team's promising freshmen, said, "The seniors were great to me and the other freshman." I found Kevin's statement to be as much a part of their legacy as the rings on their fingers.

That class didn't just lead as seniors. At the beginning of the 1989–90 season when they were juniors, freshman Erik Forselius came in "with an attitude," as Bill Teggart described it. He was partying a lot and he missed some preseason "captain's practices," when he went home on weekends. Teggart and Tony Sericolo confronted Forselius about his apparent indiscretions, and among other things, told him to get his "shit together."

"That 'attitude' needed adjustment, and it happened," Teggart said. "And when it happened, he matured and became a great person and player."

If we had big leads like we did against Potsdam, I often pulled our top players from the game. They didn't always like it, but I thought it was the right thing to do. And I didn't want to be accused of running up the score. Just as I expected guys who received less ice time to support their teammates on the ice, I presumed our regulars would be supportive when the skate was on the other foot. I didn't know it at the time, but in the future my teams would periodically suffer large-score losses. Some coaches sat their best players with a big lead against us. Some didn't. And others may not have even thought about it because they mainly won. I never said anything, but I respected coaches who pulled back when they led by a lot.

We finished 15–10–2, with five of our last six games entering overtime, and I hoped the pressure-packed aspect of sudden-death hockey would prep us for the playoffs. Familiar foe Babson was our playoff opponent again. Each player got a scouting report labeled "Points to Ponder on Babson Eve." The handout included a review of their systems, along with Larry's insight on beating goalie Joe Capprini, an Islanders draft pick: "Pepper him with shots. Shoot low to his glove side. He struggles with wide-angle shots."

The scouting report ended as they always did with the last two bullet points being, "Work Hard. Have Fun." We subscribed to the saying, "When you're having fun, all the pressure turns to pleasure."

Dan Bouchard started against his former team as he had in the 1990 semifinals, and he kept the Beavers at bay through most of the first period until they scored with a minute left. Goals in the first or last minute of a period always sting. (When my UVM teammate Tim O'Connell played in the WHA, his team fined players who were scored on in those situations.) Other than the goal, we battled and outshot Babson 13–10.

After a scoreless second period, Babson opened the third with a goal to go up 2–0. We were in a hole, and we needed to dig ourselves out in a hurry. We did. Kevin Daly found the back of the net off a goalmouth scramble shortly after, and Martin Labonte tallied two minutes later. The game remained tied at the end of regulation. Babson's Rob Tobin, an Army transfer, scored off a 2-on-1 versus Kevin Wortman only thirty-nine seconds into sudden death, and we were done. Kevin would be named the ECAC East Player of the Year that season, but the game ended with him sprawled on the ice trying to break up the play.

The loss concluded Larry O'Donnell's coaching career along with that of our eight seniors. He'd recently been appointed AIC's full-time assistant athletic director. He also owned Larry's Pro Shop at Smead and another in Springfield's Cyr Arena. (He fittingly named his two cats Koho and Sherwood.) I was surprised he didn't purchase Smead's snack bar. A fast-food connoisseur, he ranked his favorite snack bars while recruiting in rinks around New England. Two of his top choices were the Hingham Arena, where they served steak fries, and the Concord Arena, whose menu featured palate-pleasing chocolate pucks.

While Larry ran his pro shops, I wrote a book called *Pass the Biscuit*, subtitled *Spirited Practices for Youth Hockey Players and Coaches*. It described twenty sample practices with drill descriptions and diagrams, plus other practice suggestions. Bruce Johnson served as proofreader, and we often discussed the book on company time while working in the housing office. Bryon Lewis, my former goaltender, expertly drew all the drill diagrams freehand. The self-published book sold well, despite being written before the Internet age.

When Paul Cannata began coaching at AIC, he noticed that Larry and I were both involved with outside projects/businesses. Those endeavors did take some time, so we weren't always available when Paul needed us. He often said, "I get to AIC all excited about my first coaching job, and I can't find the head coach because he's writing a book, or the assistant because he's off running pro shops."

Paul had an insatiable curiosity about the game, so I'm not surprised he's stayed in coaching. He embraced our creative approach, which during his time included painted "support pucks." There were often three to four of these red pucks at practice, and if players ended up with a colored puck, every pass had to be fifteen feet or less. It emphasized active support for the puck carrier, especially short support. This added prominence to the player away from the puck, who now dictated play as much as the puck carrier. When Paul started his own hockey school, he cleverly included the rink's snack bar as a station. For example, each group might power skate, then rotate to a shooting station, followed by a prearranged snack at the snack bar, before heading to a small game station at the next whistle.

Paul liked to grab bread out of the dining commons, mount his battered old bike, and pedal to practice. There was a swampy cattail area at Blunt Park on the way to Smead Arena, and he'd stop there and feed bread crumbs to the waiting geese and the occasional seagull. The waterfowl flocked around him in a feeding frenzy, as they did around the Pigeon Lady in the *Home Alone* movie. I told Paul not to wear his AIC coaching outfit during these catering sessions, for fear he'd scare off our fans.

We completed the next season 11–13–2 and barely missed the playoffs. It didn't help that sophomore Steve Sangermano, who centered our green line, flunked off the team before the second semester started. Paul and I tried to get him to stay in school and improve his grades so he'd be eligible in the fall, but to no avail. Steve said he didn't want to be at AIC if he couldn't play hockey. He returned home and skated at Roger Williams College. He went on to play in the AHL, where he scored five goals in eleven games. When I heard that, his departure stung all the more.

Shawn Cornelow emerged as a top four defenseman after playing a lesser role during his first two years. We recruited him out of Quebec and Larry predicted that he might become the next Frenette or Wortman. That didn't happen, partly because he lacked foot speed, but he became a dependable defender. A criminal justice major, he joined the Royal Canadian Mounted Police after graduating.

I was excited to have Shawn in our program, not just because he was a good player and person, but because he was biracial. He had a white father and a Black mother. There weren't many Black people playing college hockey at the time. There still aren't. I thought being more ethnically diverse would benefit our team. On his recruiting visit he asked if "Springfield can be like *Mississippi Burning*," a new movie loosely based on the murder of three Black people during the Civil Rights Movement. I assured him that he didn't have to worry. I also pointed out that AIC was among the most diverse colleges in the country.

We did experience a racial incident during Shawn's career. After one of our games, I heard that an opposing player had used a racial slur against him. I strode over to his stall and he confirmed he had been called the N-word. I responded by saying that I'd report it to the kid's coach, but Shawn insisted that I let it go. He didn't want to make a big deal of the incident, despite my contention that the word is offensive to Black people. I deferred to his wishes, although in retrospect, I wish I had convinced Shawn that I had to report it.

Derek Decosta's decision to quit hockey also affected our season. He told me after the fall semester that he didn't want to play anymore. Derek had zero points in the nine games he dressed for, which probably indicated his apathy toward playing. But he had scored big goals for us in the past. He promised to stay in school and graduate, so I was pleased about that, as it would have been a double whammy if he dropped out. I accepted his decision and told him he could rejoin the team if he had second thoughts. He didn't change his mind, and before graduation he and his dad swung by my office to say goodbye.

That summer, I started a four-year association coaching at the USA Hockey regional 16/17 camps, held in Lake Placid and St. Cloud, Minnesota. I worked with many of the top prospects in the country, who were placed on eight teams that practiced and played games each day. Before the camps opened, our staffs attended a four-day orientation at the Olympic Training Center in Colorado Springs, where we learned about "icebreakers," which are used for team building and getting acquainted in a relaxed setting. One day Mike McShane, a fiery coach, called time-out in a game at Lake Placid and lit into his team. Then, looking up at the directors and coaches evaluating in the stands, he yelled, "How's that for an icebreaker."

We didn't need an icebreaker to begin the 1992–93 season with most of our team back. Our new assistant, Dave Guden, who played at Providence, was a teammate of Paul Cannata at Roxbury Latin. Paul had been hired as the new head coach at North Adams State. Freshman Craig Pitman led us in scoring, as we finished the first semester with a 5–2–2 record. A 145-pound dynamo, he darted around the ice making plays at every turn. He attended prep power Cushing Academy and Paul had worked tirelessly to recruit him.

When Craig came with his parents to register for courses, his mother told me she was worried about him getting up for classes. "He likes to sleep late," she said. And then his father said, "But he doesn't have any problem getting up for golf." Mrs. Pitman nodded in agreement about the golf. I smiled and told them we'd keep an eye on his attendance. I meant it.

We alternated Shane McConnell and Shawn Arcidiacono throughout a game against New England College. They each played for five minutes and sat the next five. Bill Beaney did a version of it when he coached at Berwick Academy but, for the most part, the move had few precedents. I thought there might be some merit in a goalie staying fully focused for a few minutes and then recovering on the bench like any other player. Moreover, netminders rotate in and out every day at practice. And if one goalie wasn't sharp, we could pull him knowing that the other goalie was warmed-up and dialed in. Shane and Shawn were close friends of relative ability, so that factored into my decision as well.

I explained my plan to the goalies a few days before the game, and emphasized that it wasn't anything we expected to do all the time. I also said they'd need to be strong and keep an open mind about this new way to play. I also told them that they were likely part of something that hadn't been done at the college level. To my relief, they seemed receptive to the idea. That's not to say they didn't exhibit some skepticism, but they were the kind of individuals who dared to try something different. Provided it worked, of course.

The game ended in a 7–7 tie—not the kind of score we hoped for in our first experiment with an in-game goalie rotation. Shawn had twelve saves and Shane stopped fourteen pucks. No record remains of how many goals they each allowed. They obviously weren't happy with the result, but looked forward to giving the rotation another try. We wound up going 4–2–1 in these rotation games. Ron Chimelis wrote an article a year later in the *Springfield Union-News* about our goalie switches under the alliterative headline, "AIC Shuffles Its Saves with Shane and Shawn."

A 10–1–1 run propelled us into the postseason. One of the wins came against Army, a Division I independent, who had recently pulled out of the ECAC D-I league. Craig Pitman potted two goals in the 6–4 win at West Point. Kevin Daly, our redheaded Bostonian from BC High, called it one of those victories where "you hug your teammates in the locker room." Army's historic campus, D-I status, and first-rate Tate Rink, which was a far cry from Smead, can do that to you.

We played the Williams College Ephs (once called the Elks by our student PA announcer) in the quarterfinals. They were the No. 4 seed and we were seeded No. 5. Despite our playoff-entering momentum and having beaten them in the regular season, we lost 6–2. I switched our goalies throughout the game, as I did in the Army win, but it didn't go well that night. I labored over whether to rotate them in a playoff game and then wondered after the game if I made the wrong decision.

Rob Abel, ironically a Williams grad, became our GA for the 1993–94 and 1994–95 seasons. His hiring was part of a musical-chairs scenario featuring AIC assistants. Rob replaced Dave Guden, who returned for his second year but quickly took the head coaching position at North Adams State when Paul Cannata left to become the bench boss at UMass Boston. Paul got hired in September, so I encouraged Dave to apply even though he had another year. I thought it was too good an opportunity for him to pass on, considering that North Adams was scrambling to hire a coach in the early fall. Plus, North Adams had liked the job Paul did, and their AD and Bob Burke were friends.

When Dave Guden started at North Adams, he had to wait to get materials back from their print shop. He thought he might have a solution. He had a good relationship with AIC printer Rich Hanson, an eccentric employee who, depending on his mood, either performed someone's printing needs while they waited, or told them to fill out a long order form and come back later. Rich agreed to a printing pact with Dave, despite the fact he now worked for another college. So when Dave drove to AIC to continue his grad classes, Rich did some on-the-spot printing for him. Paul Cannata always said he enjoyed the "collection of characters" that worked on our campus; there was none bigger than Rich Hanson, official printer for American International College and North Adams State hockey.

Tri-captains Kevin Daly, Mike Rood, and Shane McConnell presided over a team that took very few penalties. Our players knew I didn't tolerate bad penalties. If someone took such an infraction, or accumulated a lot of PIMs (penalty infraction minutes), he sat. It could be anywhere from a few shifts to a game, depending on severity. Ice time is precious to a player, so taking it away is the best deterrent for bad behavior, penalties or otherwise. And I held everyone accountable—the team's best player as well as the third goalie, because the players were always witness to my credibility. Marty Pierce, the

Boston fire chief who coached Matignon, a juggernaut high school team, said, "My heroes are the guys who stay out of the penalty box." He won a lot more championships than me, but we shared a disdain for dumb penalties.

Jim Greenridge wrote a *Boston Globe* story on Mike Rood, who was recommended to me by Maine great Gary Conn. Mike played at Beverly HS, and Gary coached in their league. Mike later joined AIC's 100 Point Club and he spoke about our team's low penalties in the article. "Our coach doesn't tolerate penalties," he said, "especially those behind the play, after the whistle or the high sticking ones, but it's OK if there's a breakaway and we're trying to prevent the easy goal." Mike made some good points, though Shane and Shawn probably wouldn't consider an opponent's breakaway to be an "easy goal."

We played in UMass-Boston's Twenty-Ninth Codfish Bowl in late December. It's considered the premier Division II/III tourney in the East. Held in their campus rink on the shores of Boston Harbor, the tourney didn't receive the attention of the Beanpot tournament, but it was well covered by the *Boston Globe* and *Boston Herald*. Participating in the tourney was exciting enough, and it was even more fun with Paul Cannata now coaching the host school.

On the day of our opening-round game with Salem State, we pulled up to the adjacent John F. Kennedy Presidential Library, and I entered the library on a whim to see if they'd let our team in at no cost. They said we had to pay. I headed back to the bus and Rob Abel, my outgoing young assistant, asked if he could try. I told him to go ahead, though I doubted he'd have any better luck than me. Minutes later he bounded back onto the bus.

"We're all set," he announced, "I've got us in for free." Everyone walked excitedly into the library. Well, a lot of us were excited; I'm sure some guys weren't thrilled about the visit.

Rob said afterward that he got us in by telling the administrators that we were playing in the Codfish next door and didn't have a budget for such a visit, so he asked if we could come in for a short time.

"Our players are interested in political history and learning more about President Kennedy," he said. "They're almost as excited about seeing the museum as playing in the tournament." It worked, but that reasoning might have been a stretch.

Salem beat us 5–4, and the next day we routed the UMass Boston Beacons

11–3 in the consolation contest. We unloaded forty-nine shots against three goaltenders, two of whom rotated through much of the game. Paul Cannata had left AIC by the time we started in-game goalie switches, but he knew about our approach. He inherited a fairly weak team, meaning there was only so much he could do with his new club, and only so much I could do to keep the score down, other than shorten the bench in the third period.

I told the *Boston Globe*, "We put a lot of emphasis on this game. In many respects, you can learn something about your kids in a consolation game."

Paul called and said, "Coach, I just saw the game article. Did you have to say that? I mean, what does it say about my team?" I wasn't commenting on his team, but I understood his concern. That said, I was generally circumspect when dealing with the media to avoid making comments with unintended consequences. The irony is that I've always enjoyed reading colorful quotes from coaches and others. I guess mine could be boring by comparison.

We finished a few games over .500. Bowdoin was our first-round opponent. With a veteran-laden team featuring six seniors, our playoff prospects seemed promising. They weren't. Bowdoin blew us out of Brunswick 10–0. After speaking with the team and recognizing the seniors, I slipped out the back door and leaned against a spindly tree.

"Have a safe trip home," a woman said as she walked by.

"Thank you," I whispered. We were safe enough on our trip back, but it was cold. Even the heat didn't work out right.

We struggled after those seniors graduated. To some extent it was due to our decision to drop athletic scholarships a couple of years before. This resulted from the Division III institutions in the ECAC East wanting everyone to play by NCAA D-III rules. They outnumbered Division II schools like AIC and St. Anselm's, and UConn and Holy Cross, both D-I colleges. The league adopted NESCAC (Colby, Middlebury, etc.) rules, such as starting practice on November 1, playing games on Friday nights and Saturday afternoons, and each team had a travel partner. For instance, we'd play a team on Friday and our partner UConn played the other. We switched opponents on Saturday.

The NESCAC procedures added structure to the league and their policies provided a balanced schedule where we played each ECAC East team, unlike in the past. However, our financial aid packages now had to be need-based, and our school's smaller endowment, as opposed to that of our opponents, didn't allow us to meet many families' need. But other colleges had their challenges, so we tried not to make excuses and just get the job done.

Pat Moriarty got it done as a co-captain. He was a local boy from the Hungry Hill section of Springfield. (AIC professor Mike Manley, a former policeman, said cops originally named the neighborhood because there was no place to get a bite to eat.) Pat attended Cathedral HS and received the Amo Bessone (former Michigan State coach from West Springfield) Award for the top hockey player in Western Mass. Pat was a strong student, and we landed him in part because he wanted to stay home. He was a good player, an even better person, and a leader. In fact, he evolved into a fearless leader, unafraid to call guys out when they misbehaved.

Pat coached at Cathedral before being named the baseball coach and a college adviser at prestigious Deerfield Academy, where he now lives. He reflected on his new job:

> Deerfield is a long way from the two-family, single-parent household that I grew up in on Hungry Hill in Springfield. I am not sure if you knew this, but I almost attended Deerfield, but my mother simply could not afford the tuition. So when I accepted the position this past summer, I drove my mother up here to show her the campus and our new home. She was so happy that she could not stop crying. It was a very emotional day to say the least.

Our team flew to play Alabama-Huntsville in December. The trip offered a reprieve from the winter weather back home. That was about it. We got annihilated both nights, losing 8–3 and 12–4. The song "Sweet Home Alabama" played like a broken record every time they scored. There was no joy in Mudville (I mean Huntsville) that weekend for goalie Shawn Arcidiacono, or our team, which labored in front of their beleaguered goaltender. After we got home and the dust settled, freshman Eric Lang had an idea. He called Shawn's room and when he answered, Eric played "Sweet Home Alabama" over the phone. Another time he left the song on Shawn's answering machine. It was pretty brash for a freshman, even if he was sort of a city kid from the Bronx, but Shawn took it in good humor.

We floundered down the stretch, losing to teams we usually beat, and losing by larger scores to opponents who had been our equal. We hadn't experienced that in recent years, so Rob Abel and I met with our seniors in the hockey office. I implored them to provide leadership to our younger players by staying positive and working hard. Then I asked how they were coping with the losses. Phil Saunders, a tall, soft-spoken defenseman from Michigan, said quite sincerely, "I usually go back to my room at night and have a good cry."

Our players gave Rob a send-off present for his two years of service. It was a modest yet meaningful gift. They all signed a wooden Canadian 6001 hockey stick, and some guys added a comment:

"Rob, thanks for all the great memories. John Paluzzi #11; Abe's, thanks for bringing me here. Your buddy from Da Bronx: Eric [Lang]."

The stick still hangs in Rob's garage. His son plays hockey, and I think his wife might have banned all sticks from the house, including that one, which he considers "among my most prized coaching gifts due to its personal nature." After AIC, Rob coached at Dartmouth and Brown and became the CEO of MountainOne Investments. He handles my investments.

I hired a new GA in the spring to start work in the fall. A player committee, chaired by captain Pat Moriarty, helped to interview the finalists. They selected Greg Klym as their first choice. Greg came from Ontario and played for Dick Umile at UNH. He dated one of Dick's daughters. It was an unusual situation, but things worked out OK, perhaps because Greg was an excellent player and co-captain at UNH, so he didn't have to complain to his girlfriend about her father not giving him enough playing time. I hired Greg in the end, although not without pause. He was the only candidate who didn't wear a coat and tie. Instead, he showed up in an untucked plaid shirt. We still laugh about it.

There were also the usual laughs at the Vermont Hockey School that summer. Neddie Grant was a veteran VHS instructor, and John LeClair spent a few years on staff. Having played at BFA and UVM, and being an NHL star, John was a favorite of the participants—and their parents. One year, Neddie announced to the kids that the constant requests for John's autograph were a distraction. He told them that John could hardly do his job, and the staff was even being interrupted in the coaches' room. "From now on," he said, "if you want John LeClair's autograph give me a quarter and I'll get you one."

The 1995–96 season included a return to the Codfish Bowl. Babson beat us 5–3 in the first game and UMass Boston drubbed Southern Maine 10–4 in the nightcap. My former assistant Paul Cannata, ever the wordsmith, said in the *Boston Herald* game story after his team's win, "For the first time since I've been here it seems easy. No matter what cards you throw out there, anybody can be a good coach if you have the kings and queens and aces."

The next day we visited Faneuil Hall and Quincy Market in downtown Boston. I walked around and entered a few of the stores myself, though I'm no shopper. Yet I ended up purchasing a pond hockey painting titled *Boston Twilight Players*. It was painted by Candice Lovely, a classmate at the University of Vermont. We didn't know each other personally, but I knew some of her sorority sisters. The painting hung on the wall of my hockey office. I wonder if attending UVM prompted Candice to paint a hockey scene.

That afternoon, we went up 4–1 on Southern Maine when Craig Pitman whooshed down the ice and whistled in a wrist shot. Soon after, Eric Lang collided with an opponent and slumped to the ice. He was strapped to a backboard and transported to a nearby hospital for observation. (Travis Roy had recently been paralyzed in a BU game, so that probably influenced the precautions taken with Eric.) The game resumed after a long delay and ended in a tie. Fortunately, Eric was released the next day.

We hosted St. Anselm's and New England College (NEC) at the end of the season. Led by Chris Mohney's five goals, we swept the series to end on a positive note. The Billy Idol version of "Mony Mony" blared every time he scored. The spelling was different, but the pronunciations matched perfectly.

The weekend represented the last AIC games for our four seniors: Travis Brennan, a forward, who played for Jim Tortorella at Cony HS in Maine; Les Feltmate, who rarely got in the lineup; JJ Moore, a cerebral performer who was a long-haired Grateful Dead fan; and Craig Pitman, captain and member of the career 100 Point Club, who also excelled on the golf team. Craig was the recipient of the Joe Tomasello Unsung Hero Award by the New England Hockey Writers.

I wasn't going to dress Les Feltmate against NEC on Senior Night, because we had other players better than him. Plus, he had only played a handful of games in his career. The seniors came to my office that day to ask if I could dress Les. I told them I'd already made my decision not to play him, and JJ Moore said, "If he can't play, I don't want to play."

"First of all," I snapped, "don't even think about threatening me about this."

JJ backed off, and then they went with what appeared to be a backup plan. They said Phil Langill, a sophomore fourth-liner, wanted to sit out so Les could play.

"Did you guys pressure him?" I asked. They shook their heads. I thought for a second and told them to send Phil over to talk with me.

Phil convinced me that he wanted Les to play, so I went along with it. On his first shift, Les made a nice move taking the puck down the boards, and for a moment I thought to myself, have I made a mistake not playing him all along? But his other shifts were marginal, which got me off the proverbial hook.

Greg Klym put together a highlight film which included interviews with the seniors. In it, Les gushed, "I had guys coming up to me after the game saying, 'It was a pleasure playing with you.' I mean, I couldn't believe they were saying that about me." When I watched it for the first time, I knew the seniors were right and I was glad they made me change my mind.

Anthony Giusto captained our team the next season. He transferred from UMass Amherst after playing for the restarted Minutemen program. They recruited a whole team to start with, and with subsequent recruiting classes coming in, there wasn't room on defense for Anthony. I rarely dealt with transfers, but he'd played locally for the Springfield Pics, and I coached him in the Connecticut Hockey Training Program (CHTC), a summer program for college prospects. I decided that his strong defensive play and D-I experience would benefit us, in spite of his propensity for penalties.

Anthony took too many penalties during his first season. He could also be hot-headed and borderline belligerent if I reprimanded him on the bench. Despite that, the team elected him captain for his senior year. Maybe they knew something I didn't. He calmed down, though I'm not suggesting he became a dove in the defensive zone. He gave us great leadership. Sometimes the guys you battle with as a coach can surprise you. Anthony not only altered his behavior, but he wrote me a nice letter after graduating:

I just wanted to take this opportunity to thank you for all that you have done for me and our team. You have given me the chance to play for and with some of the best people that I have ever had the pleasure to know. It takes very special people to keep a positive attitude through the tough times, and for that I am extremely grateful to each and every one of my teammates as well as the coaches. There may have been a few instances where we haven't seen eye to eye, but the discipline you have taught me will be with me for the rest of my life.

That discipline, along with effort and attitude, are three areas within a player's control. Not everyone can be a leading scorer or an elite performer, but each team member can live those three qualities. And I insisted that they did—and disciplined them if they didn't. Our student-athletes were responsible and accountable for their actions when it came to effort, attitude, and discipline. Any player who could consistently exhibit those qualities was a winner in my book.

Discipline is one of a team's building blocks. Or it should be. Showing up on time, staying out of the box, not over-staying shifts, and being dependable defensively are all examples of discipline. Discipline away from the ice is just as important. Going to class, avoiding trouble on campus and in the community, getting enough sleep, eating properly, and working hard in the weight room are crucial components of self-discipline and commitment. Renowned UCLA basketball coach John Wooden said it best: "Discipline yourself and others won't have to."

Another famous basketball coach, Pat Summit, the women's coach at Tennessee, felt that she shouldn't have to coach "effort." Systems, running effective practices, and motivational tactics are all predicated on having players who work hard. Lazy athletes are a challenge to coach. There are ways to motivate people, but the best way is to recruit committed competitors to begin with—players who "come to play" every day. A sign above our locker room door read, "Whatever you've got, we need it all the time."

Ten years hence, veteran *Springfield Republican* sportswriter Garry Brown wrote in his "Hitting to All Fields" column, "Hats off to coach Gary Wright and his hard-working AIC hockey team." I liked his catchy line because it implied notable effort in our play.

Attitude, the other category in this troika, can make or break an organization, a company, or a team. I always asked coaches about a player's attitude. If they hedged to protect him, I dug deeper, because a team member with a bad attitude can be a louse in the locker room. If teammates start to listen to that person, it can undermine team chemistry—and the coach. I disliked coaching chronic complainers. Upbeat players who love to practice and play, don't gripe about team meal menus, appreciate the equipment we provide, and are fun to play with are the unsung heroes on any team. These individuals can lift their teammates from the depths of defeat, as Anthony Giusto did. I always told our guys: "When I run into you on campus, I want to be glad to see you."

Following his success at the end of the previous season, senior Chris Mohney's career ended differently when he butt-ended an NEC player behind the play in the closing minutes of our last game. The kid had to be helped off the ice. Chris had been unhappy with his ice time, so the incident was likely related to frustration. I wasn't happy about it, and for years to come I warned our players not to do something stupid in the last game. "You don't want to burn bridges at the end," I persisted, "particularly if you're a senior, since it's hard to redeem yourself when you're done playing."

We moved to the Olympia Ice Center in 1997–98. Barry Tabb, the owner, had reached out to me and Bob Burke to see if we wanted to change rinks. The Olympia was farther from campus than Smead Arena, but it had more to offer, and they agreed to build us a new locker room. It even had a bathroom and showers. Our maintenance department then constructed birch player stalls with wooden Shaker pegs for hanging equipment. The floor carpet featured our logo. Assistant Captain Ben Ballou ran around like Bob the Builder and made us a stick rack.

I held my breath when certain players returned each fall. Bill Daley, a lunch-pail player who became a high school math teacher, had been too heavy in past seasons, so I was relieved when he came back in better shape. The year before, I asked him about his eating habits and he told me he went to Burger King every night, because he got tired of eating "the same old food" at the dining commons (DC). Our talk ended up like this:

Me: "What do you order there?"

Bill: "I usually get two Whoppers, a large fries and a coke."

Me: "So you go to Burger King because you're tired of the DC food, yet you eat the same meal at BK night after night."

He just shrugged his shoulders.

Eric Lang wore the C for us after assisting Anthony the year before. There were already indications that he might make a good coach someday. He read Pat Riley's book, *The Winner Within*, and handed out copied excerpts at a players' meeting, including Riley's belief that each player has more to give, thereby strengthening a team that has endured the losing-before-winning process. I often quoted retired Boston Celtic Don Nelson to support that idea: "I never had speed, size or jumping ability, so I looked for little ways to make up for that and I found hundreds."

Greg Klym coached Eric his first two years and said he was the kind of player who "stood out to me, because he was always picking my brain about ways to improve his game." Eric in turn mentioned that during his freshman year, Greg told him to play tougher and be less of a perimeter player. "That's a sensitive subject for any player," Eric said, "but Greg had such a nice way with words that he made his point without offending me, or any of my teammates for that matter."

One of Eric's buddies was fellow New Yorker and teammate Peter Szymanski. Peter lived in a high-rise in neighboring Hell's Kitchen and, like many Big Apple kids, he played roller hockey. He also skated with the NY Junior Islanders prior to attending AIC. Built like a bodybuilder, he bowled over opponents on his way to the net. Peter's sense of humor showed when he came up to me during an outdoor off-ice training session and said, "Coach, I think you dropped this," as he handed me a small Ziploc bag stuffed with grass he'd pulled from the ground. I didn't ask him if he'd also seen a pot pipe lying around.

In addition to Eric's leadership, the move to the Olympia gave our program a big boost. We'd had some great years at Smead, but the Olympia featured a more modern and professional environment. And there was another big move coming to our program that changed the course of AIC Hockey.

Chapter 10

Going Division I

We entered the 1998–99 season as a charter member of the Metro Atlantic Athletic Association (MAAC) Hockey League. Quinnipiac AD Jack McDonald was the brainchild of the new league, which became NCAA hockey's fifth Division I conference. The MAAC started with eight D-I and D-II institutions who, like us, had been playing in leagues that were predominately D-III. Bentley and Mercyhurst joined a year later. Ascending to that level meant we would be operating our program under Division I rules and could offer scholarships again. The NCAA allowed for eighteen athletic scholarships, but the school's athletic directors agreed to eleven grants as a cost-effective measure. The MAAC also offered an opportunity for teams to play in the NCAA Tournament, and the league planned to apply soon for an automatic qualifier berth.

Going D-I represented a big step for AIC and our hockey program. Bob Burke worked hard to get us into the league and to convince President Harry Courniotes that it was the right choice for us. Burke emphasized how D-III was trending toward leagues with like schools, and that our best chance to join the MAAC was now. Bob told me that although we'd be spending more money to participate in the MAAC, it didn't mean there would be big increases in the future. "In other words," he said, with a pointed wave of his right index finger, "I don't want you coming into my office next year looking to spend a whole lot more money."

"Do you really think I'd do that?" I said with a grin."

"Yes, I do," he said.

The MAAC Hockey League held its media day at UConn. The Huskies left the ECAC East with us and Holy Cross to join the new conference.

Bob and I attended the event with team captain Mike Sowa. Commissioner Rich Ensor spoke, along with each head coach. The next day a Ron Chimelis article appeared in the *Springfield Union-News*. Headlined, "AIC Takes New Path in Hockey," it had a creative opening:

> That American International College is a Division I hockey school probably seems no more incongruous than the fact that AIC is a hockey school at all, even though the Yellow Jackets have been dropping the puck since 1948. The college is nestled in a predominately urban environment, quite unlike the snowy, picturesque backdrops of the Bowdoins and Colbys that AIC has been playing.

When Mike Sowa visited campus with his mother during the recruiting process, I worried about what he'd think of our inner-city setting. He graduated from Culver Military Academy in Indiana, where he lettered in hockey, football and golf. Culver has a beautiful lakeside campus that includes nearly one hundred horses, which are ridden as part of the Black Horse Troop that participates in most presidential inauguration parades. I mention this not because horses are necessarily hockey fans, but to underscore how different his prep school environment was from our city campus. But I needn't have been worried.

I brought up our location during their visit, as I always did with recruits and their parents, knowing it was on their minds anyway. To my relief, Mrs. Sowa weighed in and said that Mike was looking for a different experience by attending college in a city. I was relieved to hear that, and it spoke to Mike's enlightened view of things. He majored in psychology at AIC and was a dean's list student. Richard Sprinthall, an AIC professor who authored a psychology textbook used by more than two hundred colleges, tried to get Mike to stay at AIC after graduation and work toward a PhD in clinical psychology, but he decided to move on.

The MAAC had a major league feel as a Division I conference. A MAAC banner hung in the three-rink Olympia Ice Center in West Springfield and the league logo was on the ice. The MAAC plastered their logo on everything: jerseys, jackets, pucks, clocks, and whistles. During our opening practice, I watched a 4-on-4 scrimmage from the stands with returning assistant Frank Genovese as manager Amy Kirrane blew my new MAAC Fox 40 whistle every forty seconds to change players on the fly. It screeched like a dog whistle, so I sent Frank down to the bench to investigate. He came back soon after to tell me he'd checked it out and even blown it himself, and there wasn't anything wrong with it. "But it sounds different, because it's a pea-less whistle," he said. Pea or no pea, I eventually adjusted to the newfangled device, which allowed me to whistle while I worked.

Amy Kirrane did more than blow whistles. She may have been the best manager we ever had. And she came from good hockey stock. Her grandfather, Jack Kirrane, captained the gold-medal-winning 1960 U.S. Olympic Hockey Team. Amy was a physical therapy major who played on the tennis team and served in student government. She managed our team like a general manager. She performed office work, oversaw practice and game management, and helped with trip planning. Amy not only had a good rapport with our players, but she had their respect. Eric Lang remembers the team "watching over her like she was our little sister."

We opened with a home-and-home sweep of Fairfield University and then took on Bruce Marshall's UConn Huskies. They were playing their first game in the newly constructed Freitas Ice Forum, which replaced their outdoor rink. Mike Sowa represented us in the ceremonial puck drop to open the new facility. The game ended in a 2–2 tie. It wasn't pouring that night like it did in 1990, and even if it had been, I had no reason to walk in the rain after a hard-fought tie and a 2–0–1 start in the MAAC.

I kept Middlebury and Williams on the schedule in our last season playing non–Division I teams. Ben Ballou got the game-winner in a 2–1 win over Williams, but Middlebury blanked us at their place. We'd been playing the Panthers for years, and of all the teams we competed with in the ECAC East, Middlebury was the hardest team for me to drop from our schedule. Besides my Middlebury-area roots, we had a nice rivalry with them, in part, I think, because Bill Beaney and I have similar philosophies, though he was more successful than I. His use and promotion of small games, and his unique system that utilized two forwards and three "backs," as opposed to the traditional three forwards and two defensemen, differentiated his teams from all others. I coached against some of the finest Division I coaches in the country, but none were better than Bill.

There are photos in Bill's office of the Middlebury coaches and close support staff, pictured with the various national championship trophies. I was surprised to find that I couldn't identify one particular person in the pictures, until I learned it was bus driver, Gary Forcier, considered to be a big part of the team's success.

We occasionally visited at my parents' Cornwall home when we played at Middlebury. One year my mother oversaw the pregame meal, but it was a short-lived experiment. Better known for her academic pursuits than culinary expertise, she catered in a meal, and although I cautioned her about our players' ravenous appetites, we ran out of food by the time our last few guys got to the makeshift buffet table. My frazzled mother then dashed into town to pick up some emergency pasta.

I usually took our players down behind our Cornwall house to see the beaver pond. It was frozen most years when we went to Middlebury, so guys slid around on their shoes. Well, everyone except Peter Szymanski; he didn't trust the natural ice. Apparently Hell's Kitchen ponds don't freeze over.

Senior Matt McCormick was nicknamed "Mattie Mayhem" by his teammates. A Springfield native, he played for former AIC star Edgar Alejandro at Cathedral HS. Matt's nickname referenced his tendency to occasionally mess up in drills. He'd go the wrong way and collide with another player or forget to pass to the next guy in line. At worst, he caused enough chaos to disrupt the drill. Undeterred, he often headed right back to the front of the line.

Our regular season ended with back-to-back 5–4 OT losses to league-leader Quinnipiac. As the No. 5 seed, we were bound for Buffalo to battle the No. 4-seeded Canisius Golden Griffins. We departed the day before the game and stopped to have a pasta dinner en route. This deviated from our normal routine of eating at a rest area. Mike Sowa had approached me about scheduling a more formal sit-down meal since we had a playoff game the next day and the food would be better. I went along with his idea. I always tried to consider requests from captains if they were reasonable and infrequent.

We entered the Canisius contest in good health, except for assistant captain Rob Murphy who'd been playing with a high ankle sprain. It nagged him for weeks, despite the efforts of trainer Barclay Dugger, who allowed Rob to play through the pain, since it wasn't a serious injury. The best solution was for him to sit out awhile, but Rob didn't want to do that late in his senior year. Thus he soldiered on, sometimes making it through half a practice before a random movement caused a sharp pain. Whatever the pain, he felt that sitting out would be worse.

I was surprised to see MAAC Commissioner Rich Ensor at the game, considering the league sent a rep to cover each quarterfinal game and the other contests were closer to the conference office. Assigning himself to the longest trip indicated his strong work ethic. A heavyset man, he had an air about him that suggested a big-time CEO or commissioner. He backed it up when, as the head of the multisport MAAC conference and a member of the Division I NCAA Management Council, he spearheaded the increase from twelve to sixteen teams in the NCAA Tournament.

Canisius built a 3–2 lead in the first period. Joe Wlodarczyk had our goals. He notched another in the second stanza and assisted on Kevin Fournier's goal, but the Griffins had two of their own. Play went up and down in the third and it remained a one-goal game until Canisius scored with a minute left to go up 6–4. Then they added an empty net goal to seal our fate.

Joe's hat trick wasn't a shocker. He led us in scoring as a sophomore, but his eligibility ran out after the playoffs, making his situation one of the few negatives from our move to Division I. His two years at AIC, combined with full-time enrollment at a previous college, meant his D-I career had ended. Still eligible to play D-III, he transferred to Potsdam State, one of the schools I recommended he consider. We missed having him in the lineup the next two seasons.

I returned to the Vermont Hockey School (VHS) a few months later. I'd been working there for twenty years, and during that time I had to listen to former Maine and UVM assistant coach Ted Castle mention my name when he demonstrated a skill to the kids. It might be, "Don't slap at the puck when you stickhandle, that's the way Gary stickhandles," or, while demonstrating with a stumbling skating stride, he'd say, "Don't skate this way, that's the way Gary skates." Unfortunately, there was an element of truth to Ted's whimsical assessments of my hockey skills. Most of what he said, however, went over the heads of the younger kids, who were often focused on other things, like whether or not the snack bar would be serving curly fries.

While I worked at the Vermont Hockey School, co-captains Aaron Arnett and Zac Kalemba sent a letter to their teammates. I asked our captains to do that every summer so players heard from someone besides me. A section of the letter provides a peek at their leadership:

It doesn't take much out of the day to go workout for an hour. So just get it done, so we don't have to put up with the bullshit of some of our best guys sitting out of important games (penalty for failing fitness test). We need to be stronger and more physical next season, so hit the weights hard and get on the ice as much as possible.

In addition to sharing encouraging words, they also told the team to "be smart and take it easy with the partying," because there's always some guys who "come back fifteen pounds heavier and it's not from working out."

Aaron and Zac impressed Jeff Matthews, my GA at the time. Aaron stayed after graduation to get his master's in forensic psychology at AIC, and then joined the Ontario Provincial Police. Jeff, who in time became head coach of women's hockey at Amherst College, recalled their captaincy:

They were tremendous leaders and captains. Their maturity level was impressive and they were willing to work in the shadows, doing everything necessary to keep the team together, and everyone else happy, but they weren't afraid to exact tough love. They did the grunt work, without looking for praise or accolades. Those two were big-time competitors, who were consistent in their performance and demeanor. And they were rarely moody and highly trustworthy. I'll never forget them.

I had Jeff refinish our office desks when he started work. He played at Deerfield Academy and RPI before entering the business world, so he made a brave decision to switch careers with no guarantee he could get a full-time coaching job after his two-year GA position. He passed on the dorm-room option to stay with his parents in nearby Westfield. They were surprised to hear that he spent time refinishing desks, so the next day I told Jeff to tell his folks that now he had to mow the athletic grounds. That understandably shocked them, and his mother was afraid that his new job might be more of a maintenance position. The mowing part was just a joke, and Jeff soon learned that other than his schoolwork, his focus was all hockey, all day and into the night.

And sometimes it was all night. Jeff recalls watching a junior game in the Chicago area and then driving nine hundred miles through the night to get back for practice and a test in his educational psychology master's program. He studied for the test as he drove, which he admits probably wasn't the "safest or smartest move." He stopped along I-90 for coffee and gas and to take a catnap in his car. The next morning, he pulled wearily into the hockey office and I put him right to work.

Jeff's predecessor, Frank Genovese, had his own recruiting story to tell. He was in the Ottawa area watching Junior A games, and on his final day he went to a game in Kanata, only to find out that the contest had been canceled due to a burgeoning ice storm. He then drove onto the icy Queensway to begin the long drive home. He didn't get far. Cars spun out everywhere and soon Frank's 1996 Nissan Sentra suffered a similar fate. He finally got towed out and found his way to a hotel, where he waited in line for the last room. He holed up in the hotel for the next three days, unable to leave because the Ogdensburg Bridge, which crosses the border, was also closed. The hotel lost cable service due to the epic storm, so Frank hung out across the street at East Side Mario's restaurant and bar, where he fit in fast with the regulars. When the bridge reopened on Saturday morning, he sped back to Springfield and arrived just in time for the Colby game. His presence didn't save the day. We lost 6–5.

Another recruiting adventure involved Larry and me in the late 1980s. We drove ten hours to see one of his recruits in Michigan. The kid knew we were there, yet still managed to get DQ'd for spearing in the first period. There was an awkward silence as we watched him head to the showers. Awkward, because I had come all the way out to see a kid Larry may not have properly vetted. Thereupon we left and set out for Springfield in Larry's dilapidated Datsun with the tied-down hood. The plan was to drive straight home. We got onto Ontario's Highway 401 in a blinding blizzard that blew snowdrifts onto the road. Larry kept complaining about the driving conditions. I implored him to keep going and promised to take the wheel soon. Two hours later we switched positions. I drove for a short time before pulling into a motel.

"What are you doing?" Larry asked as he woke up.

"The driving is impossible," I said, "we'll never make it home tonight."

"No shit," he muttered.

My summer letter to the team the ensuing season ended with a potpourri of AIC hockey happenings:

> The ongoing Olympia renovations look super. We have a great
> group of returnees. We anticipate a terrific recruiting class.
> The MAAC is receiving an automatic qualifier to the Division I
> NCAA's. The locker room has a new life cycle. We hit the ice in
> three months. And fly to Colorado in October. How sweet it is.

Senior goaltender Chance Thede was pumped to play Air Force. Chance
lived in Westminster, Colorado, not far from the Academy's campus. He
played well in a 4–2 loss the first night and not so good the next night. He
was All-MAAC Second Team as a sophomore, and his .907 save percentage
his senior year placed fourth in the league. In a *Springfield Republican* article
prior to our series with MAAC newcomer Army, staff writer Dick Baker
referred to Chance as a "stone-faced finance major, who could easily pass for
a member of the [Army] Cadets." Chance's serious, technician-like approach
to his craft meant he rarely took a shot off, whether it be a game, a practice,
or warm-ups.

Chance mentioned to my assistants once that he couldn't help glancing at
me after he let in a goal. He said I sometimes had a look of disgust on my
face, or appeared to be mouthing frustration about the goal, as if I thought
he should have stopped the puck. I didn't realize my body language was
that overt, so I curbed my behavior without saying anything to Chance.
Goaltending is a hard enough position as it is, without being second-guessed
in real time by the head coach.

Chance was a workhorse for us and played 1,800 minutes in net, which
left a mere 100 minutes for backup Tom Patty. But Tom didn't let his senior
season go to waste. He knew he wanted to teach and coach after graduation, so
he listened up, instead of tuning out like some goalies do, when we discussed
forechecking and other systemic subjects. He's since had a career as a prep/
public school educator, including coaching stints at the Winchendon School
and Fitchburg State University. Not bad for a kid who once played between
the pipes for Smead Arena's next-door neighbor, Springfield Central High
School, a city team that barely fielded a full roster.

We finished with a 10–15–1 MAAC record. Two of our wins came against
Holy Cross by identical 4–3 overtime scores. Not only that, but they were

scored by the same player: Trent Ulmer. The first win came on the road, and
the second contest was played at the Olympia. In that game, Trent crossed
the blue line near the Crusaders' bench and unleashed a long top-shelf laser
at 4:58 of the extra frame. Our team abandoned the bench and sprinted to
celebrate with Ulmer. The press guide included a picture of the celebration
the following year. In the scrum, you can see Quebecker Kevin Fournier
with his right glove planted warmly on the head of Trent Ulmer. Guillaume
Caron, Jeff Matthew's prized recruit, hugs winning goalie Chance Thede.
There's a big smile on Tom Patty's face. It's easy to see because he doesn't
have his mask on. It's heartwarming to see because he's elated, even though
he didn't play. I saw the picture again seventeen years after it was taken. It's
pure bliss to look at. In a way, I guess you can say the thrill of an overtime
win is everlasting.

Richard Novak, our grad assistant for the 2001–02 season, came from
Switzerland armed with a one-year visa, hoping to find a college team that
would have him. Richard also visited BU's strength and conditioning guru
Mike Boyle and Harvard coach Mark Mazzoleni, where he learned about
our GA opening. I hired him even though he could only do a year of the
two-year grad program. He had a strong coaching résumé, and I thought
he'd bring fresh Swiss ideas to AIC Hockey. He did. Richard's specialty was
dryland training and conditioning, and he had a master's degree in physical
education. When our players first reported to his preseason conditioning
program, they thought this boyish, mild-mannered individual with an
accent might be a pushover. They found out differently. He worked them
hard and impressed them with his European conditioning ideas. One of
his exercises involved throwing a ball up in the air, doing a somersault and
then catching the same ball before it landed. He also excelled on the ice
(where he wore mittens), and oversaw our defensemen and defensive zone
coverage. Maintaining defensive posture from the "inside" was one of his
chief concepts, and he emphasized how smart positioning could "keep us
safe," while still playing assertively.

I had minimal familiarity with Swiss hockey prior to Richard's hire, other
than the witty response of crusty Boston Bruins GM Harry Sinden when he
heard that Bruin Joe Juneau was considering playing in Switzerland: "Well,
he better learn how to yodel."

I don't know if Richard could yodel, but he did experience a few language and cultural barriers. After his first solo drive to watch Albany Academy play, I asked how his trip went, and he said he saw some good players, "but I felt like a criminal." When I laughed and asked why, he explained that people in Switzerland tend to carpool to protect the environment when driving longer distances. Then there was the time I told him we were going to have a "meat and potatoes practice."

"Meat and potatoes?" he said with a puzzled look on his face.

I explained that the expression meant we were having a hard, no-frills practice, not a meal.

Richard did a stellar job with our defensemen. Those of us in North America have long associated the Europeans with their offensive proficiency, but he was proof of their commitment to defense. He awarded our first USHL player, Mike Bujdos, with big minutes, and he respected full-bodied Kevin Fournier, a smart, stable defenseman who made simple outlet passes, while playing a defense-first game. One of our D's, Mike Liebro from West Springfield, was the Eddie Shore recipient as the top defenseman in Western Mass HS hockey. Mike was a fifth- or sixth-type defenseman on our team. Richard counseled him on accepting his new and unwanted role.

We sunk to a seven-win season. Losing is tough on players and coaches. It can eat you up if you let it. Ironically, as head coaches, we often do our best job when we're losing, at least with respect to our day-to-day coaching efforts. It forces us to find additional ways to win. For instance, I spent more time planning practices that season than other years when we had stronger teams. It was small consolation, but our seven-win season could have been worse, and we'd have lost by bigger scores, if Richard and I didn't come to coach every day. The expression "winning isn't everything, but wanting to win is" speaks to the importance of competing hard and not succumbing to loss. So, while losing hurt, learning from those losses inspired us to strive for more wins. The Dalai Lama says, "When you lose, don't lose the lesson."

Back In 1997, I spoke about losing at the American Hockey Coaches Association (AHCA) convention in Naples, Florida. Executive Director Joe Bertagna allowed me to choose a subject, so I came up with "Winning While Losing: Progress During the Tough Times" as my topic. Speaking in front of one's peers can be intimidating, so I hoped that my voice wouldn't quiver, my hands wouldn't shake, and my legs wouldn't buckle. None of that happened, though I did feel a little hurry in my heart. I received several compliments from coaching colleagues, which I appreciated.

My presentation covered thoughts on dealing with a losing season. I talked about how losing can threaten a team's psyche and that strong leadership is a coach's greatest gift during adversity. I emphasized that leadership must be steeped in honesty, persistence, and dedication to the profession, and that there can be no quit in the coach. Furthermore, maintaining a good rapport with players is essential, because a coach who is too dictatorial is often less tolerated during the tough times. I discussed the importance of having dedicated assistants and strong captains, the type of individuals you'd "want to be in a foxhole with," as aptly described by former Maine admissions counselor Bill Bryan.

I spoke about showing no letup when it comes to planning practice during the difficult days; how practice should be spiced with fresh drills; and to include small games, because they're fun and competitive and the "play instinct is a powerful instinct." Discipline, I stressed, is critical during a losing season. If it's not enforced, progress is negligible and the season can trend downward. Not letting the little things slide is paramount: starting practice on time, no shooting pucks after the whistle, new information on the bulletin board, skates sharpened on time, etc. My last point was, "If a player stays strong and maintains an upbeat attitude, he or she will be a winner in life."

Richard returned to Switzerland following the season and, years later, we talked again. He reflected on his time at AIC, stating that toughness was an important characteristic he took from AIC. He said he learned a lot, but the overall coaching experience proved to be hard. The game and practice demands, recruiting responsibilities, overseeing our conditioning program, and taking classes all added up to long hours. And he was the only assistant. Those challenges were compounded by his unfamiliarity with a different country. He said the whole experience helped him to "become a stronger character and a better coach."

The 2002–03 season featured two games at WCHA member Minnesota State-Mankato on December 27 and 28, 2002. The Mavericks would be nationally ranked for most of the season and their final 20–11–10 record included a seventeen-game unbeaten streak. They participated in the NCAA Division I Men's Ice Hockey Tournament. We were not only playing a team from the prestigious WCHA conference, which included that season's national champion, the University of Minnesota, but we were going up against a formidable opponent in Minnesota State.

I spent Christmas in Cornwall, Vermont, just outside of Middlebury, as I always did. We celebrated earlier, so I could leave at 3 p.m. and get back for an evening practice at the Olympia. The late session allowed most of our players and staff to spend a few hours of the holiday at home before heading back to Springfield. Scattered snowflakes started to come down as our family members ate dinner and opened presents. At first, the light flurries provided a nice white backdrop, but when they started to fall faster, I elected to leave early. If there's one person who can't be late for a team's first practice after the break, it's me—the head coach.

The three-hour drive to the Olympia took much longer. The snow pelted my windshield and the nearly whiteout conditions slowed my car to a crawl. Five hours later, I arrived at the rink and saw six cars. Not a good sign. I soon found out via various cell calls that we had some guys still navigating the storm, some stuck on the highway, and others stranded in airports. We practiced with only twelve skaters and no goalies. That gave us more the appearance of a youth hockey team than a D-I program preparing to play one of the nation's top college teams in forty-eight hours.

Meanwhile, we had guys grounded at the Detroit airport, including Chad Davis and Frank Novello, our top two goaltenders. Their group was unable to fly east due to the wide-ranging snowstorm, but that night they caught a break and rerouted west to Minnesota. They arrived in Minneapolis just before midnight, got a room near the airport, and joined the rest of us when we landed the next day.

After busing to Mankato, we skated at Minnesota State's home rink, then called the Midwest Wireless Civic Center. Everyone was there. Our goalies were practicing in net for the first time in nine days, but one of them had to start the next day, so I chose Chad. Regardless, we were all pumped up to play the multitalented Mavericks. "We wanted to prove ourselves against the WCHA," Ron Miller wrote, "and I can say that I've never looked forward to a weekend series like that, ever." I just wished at the time that the storm hadn't disrupted our practice schedule and provided a distraction that all head coaches dread. As it was, we had enough of a challenge against Minnesota State without having to play them with nary a normal practice.

We lost 7–3 on Friday night. Late goals by Andy Walbert and leading scorer Guillaume Caron made the final score more respectable. Guillaume's second tally came with thirty seconds remaining, so I hoped his no-surrender goal would provide momentum for the second night. Considering we got bombarded with sixty shots, any mention of momentum may have seemed like a reach, but a goal like that can have a carryover effect. And an overall play-to-the-buzzer mentality might also lead to some late-game heroics somewhere down the line. In any event, we got through the game without embarrassing ourselves, and our conditioning had been OK in spite of our recent calamities.

Chad played well under the circumstances, and he was coming off an old-time 0–0 tie with Sacred Heart and an OT win over UConn, so I went with him again. I told Frank Novello my decision before announcing the lineup, because I originally planned to give each goalie a start, and knowing how badly he wanted to play, I thought he deserved to hear from me directly. Frank took the news well. He was a team player. So was Pat Forte, one of my first recruits, who often wrote his surname, Forte, as the number 40. He returned to Minnesota after a rare knee disorder ended his AIC career and led to multiple surgeries. He became a teacher and coach. Pat visited me at the hotel and came to Friday's game.

We began better the next night and halfway through the first period, co-captain Andy Luhovy scored off a pass from Ron Miller on a 3-on-2 rush. A too-many-players on the ice penalty with twenty-five seconds left put us in peril because it allowed Minnesota State's power play to continue on fresh ice after the intermission. And their PP had Shane Joseph and Grant Stevenson, who became All-Americans that season with twenty-nine and twenty-seven goals, respectively. Those totals included a pile of power play goals. We killed off the penalty and I breathed a brief sigh of relief. Barely ninety seconds later, like a good captain should, Andy Luhovy struck again when he blasted the biscuit over goalie Jason Jensen's left shoulder. Miller and Guillaume Caron assisted. We were up 2–0. Chad Davis continued to hold the Mavericks scoreless with several scintillating saves, until they finally lit the lamp with 1:42 left in the second to make it 2–1 going into the third.

I seem to recall it was during this game, although it might have been the night before, that at one point I sent our best faceoff forward, Trent Ulmer, out to take a PK draw in our end. He didn't kill penalties for us, so I gambled that he'd win the faceoff and come right to the bench. It didn't happen. He lost the draw and couldn't get off the ice. The Mavericks zipped the puck around and fired off rockets from everywhere, as Trent, slow afoot and unversed with our PK system, struggled to keep up. It probably didn't help that frantic cries of, "Get on him, Trent," "Behind you, Trent," and "No, Trent, no" were shouted by a chorus of coaches and players. This went on for an interminable two minutes and thankfully they never scored. It wouldn't have been good if my faceoff move backfired into our net.

Chad stood firm in his six-foot-two frame as Minnesota State showered him with shots to start the third period. Then they scored near the nine-minute mark to make it 2–2, but we didn't crack. Four minutes later, fourth-liner Todd O'Neil, who had three goals in his entire 112-game career, scored. Anthony Rufrano had the helper. He centered the second line, but I sent him out for a shift with O'Neil and linemate Patrick Tabb to give a break to our other forwards, as we mostly rolled three lines. I knew they could be depended on defensively. Their goal electrified our bench.

If only the game had ended right there. It didn't, though, and they tied it with a minute left. Play continued into OT and we almost had the winner when Ryan Robin plowed into the cage with the puck. Referee Marco Hunt waved it off, and the game ended 3–3. The overtime raised the Maverick's shot total to sixty again, and in a U.S. College Hockey Online (USCHO) article titled "Netminder Davis Leads AIC To Tie," Chad quipped, "Usually not quite as many," when asked if he was used to so many shots. "I think it was a good weekend for the team and the boys," he added. "Obviously we wanted the win, but we rebounded and gained a little respect after last night, and that's what we were looking for."

Following the season, MAAC Hockey became Atlantic Hockey. Fairfield and Iona both dropped the sport, leaving only Canisius as a full-time (all sports) MAAC member. That initiated the formation of the Atlantic Hockey Association (AHA). Former Merrimack AD Bob DeGregorio became the new commissioner. Bob's nickname is Barney, which stems from *The Flintstones'* Barney Rubble, because they're both short and stocky. His nickname isn't included on official Atlantic Hockey releases.

Bobby Ferraris came in as my new GA. He skated at St. Anselm College and played professionally, mostly in the United Hockey League. One of his UHL teammates was Glenn Stewart. Bobby told me that Glenn, a UNH alum who played thirteen years in the pros, including twenty-two AHL games, wanted to coach. We still had only the one grad assistant position available, so Bob Burke worked out a way to (sort of) compensate Glenn. In the end, he agreed to a free lunch deal. Each Monday, he'd pick up five complimentary lunch tickets to the campus dining commons. It wasn't much, but Glenn made the financial sacrifice to get into college coaching.

Glenn worked with the forwards, and Bobby ran the defensemen. They were older and more experienced than my previous assistants. Glenn and I oversaw the power play and we tried something different, where he directed the first power play, called the Snipers, and I oversaw the second unit, named the Sharpshooters. (A third group was called the Lamplighters.) I used those names as a semi-psychological ploy to foster a goal-scoring mindset.

We had moderate success on our power play, but we also struggled to score 5-on-5. With Glenn and I each running a PP unit, we were able to show completely different looks to our opponents. Because we both worked with a smaller number of players, we could easily grab our respective power plays for extra work, either before or after practice. It also allowed us to focus in on the guys we were working with.

Our tri-captains were seniors Guillaume Caron, Jay Fennessy, and Anthony Rufrano. Anthony is among the best defensive forwards I've coached. Shawn Walsh's "Recruit offense and teach defense" philosophy didn't apply to Anthony. He was so dependable in the D-zone, he even covered the referees. Jay was a dedicated player and a popular teammate, though he thought he deserved more ice time. Some guys eventually come to terms with that, some don't. This can adversely affect a player-coach relationship. It's also not good for the player, because the ongoing disappointment can sap some of the joy out of playing. I think that happened to Jay and others a little bit.

Guillaume made the MAAC All-Rookie Team as a freshman and Atlantic Hockey First Team All-Conference after the season. He was our first Division I player to score one hundred career points, ending up 52–56–108. Jeff Matthews recruited him from the Quebec City area, which is noteworthy, because we usually recruited nearer to Montreal, where the drive is shorter and more English is spoken. "I still can't believe we got Guillaume to come to AIC," Jeff said. "He could have played anywhere."

Assistants can help solve problems behind the scenes, or correct a player's behavior. Glenn noticed that Guillaume didn't always look up at the board when I diagrammed practice drills. Guillaume claimed it was because he knew most of the drills. Glenn told him that didn't matter. He said that he had to show respect for my position as the head coach, and as a captain, he needed to set an example and pay attention. Glenn made his last point with an edge: "If you do that in the pros, you won't be around long." Guillaume got the message and continued producing on the ice.

We played at Union in late October. Nate Leaman was the new head coach of the ECAC opponent. The Dutchmen notched two backbreaking shorthanded tallies and an empty-netter against us on their way to a 6–3 win. Freshman Jeremy Leroux, who played his junior hockey with the Cornwall Colts, scored his own shorty and later fired a low blocker shot past the Union goalie. Jeremy's parents and grandparents drove down to the game from the Ottawa area. He remembers it as a very special night. "In addition to scoring two goals, my grandfather and grandmother, who are no longer living, got to see me play."

After finishing 10–20–2 (9–16–1) in our final season of MAAC action, we came in dead last in our new league. In Atlantic Hockey, however, every team makes the playoffs, and we beat tournament host Army 4–3 at Tate Rink. The next night we lost to top seed Holy Cross 5–0. They kept winning and became Atlantic Hockey champions.

Our post-season win ended up being Rob Riley's last game as Army head coach, and his brother, Brian, took over for him the following year. Now and then Rob reminds me that he lost to AIC in his last game as the Cadets' coach. I usually nod modestly, knowing he beat us more than we beat him.

Around the time of our league playoffs, the Middlebury College men's and women's hockey teams both became 2004 National Champions. Spencer Wright, my father and coach at Proctor, followed them all the way. He came to embrace the women's game, as did former Holderness coach George "Rip" Richards, who volunteered as a goal judge for the Dartmouth women's games. These two eighty-something old-school coaching rivals grew to love the brand of hockey that the women play.

We received the first Atlantic Hockey Sportsmanship Award, which goes to the team with the fewest penalty minutes. It was a notable accomplishment and a credit to our players. Glenn Stewart's venture at AIC paid off for him in more ways than one. Bruce Marshall hired him at UConn, for a lot more than lunch tickets. "I remember being very happy for Glenn when he got the job at UConn after AIC," Bobby Ferraris said, "and for you to be part of that process year after year must have been bittersweet but satisfying as well." Bobby's "bittersweet" reference spoke to the fact that the two-year GA position meant that I had to hire a new assistant every other year, and part-timers like Glenn could often only afford to stay one season. The constant turnover was challenging, but I enjoyed sending my assistants on to other programs.

Bobby returned for the 2004–05 season. With Glenn gone, we both had more to do. "On top of the usual academic and professional obligations of being a graduate assistant," Bobby said, "I couldn't care less that I had to be the strength coach and part-time equipment manager/resident skate sharpener; I was very proud to be a college coach." Bobby's quote is telling. I had to hire coaches who weren't afraid to get their hands dirty and who deemed no task to be beneath them. That type of person is an asset to any organization.

We wrote up a "Some Keys to Winning" laminated poster and hung it on our locker-room wall. I told Bobby to come up with a key specific to defensemen. That's not an easy assignment considering the complexities of the position, but he handled it nicely as seen on the fifth line below:

- Players who always compete
- Best "loose pucks" team in the league
- Strong puck possession and pursuit
- Forwards who care about defense
- Defensemen good enough to make simple plays
- Game-breaking specialty teams
- Minimal odd-man rushes against
- Consistent goaltending; save percentage over .910
- High-energy shifts and D-I hockey's best changes
- Discipline, discipline, discipline

Bobby eventually emailed me a quote from former comic actor Charlie Chaplin where he said, "Simplicity is not a simple thing." He said it instantly reminded him of the key for defensemen line he wrote. That in turn made me think of a related quotation I shared with my players: "Hockey is a simple game, but it's not easy."

Frank Novello started all of our games and met the consistency key with a .913 save percentage. He was a pint-size goalie with cat-like quickness and a puck-gobbling glove. He came from Sault Ste. Marie, Ontario, and played for the Soo Thunderbirds. After questioning the Soo goaltending coach about Frank, I asked if he had anything else to add.

"Yes," he said, "He'll be a steal for you."

He was spot-on. Frank became a First Team All-Conference goalie.

Frank blanked Army 2–0 at the Olympia in November. We held a team meeting earlier that afternoon as we often did on game days. Our staff would review the scouting report and/or show film clips, and then I'd share something with them. It might be a reading from Ken Dryden's *The Game*, notes from a Roger Neilson seminar, a poem, quotes from NHL players, or an online hockey article. Sometimes we watched Internet videos, like "Lessons from Geese," which shows how geese display teamwork when they take turns flying at the front of their V formation, flap their wings to provide uplift for the flock, and honk to offer encouragement. Preparing for the game was a central purpose of the meetings. We usually met in a classroom in Amaron Hall; college hockey, after all, is an extension of the classroom.

We scrimmaged the St. Nicks Hockey Club, a group of former college hockey players who work in New York City, to start the next season. Their players talked to our team in the locker room afterward about their hockey experiences and gave advice on job networking. St. Nicks is no fly-by-night operation. Hobey Baker skated for them after he graduated from Princeton and prior to becoming a World War I pilot. Sportswriter Ron Fimrite wrote a poignant piece on him in *Sports Illustrated* titled "A Flame That Burned Too Brightly," where he mentioned how the marquees announced "Hobey Plays Tonight" before St. Nick's games.

Interestingly, we visited Princeton's Hobey Baker Memorial Rink the previous year. As we entered their impressive Ivy League campus, Bryan Jurynac yelled, "Hey, there's a castle," as his teammates crowded to one side of the bus for a better look. Princeton coach Guy Gadowsky later confirmed it was a real castle. We ended up losing 4–2. Junior Preston Cicchine scored at 18:00 of the third period to bring us within a goal. That tightened things up until Princeton got one by Frank Novello forty-two ticks later to torpedo our upset bid.

Preston captained our team as a senior. He also golfed during the years

I did double duty as the golf coach. I received a letter from an alum who marshaled at a tournament we played in. He met Preston briefly on the course and Preston flipped him the AIC hat right off his head. "His spontaneous act was one of the highlights of my golfing experiences," the man wrote. That's a letter you save as a coach.

Preston's assistant captains were Ryan Robin, a sturdy skater from Saskatchewan, and Cape Codder Jeff Valdez, who played for former AIC assistant Jeff Matthews at Northfield Mount Hermon. Coach Matthews also sent Ben Ellsworth and Brent Griffin to AIC. I considered his confidence in recommending us to his players a big compliment. Having spent two years in the trenches at AIC, as both a coach and a graduate student, Jeff knew us well. I also knew him well, which is why I trusted his recommendations.

Joe Exter became our new GA. A former captain and goalie at Merrimack, he coached the defensemen and penalty kill. He also schooled freshman goaltender Tom Fenton. We were lucky to have Joe, not only because he was a talented young coach, but also considering that he nearly lost his life in a collision with Boston College forward Pat Eaves. On an ESPN special, Joe described the injury as feeling like an "earthquake going through your head." He was listed in critical condition as a result of a severe concussion and skull fracture and placed in an induced coma. He likened the experience to "living through your own wake." Initially expected to spend up to four months in rehab, he was discharged in eight days.

Joe's work with Tom Fenton began to pay off. We defeated Canisius 2–1 on the first night of a home series when defenseman Matt "Woody" Woodward whacked in the game winner. Then we beat them 5–2 in a Saturday matinee. After the game, I congratulated our team and Fenton on the win, yelling, "These sweeps are sweet," and dived into a trash barrel, which our players had conveniently placed in anticipation of my zany celebration. I spilled myself onto the floor along with balls of used tape, broken stick blades, crumpled scouting reports—and spit. Everyone hooted and hollered. We were a buoyant bunch.

We hosted UConn on Friday, February 10. Ryan Robin recorded an empty-netter at 19:04 of the third period to presumably ice the game for us. At 19:10, Husky coach Bruce Marshall, who didn't like referee Pete Torgerson's calls that night (and didn't like him to begin with) started giving it to the ref. Torgerson slapped him with a bench minor for unsportsmanlike conduct.

When the call was made, Coach Marshall really blew his top, his referee reprimand reverberating through the Olympia as if blasted through the PA system. For that, he received an additional ten-minute game misconduct. He then stomped out of the rink. We won 7–5, and as I walked outside the glass behind our bench at game's end, Bruce snuck around a corner and shook my hand.

Bruce called the next morning: "Gary, you didn't get a call from the commish, did you?"

Me: "No. Why, should I have got one?"

Bruce: "I could be in trouble with Bob and Gene because Torgerson threw me out of the game. But I was a good sport and shook your hand after, right?"

Me: "Yes, you did. And, I doubt they'll call me, but if they do, I'll tell them you graciously shook my hand after. Besides, it's not that big a deal, you just got a little excited."

Bruce: "Noooo, don't say that."

Me: "Don't worry, I just said the 'excited' part to you."

Bruce: "OK, thanks. Hopefully I'll be back on the bench tonight."

Bruce was on the bench and he behaved himself. It didn't hurt that his Huskies bageled us 6–0. I didn't hear from Commissioner Bob DeGregorio or Gene Binda, the director of officials. We visited in Bruce's office before the game as we always did, and he was relieved that he didn't receive supplementary discipline. I joked with Bruce that we'd have to beef up security the next time he came to the Olympia.

I never got thrown out of a game like Bruce, but I did make my share of bonehead mistakes on the bench. One of them involved calling out the names of the next two forwards to replace our penalty killers. I usually changed the forwards and, for instance, I might say, "Jurynec and Sullivan are up next." Then someone on the bench would say, to my dismay, "Coach, Jurynec is in the box."

We held Senior Night at the Olympia, where we introduced each senior in lieu of the starting lineup. Army had players out due to an uncharacteristic line brawl with Mercyhurst the previous weekend, but we still lost 6–3. The next evening, the Cadets had their suspended players back for Senior Night at Tate Rink. They also introduced our seniors, which was a nice touch. Despite the added obstacles we prevailed 4–2, aided by leading scorer Jeremy Tendler's game winner in the third. I often pointed to that weekend as proof to our players that "there's nothing that says the home team is supposed to win on Senior Night."

Holy Cross beat us 3–1 in the playoffs. They went on to be Atlantic Hockey Champions and defeat mighty Minnesota 4–3 in OT in the first round of the 2006 NCAA's. In an article titled "Remembering the Holy Cross Upset 10 Years Later," sportswriter Chris Dilks called the game a "cultural moment," and described it as a "Where were you when . . ." moment. Well, I was watching the game just over the state line in an Enfield, Connecticut, bar, and what a marvelous moment it was for Holy Cross, and our league—and for college hockey in general. During the twenty-minute ride home, I exalted about the upset and imagined my team winning such a game someday. We don't just dream when we're young.

Chapter 11

Honking Horns

The 2006–07 school year started with significant administrative changes. (Air Force and RIT also joined Atlantic Hockey.) Vince Maniaci had replaced Harry Courniotes the year before. President Courniotes was in his eighties and was believed to be the longest-serving college president in New England when he retired. President Maniaci, who goes by "Vince," proved to be an accessible administrator, with a student-first philosophy, something the college needed. Remarkably, he learned the names of nearly one thousand students. He memorized some of those names on Friday mornings when he threw a football to passing students in front of the Campus Center building. The students always smiled—even when they dropped the ball.

Rich Bedard replaced Bob Burke as athletic director. Rich was a longtime assistant to the president under Harry Courniotes, and earlier served as AIC's baseball coach. He played the sport at Amherst College and spent time in the New York-Penn (Single-A) League, where "the curve ball got the best of me too." I knew Rich well, so it turned out to be an easy transition when he succeeded Bob. Still, Bob had been my boss for over twenty years, and he had stuck with me through thick and thin. He was a good AD and a good friend. I missed him when he left.

Our team flew to Detroit in October and then bused north to Sault Ste. Marie, Michigan, to take on the Lake Superior State Lakers, a Central Collegiate Hockey Association (CCHA) member. Two of our young forwards, David Turco and Mike MacMillan, lived on the Canada side of the similarly named but separate city of Sault Ste. Marie, Ontario. I met with Mike personally at the hotel, given that he lived locally and we wouldn't be dressing him the first night. He took the news stoically, but for a wee wince. David's parents hosted a postgame meal after the second game. His dad, Mario, was superintendent of schools. David stayed in education, too, and he would one day become head women's hockey coach at Manhattanville College.

After suffering a sweep, we headed back to Detroit on a wet and windy morning. That was another problem. The Mackinac Bridge is one of the longest suspension bridges in the world and high winds can cause the five-mile structure to be closed. We were due to cross the slightly swaying bridge during our drive to the airport. I sweated it out when we were held up for an hour, before they let us through behind an escort vehicle. When it became evident that we'd make our flight, I went back to lamenting the losses and trying to figure out how to get better.

Eric Lang and Trevor Large, our recently hired grad assistants, were aboard the bus. There are always changes with a new administration, and getting a second GA was helpful. The fact that Eric played at AIC meant our players would be mentored by someone who had literally walked in their shoes— or skated in their skates. Eric taught and coached baseball at Stepinac HS in White Plains, New York, while coaching HS hockey at another school. Trevor played at Ferris State, where he'd met his future wife, Molly. They were quite the winter sports couple, as she played on the women's basketball team. He worked at Jasbro Truck Leasing in his hometown of Brampton, Ontario, prior to coming to AIC. Trevor soon learned that my assistants logged truck-driver miles when motoring everywhere in a never-ending search for blue-chip recruits.

Eric's wife, Chris, who earned a PhD in her late twenties, discovered that Eric wasn't around much. She was back in White Plains, New York, with their penalty-prone dog, Puck, while Eric lived in a bare room above our office in the former TKE fraternity house. (Joe Exter stayed there the year before to avoid dorm life.) Eric told me things were getting "really bad," with Chris, because he was always away. It didn't help that he gave up a full-time job to be a GA. Realizing that Eric's marriage might be on the line, or I might lose an assistant—or both—I agreed to let him spend two nights a week at home. It worked out, and he got a lot done on his laptop.

Another assistant had joined our staff the year before. A College Hockey News article artfully titled "AIC Tabs Tabb" announced the hiring of Patrick

Tabb to serve as our volunteer coach. Patrick said that being on the ice for Todd O'Neil's goal at Minnesota State "was among the most memorable moments of my career." His dad, Barry, owned the Olympia, so I dealt with Patrick on everyday rink matters. We didn't recruit him out of Avon Old Farms School, but he wanted AIC, and I hesitatingly gave him a roster spot. I worried that he might not play much, which could affect our viability at the Olympia with his father owning the rink. He didn't always skate a regular shift, but his dad never complained. I mentioned that fact to Mr. Tabb after Patrick graduated.

"I've been around enough hockey parents in my life," he said, "to know that's not the way I want to act."

We stressed the importance of emotional self-control to our players. Emotion is critical to athletic success, as long as it doesn't adversely affect the player or the team. We considered our bench to be a sanctuary, where calmness and positiveness prevail, as players prepare for their next shift. When guys exhibited disruptive behavior, I often had them write out their own solutions to it. Vezio Sacratini previously wrote a thousand-word "My Behavior" paper. Mark Pavli, a tempestuous left wing on our green line, constructed this impressive "Emotion List":

1. Relax on the bench, don't be so outspoken.

2. Breathe better to realize it isn't as big a deal as it seems to be—everyone else is going through the same thing.

3. Talk about positive situations with my linemates.

4. Turn my negative aggregations into production.

5. Remember that I love to play hockey and just play instead of worrying about all the extra stuff.

6. Know that everyone is working hard so our team can win.

7. Model myself after our captains.

We usually had good captains. Senior Jeremy Leroux wore the C, and juniors Bryan Jurynec and Jeremy Tendler donned the A. They became co-captains the following year. Tendler was in his second straight fifteen-goal season, and in the press guide I called Bryan a "veritable tornado, who competes ferociously in every practice and every game." Versatility was among Jeremy Leroux's many attributes. He came to us as a forward, and during his freshman year, we had some injuries on defense. Bobby Ferraris suggested we put him back on D in a game against Mercyhurst. Jeremy was one of our best defensemen that day. He played professionally after college, where he noted, "My versatility made me more marketable."

Jeremy did have a mishap as our captain. One time we were practicing specialty teams, while everyone else stood outside the zone. Jeremy iced the puck, but it hit Eric Lang in the head. He bled all over his black and yellow sweats as the ice turned bloodred beneath him. He ended up with twelve stitches. Patrick Tabb laughed when he recalled my sending him off the ice to stay with Eric, as practice continued.

The next day, I told Eric to run the first drill at practice, because "it will be a great thing for the team to see." I announced to our guys that having Eric right back and running the drill was an example of AIC toughness. His face was swollen like Rocky Balboa, and our players banged their sticks on the ice like maniacs as his drill started. It was great—there's nothing like starting with a big bang. Coach John Wooden pointed out that coaches should "end practice on a happy note." If that's the case, perhaps practices should start snappy and end happy.

Eric greeted our players with an elaborate PowerPoint presentation when they returned after Christmas. It introduced a new defensive zone coverage (DZC) system that featured zone as opposed to man-on-man coverage. We utilized zone coverage for years before Bobby Ferraris convinced me to go with man-on-man, which had become popular. Eric, a natural networker, got to know Ranger coach Tom Renny while working as an off-ice official at Madison Square Garden, and brought Renny's DZC system to AIC. It featured such terms as "attack zone," "support zone," and "net zone." When Eric arrived at AIC in the fall, he remembers me picking apart some of his DZC ideas. Now he was confidently in charge.

On Saturday, March 2, we played Canisius in the opening round of the playoffs. Canisius coach Dave Smith told me before the contest that our game film had only included the first two periods. He was nice about it, but Dave said that he barely saw our power play, as most of them were in the third period. I called Eric over to discuss it with us, as he and Trevor handled film exchanges. I felt awful about the mix-up and grilled my assistants about how the third period came out as a grayish blur on the film. And then I came up with an unusual solution. I told Eric to get the board and diagram our power play to one of their assistants. Eric found Greg Fargo, just a year out of Elmira College, and as the aghast young assistant watched, Eric proceeded to diagram our power play in detail, right down to where Jeremy Tendler picked up the puck behind the net. Greg likely learned more about our PP than if he had watched the third period.

Our players wore their game faces prior to the opening faceoff. The visitor's locker room was split, so everyone crammed into one side for my pregame remarks. I reminded them that if there was a Color Guard for the national anthem, we needed to stay on the blue line until they exited the ice. I made a few Xs and Os points. Then I stepped away from the white board:

> "We are the visitors tonight, but in a way we're leasing this rink to start. This is "our" locker room. We have our own bench. It's our zone and our net. Our fans are in the stands. It's our score on the scoreboard. Our starting lineup will be announced, as will our goal scorers and assist makers. We've come all the way to Buffalo to take over this building—and therefore the game—because we're here to win."

When our guys gathered in the hallway until the buzzer sounded, Jeremy Leroux said, "You had an interesting speech there, coach," as he walked by. It's not something I heard very often from a player, but I appreciated his compliment. Jeremy was mature beyond his years and possessed a professional demeanor. I'm not surprised he became a high school administrator. Eric Lang to this day ranks his captaincy as a "ten on a scale of one to ten."

Play started and we took three straight penalties at one point. It meant more ice time for our top penalty killers, Mike Field, Jeason Lecours, and Bryan Jurynac. Sometimes they jumped over the boards before I even called their names. Normally that would irritate me, but I let it go, as they were usually right and couldn't wait to kill. Mike and Jeason didn't get much power play time, so they took particular pride in their PK role, just as I did at UVM. Leading goal scorer Jason Weeks finally finished for Canisius on their third attempt to go up 1–0.

Mark Pavli's second-period goal evened up the score and we entered the third tied 1–1. We didn't know it then, but when we watched the game film later, the person doing color, who I believe was an injured Canisius player, said halfway through the period that it made him nervous that AIC kept hanging around. His words turned prophetic when rookie Mike McMillan, the same player I didn't dress at Lake State, wristed in a shot from the high slot at 12:25 of the third. AIC 2, Canisius 1. And that's the way the game ended.

The bus trip home felt like a ride down the happy highway. A former college hoop coach once said, "Happiness in sports is winning on the road." Most would argue that wins before the home crowd are also pretty special, but the road point is well taken. Winning on the road, according to NHL coach Ken Hitchcock, "takes mettle, courage, and chemistry, and it may be the hardest thing to do in sport." Our bus was abuzz with the high-spiritedness that comes when a team knows that it's won a big one—and will live to play another day. The playoff win made the postgame pepperoni pizza taste perfect. A congratulatory call to Eric's cell from new Mercyhurst assistant Bobby Ferraris felt good, too.

Bear Trapp (real name) scored twice as Sacred Heart beat us 4–0 the next weekend, despite a productive week of practice following our first-round win. We even drove down and back to practice at their rink on Wednesday. While we were there, former goalie Buck Buckley delivered sticks to my office—and he walked the dog. Buck worked for Larry O'Donnell at CCM and rejoined him after Larry became director of hockey at Warrior. They met at AIC. We bought a lot of our hockey equipment from CCM and Warrior, including deals that allowed us to stretch our equipment budget. We needed the help because we were the only Division I team in the country that didn't supply skates.

My dog's name was Ebbie, and Buck took her out so she could pee. Unlike Hester, Ebbie never went to a game or practice, since we played indoors. She did appear in this "Musings from Coach Wright" section of our press guide:

My black lab, Ebbie, comes to the hockey office with me every day. She's not much of a hockey fan, but she's always up for a big hike. She has an energetic, spirited and dogged approach to hiking and she brings it every day. We want our players to bring that same mindset to the rink.

Early the next season, we battled the Quinnipiac Bobcats, now an ECAC team. Mike Field took two penalties in the second period. They were otherwise innocuous PIMS, but then he had a borderline late hit in the third. I didn't see the play clearly; however, I saw enough to know the check was marginal, and I reduced Mike's ice time based on his two penalties along with the hit that he got away with. When we arrived back at the Olympia after losing 3–2, Mike asked to speak with me, a rare request on his part. We met in the shadowy rear parking lot. He wanted to know why I benched him in the third. I admitted to some ambiguity because there was no call, but even so, I told him, he'd already taken two penalties and shouldn't be risking another with an over-aggressive play that wasn't preventing a goal. I also reminded him that prime penalty killers can't be taking penalties. I don't recall the exact context, but at one point Mike said, "So what should I do?"

"Deal with it," I said. "Just deal with it."

With that, we headed to our cars. It was getting toward midnight anyway.

The following Friday, we tied Bentley 1–1. Veteran officials Mike Taddeo and Jim Doyle did the game. Doyle, a squat man with a roundish face, who could have been a central casting candidate to referee in the movie *Slap Shot*, was referred to as "an old-time hockey referee" by Jeremy Leroux, because he didn't call many penalties. Maybe that's why I liked him. But he and Taddeo whistled two on Mike Field. That came to four in two games, plus the other close call, so he sat out the next night.

Mike got in a brief shoving match at RIT a few weeks later. A referee started to call matching penalties, when Mike pleaded for a break. He said another penalty would land him in big trouble with me. "If you don't make the call, you won't have to give him a penalty either," Mike said, pointing to his astonished adversary. The ref asked his partner if it was OK with him, and he kind of nodded. The two players got off with a warning to behave themselves. Mike told me the story ten years later.

We put a page from a Roger Neilson clinic in each player's notebook. At the top it read, "What it takes to be successful," and underneath, "compete" was typed sixty times in neat rows. My work-study students randomly highlighted four to six competes on each sheet with different colors, to brighten it up and add mystery to the handout. Unbeknownst to me, Bryan Jurynac and fellow senior Chris "Bolo" Bolognino started analyzing the sheets of our freshmen. It went something like this: "You've got two blue competes and a green one, which means you are not competing hard enough." Or, "That red compete is bad because it's on the third row." Some guys became quite concerned about their made-up analysis.

Atlantic Hockey added a best-of-three format to the quarterfinals. We played at No. 1 seed Army, where we were eliminated in two games. As we stood outside the locker room before the first game, Trevor Large rubbed his hands together and said, "Isn't this great," and, "I just love the playoffs." His perkiness pumped me up.

The second game included a half-hour power outage in the first period and a disputed goal, and Army sniper Owen Meyer scored on a penalty shot. We led 2–1 after the first on goals by Mark Pavli and Greg Genovese. The crusher was an Army goal that we thought hit the outside of the post and didn't go in. A referee felt otherwise, as did the goal judge, who flashed the red light. There's tremendous history and aura at Army West Point, and I thought some officials could occasionally be affected by it when forced to make a close call.

In a *Times Herald-Record* article, Ken McMillan quoted coach Brian Riley:

> We just couldn't get much going and a lot of that is a credit to AIC. They trap and don't allow you to come through the neutral zone with any type of speed so they were well prepared.

Now, we did lose both games, but Trevor Large deserved that credit. He stayed home from the previous week's Air Force trip to watch ten Army games on film. The bleary-eyed Large developed an extensive game plan to "hush the Army rush" and help us win. It didn't happen, but his efforts helped land him on Riley's staff the next year.

Intramural softball started soon after the Army series. I ran a team called the Coaches, consisting of coaches and college employees. Women's basketball coach Kristen Patterson, one of the best athletes in AIC history, played with us, as did assistant AD Matt Johnson and Dickie Lenfest before him. Soccer coach and Big Papi look-alike Kevon Isa handled first base. Popular English professor Bruce Johnson, my former assistant in the housing office, pitched and played shortstop. Bruce kept telling his students how great we were, and he often mixed up, or purposely exaggerated, the number of softball championships we won. His jocular trash talk riled them up to beat us.

Eric Lang and Trevor Large participated, as did my other assistants through the years. We faced the hockey team in the championship game. The matchup suited both teams. I loved playing my players, as they normally dealt with me in a player-coach relationship, so softball gave us a chance to compete against each other. Hopefully, they could see I still had game. My assistants also embraced the competition. Bobby Ferraris emailed me three pages of his recollections for this book. He even brought up softball:

> You, me and Glenn (Stewart) hammering home runs over the fence behind our office, the student intramural teams, especially the hockey team, had zero chance of beating us.

But then they beat us. As I walked back to my office following the game, Jeremy Tendler flashed me the Nixonian two-fingered victory sign from his car. I heard these sounds as I arrived at the hockey office: Honk, honk, honk. And it wasn't geese. Our players, Tendler, Mike Field, Greg Genovese, Mark Pavli, Bryan Jurynec, and all the others, paraded round and around in a circle, honking their horns with glee. And much of it was meant for my assistants and me. I stood on the porch and waved with a wavering smile. Then I hid back in my office with little reprieve. The loud honks still hounded me.

Ben Ellsworth remembers some of the small yet significant moments at AIC in that era: Chirping with teammates while waiting in line during practice drills and catching a whiff of the "previous night's alcohol" on their breaths; warming up with hacky sack before games; visiting the Mountain Zoo near Air Force; and watching Ryan "Rodeo" Robin put up four-hundred-pound bench presses in his boxing shoes; deejaying at a downtown bar and announcing, "Here comes the Springfield Falcons" when his AIC teammates walked in (a group of local girls rushed to greet them); hanging out with teammates at their rented house.

We opened the 2008–09 season with a full-time assistant, making us the last D-I team in the country to add a full-timer. And we retained a

GA position. Thanks to President Maniaci and Rich Bedard, we now had a salaried assistant with hockey-only responsibilities. It allowed us to hire someone with coaching experience and, importantly, the assistant could stay more than two years. Brian Bova became our first full-time hire. He played at UMass Lowell and assisted at St. Michael's College. He also skated for Jeff Matthews and the rather refined Hoggers at Northfield Mount Hermon.

Brian had to adjust to working with me, as did all of our assistants. I expected a lot and insisted that they be organized with good follow-through. I also didn't want to see any grammatical errors in their recruit letters or general correspondence. In addition to assigning to-do lists, I encouraged them to write tasks down so they wouldn't forget. Like most of our new assistants, Brian initially felt overwhelmed by his never-ending responsibilities. He came up with an unusual solution, whereby he wrote reminders on his hand.

My assistants generally considered me to be demanding, if not overdemanding at times, and a few years later several of them who had moved on to other college coaching positions were all talking together at a junior tournament in Minnesota. My mop-haired former assistant Joe Exter, then coaching at Ohio State, saw them and said, "Group therapy session," as he walked by. They all cracked up.

The previous spring, I got a letter from NCAA President Myles Brand. It was sent to teams in the top 10 percent of the Division I Academic Progress Rate (APR). The APR combines semester to semester eligibility and graduation rates. One sentence read, "The academic success of your team demonstrates your commitment to putting the student-athlete first." The honor was also a credit to our players and college.

Our APR rating reflected our quest to recruit good players who were serious about their academics, so it was frustrating when we found out in August that Richie Leitner didn't get through the NCAA Clearinghouse/ Eligibility Center. The center evaluates prospects' academic records and SAT/ACT scores, and they deemed him a non-qualifier, meaning he couldn't practice or play as a freshman. His solid freshman grades allowed him to became eligible as a sophomore. Bob Burke used a line with us coaches about ineligible athletes: "He (or she) is agile, mobile and ineligi-bile."

We played the Holy Cross Crusaders again in the playoffs. The short drive down the Mass Pike to Worcester meant we didn't need to stay over. Former Yellow Jacket Mike Field had joined us as a grad assistant, and he said that "playing Holy Cross is like playing ourselves," as Coach Paul Pearl and I have similar philosophies. I liked Mike's observation, due to my respect for the way Holy Cross plays the game. After giving my playoff-ready team a few pregame reminders in the locker room, I did something I rarely do—I read what I had recently written:

> There is a box of pucks sitting somewhere in this building, and some of those pucks will be used in tonight's game. For as long as each puck is in the game, we must own it, protect it, pass it, receive it, forecheck it, ice it on the PK, move it on the PP, block it, flip it, chip it, tip it, battle for it, share it, support it, get it through, get it in, get it out, get it deep, get it to the net, keep it out of ours, and shoot it into their net.

We stormed out of the gates and the puck was mostly ours, as we finished the first with a decisive 13–4 shot advantage, but only a 0–0 score to show for it. The game remained scoreless over the next two periods and we entered the first sudden-death frame. At 8:24 of OT, Everett Sheen scored on Fenton and sent the celebrating Crusaders into the next round. When a game goes that deep without a goal, it starts to feel like no one will ever score. But they did, and we didn't, despite a valiant effort.

On an early Sunday morning in late September of 2009, I pressed the overhead garage-door button while preparing to leave for an over-35 wooden bat baseball league playoff game in Vermont, where I played for the Burlington Cardinals with my brother Donald. (I probably should have been in an over-50 division, nearer to Springfield.) I drove the car out of the garage, got out and closed the garage door since my handheld remote didn't work. The machine hummed, but the clumsy door jammed on its rickety old track. While fumbling to fix the problem, I felt distracted by my thoughts about needing to be at the game in four hours. Then the door rolled down and hit me in the head. I fell to the floor with bilateral ruptured quadriceps tendons. That's a nasty injury.

The next week Mike Field, who had just moved from GA to full-time assistant, dropped me off at Saint Francis Hospital in Hartford, Connecticut, to have surgery with Dr. Jay Kimel. I left with thigh-high braces that immobilized both legs for ten weeks. I never got on the ice that season, although I confidently told people that I'd be skating after Christmas. However, I eventually ran parts of practice from the bench and stood near the backup goaltenders during games. Mike, just a year removed from being an AIC player, was thrust into a head coach role for a while. Listening to our games on the radio or simply waiting to hear a final score was a surreal experience. I had never missed a practice or game in my coaching career due to sickness or injury. At first I felt distant and detached from my team. And in general, I felt helpless and unhelpful, until I slowly regained mobility in the ensuing months.

Mike acquired invaluable on-the-spot coaching experience in my absence. We stayed in contact until I began going to the office again. Numerous friends gave me rides before I started driving in December. I sat sideways in their back seats with my bulky braced legs spread along the seat. After wiggling my way out of the vehicle, I'd head into the office with my walker, teetering along like the Tin Man. It wasn't a good look.

The season opened with a 4–2 loss at Union and a 3–2 loss at RPI the next day. Freshman Adam Pleskach scored three of our four goals. It was a respectable showing against two ECAC foes, and Mike handled himself well. Another freshman, goaltender Ben Meisner, recorded a 3–0 shutout against Holy Cross in our home-opener at the Olympia. I watched from a room above the ice with Bruce Johnson and John Debonville, my closest colleagues at AIC. We didn't talk much. Watching my team but not coaching them was nerve-racking. There are nerves on the bench, but most of them are displaced by focusing on line changes, tactical decisions, and generally managing the ever-changing moments that make up a hockey game.

Our locker room was named for Chris Mikula, who had recently died from cancer in his thirties. He's one of the nicest boys I've ever coached. His teammates would attest to that. His parents started a memorial fund at AIC where people could donate to our locker room in his name. They originally wanted to fund a scholarship in Chris's honor, but I suggested the locker room instead, because all players can benefit from it. The Mikulas drove down from Montreal to help dedicate the room. In a simple ceremony, I said a few words, as did Mr. Mikula, and we unveiled the Chris Mikula Locker Room plaque. His legacy lives on in a very lively place.

I say that because the locker room is a special spot for players. It's a space where the team is all together, be it before and after practice, when the mood is generally jovial, or before, after and between periods of a game, when the room hosts a range of emotions. There's the intense focus and excitement before a game as each team member dresses and prepares for the contest. Between periods is a time to regroup and re-energize. And if the previous period was poorly played due to an indifferent effort, coaches can lose it in the locker room. A few times each season, I'd go on an earsplitting, trashcan-kicking, profanity-laced tirade in front of the team. (Thankfully, they weren't recorded.) Postgame the room can be morgue-like, or the happiest hangout in hockey; winning and losing molds the mood.

A locker room can also be a prank-filled play area. Our freshmen picked up the laundry at the gym and brought it to practice in a big bag. One of the smaller guys would lie under the "gitch" (hockey slang for undergarments) while everyone waited anxiously for the next player to arrive. When that person came and started digging in the bag for his stuff, the submerged player popped up like a jack-in-the-box, scattering socks, jocks, and T-shirts everywhere as the startled player stepped back and loud laughter erupted in the room.

Nielsson Arcibal, who was a sophomore when I had the injury, spoke with reverence about the locker room (also called a dressing room) when we met about this book at the new MGM Springfield casino and resort. It's located near his office at the American Financial Network. "The time spent in the locker room is among the fondest memories of my college career," he said. "It was a central piece of my hockey experience. My teammates and I spent hours there, joking around and telling stories, and just hanging out."

Perhaps one of the best lines I've heard about the spirit of locker room life comes through a player from a different sport. Dan Quisenberry, a relief pitcher who helped the Kansas City Royals win two pennants and a World Series back in the 1980s, said, "I'm here! It's Merry Christmas! There are toys in my locker. Gloves and bats and balls." For a hockey player, that would be gloves and skates and sticks.

The Wally Barlow Fitness Award was the only other plaque hanging in our locker room. It listed the top three fitness test winners for each season. Mike Field won it three times. It's one of the reasons I hired him to become the full-time assistant at such a young age. Mike was a very dedicated player who worked out diligently during the sultry days of summer. That commitment served him in good stead when he ran the team in my absence.

But it wasn't easy at first. "Everything felt overwhelming from a logistical standpoint," Mike recollects. "It seemed like I woke up 100 times a night, trying to remember if I had ordered postgame food for the bus, packed the skate sharpener, given the dress list to Lou Topor in the equipment room, and printed directions for the bus driver." He felt like the hockey side of things from a coaching/recruiting perspective was hard enough, "but at least I knew the systems and values that you wanted instilled in our group, so I had a better comfort level there." And he faced some awkward moments, like when he sat out his former teammate, Dean Yakura, because he felt other guys were playing better. Barely eighteen months earlier, Mike had gone to Florida with Dean on spring break. Now he wasn't dressing him.

Dean finished first in his class with a 3.94 GPA and gave the valedictorian address at commencement, where he joked that I was the only person to ever manage to tear both quadriceps tendons while at home in my garage. And he thanked our staff for recruiting him to play Division I hockey at AIC. "You allowed me to fulfill a lifetime dream," he said. He also spoke to the close friendship he had with two of his fellow graduating teammates, Josh Froese and Mike McMillan, when he humorously half-sang a line from Alan in the recent comedy film, *The Hangover*: "We're the best three friends that anyone can ever have."

We had much to be thankful for as we began the next season. I was coaching a sport I loved, at a very high level and at a school where I enjoyed working. I liked the people at AIC, my coaching colleagues at other colleges, and my players, who were coachable and committed. That said, our program still lacked a critical element: we needed more wins. Coaches are largely evaluated, fairly or unfairly, by their won-lost record, and our record needed improvement. I entered most seasons believing that we would be better, that the wins would come and we'd go on a playoff run, but too many defeats always seemed to drag us down. I found those losses made it harder to be happy. They affected my psyche, though I tried not to show it. And they filled me with fear that I would be fired. Now we were coming off three strong recruiting classes. Our future felt promising.

Tom Mele succeeded Chris Campanale as captain; Eric Lang recruited him. Eric searched for players everywhere and even brought in Tomas Benovic, a Slovakian compatriot of New York Islanders star Zedno Chara. For Eric, the recruitment of Tom Mele was special; he came from Eric's hometown, the Bronx, where college hockey players are as rare as big backyards. Correspondent Bob Snow quoted Mele in an NHL.com article on our team:

> Best thing is the honor to wear the 'C' on your sweater [jersey] every day. I'm just grateful to be playing D-I college hockey, getting my education paid for, and being just two hours from home, so my family gets to come to games. And my younger brother [Steve] is on the team.

Our bus left for Erie, Pennsylvania, on Thanksgiving for a series with the Mercyhurst Lakers. We stopped at the Cracker Barrel restaurant near Rochester, New York, to enjoy a prearranged turkey dinner. New GA and Prince William look-alike Casey Balog planned the meal, and considering our eight-hour drive offered few options to celebrate the holiday, its folksy feel and menu made it a good fit. Later, we skated at their rink. We hung our equipment in the visitors' locker room afterward and left our laundry to be washed by their staff. Then we drove to the Quality Inn and Suites and also ate a light meal. A big dinner was unnecessary. Many of us could still taste turkey.

Seth Dussault enjoyed the turkey. He was a senior at AIC and had worked with our team for four years, helping our SIDs and broadcasting games on the radio. We weren't supposed to take him on overnight trips due to the budget, but I badgered Rich Bedard until he allowed it, providing we didn't rent an extra room for Seth. Thus, we squeezed him in with players or athletic trainer John Culp. He dined with us, and Seth, an eager eater, never missed a team meal. It was his first trip to Mercyhurst, and he was excited to find a Tim Hortons restaurant close by. (Former NHLer Tim Horton founded the restaurant chain.)

The year before, my former player and assistant Don Moorhouse started broadcasting our games on WAIC, so Seth slid into the color commentator spot. Don was the voice of UMass Hockey until they switched stations. (He later went back to broadcasting UMass games.) When Moorhouse started, Seth, a fine play-by-play announcer himself, told Don that he'd fill in for him if he ever needed a "mental health day." Don grinned and said, "Hockey is my mental health day."

The next night, I addressed the team before the game. Pat Burns had recently died of cancer, so I shared a line he used near the end of his life: "Don't cry because it's over, be happy that it happened." I then explained that once when the Montreal Canadiens were struggling and perhaps not competing hard enough, Burns canceled practice and ordered everyone onto a waiting bus. They drove around working-class neighborhoods in Montreal, where many of their fans lived, and he noted how the people residing there didn't get to live the "good life" of an NHLer. Burns spoke of the reverence they showed toward the Montreal Canadiens. How rooting for the Habs brought joy to their lives. And he talked about how much his players owed those fans. I told my guys there was a lesson here for us: "Maybe we don't have all those followers," I said, "but every one of you has parents, coaches, teammates, and others who have supported you along the way—and you owe them your best effort tonight and every night."

There was no questioning our first-period effort, as we outshot our opponent 16–7, but Mercyhurst scored the only goal. After trading tallies in the second, we entered the third frame trailing 2–1, and we still had four minutes left on the power play, following a five-minute major to the Lakers. Forty-five seconds later we were two men down and killing a 4-on-3 power play. Not smart. But at 6:44, defenseman Tomas Benovic fired in a goal, and since he rarely scored, he also fired up our bench. The floodgates opened. We scored three more, two by Adam Pleskach, to win 5–2.

We ate our Saturday pregame meal at Nunzi's, a restaurant my former assistant, Greg Klym, discovered when he coached at Mercyhurst. Both he and Bobby Ferraris started at AIC and ended up working for coach Rick Gotkin. Nunzi's looks run-down from the outside, but the food inside is delicious. We preordered the Italian Platter for everyone at a group rate. Spaghetti, rigatoni, cheese shells, and lasagna, along with a big meatball and sausage, are piled onto each plate. Even Seth had a hard time eating everything.

That night, we jumped out to a 2–0 lead in the first period. Captain Tom Mele scored off a nice feed from Richie Leitner, and Jon Puskar notched a beauty at the ten-minute mark. He split two defenders while fending off with one arm, and pushed the puck into the net with just his top hand on the stick. (You can hear the Mercyhurst announcer exclaiming, "What a goal by Puskar" on YouTube.) We survived Jon's five-minute checking from behind penalty late in the game, thanks to key saves by Ben Meisner. He got the 3–0 shutout, and we all savored the sweep.

Our team readied for an off-the-wall celebration from me, and they got it. I danced around squirting a water bottle, slammed my notebook on the floor, and belly-flopped onto a trash barrel. I scrambled up, playfully shoved a couple of players, and ran out of the room. I left laughs and claps behind. The boys were ecstatic, as was our staff. We had never swept the perennially strong Lakers before, much less on the road, but this trip to Erie amounted to mile-wide smiles over many, many miles.

As we pulled out of the parking lot, guys started yelling, "Four honks, four honks." They wanted the bus driver to blow his horn for the four points (two per win) we had earned. I announced that we'd wait until we got to the bottom of the hill, because I didn't want to rub it in to Mercyhurst. There were a few mock boos from the back of the bus. They didn't want to wait one second. But when we reached the bottom, I gave our driver the OK, and he blasted his horn four times. Now everyone cheered like crazy.

Earlier that month, we hosted the USA Hockey coaching certification program on the AIC campus. Seventy youth hockey coaches attended the five-hour session. I brought in most of the speakers, and my assistants and I were among the presenters. I was involved in the program other years, too, and during one three-year period, Rick Bennett, Red Gendron, and Rob Riley all volunteered to speak. Rick and Red were coming off NCAA national championships at Union and Yale respectively, and Rob coached the Springfield Falcons, meaning the coaches were treated to interesting talks. Al and Barbara Wright (no relation) served as USA/Mass Hockey registrars. Not many people have heard of them, yet they were (w)rightly inducted into the Massachusetts Hockey Hall of Fame. There are thousands of unsung heroes in hockey.

The clinics covered critical topics. Dealing with difficult parents is an issue that concerns youth hockey coaches, especially in these days of helicopter parents who hover over their kids' hockey matters. It used to be that stage mothers and Little League parents were the "poster children" for this type of behavior, but I'm afraid that hockey moms and dads may have assumed that ignominious mantle. While there are plenty of parents who have the game in perspective, too many others don't.

Many kids enroll on travel teams at a young age, involving long drives and overnight stays. (I'm glad I didn't spend my weekends in cars as a child.) Parents pay the high cost of having their children in hockey: registrations, team fees, costly ice times, equipment, travel, hockey schools, and even private lessons. This excludes poorer families from participating, and parents paying these large fees tend to develop unrealistic expectations for their son or daughter. The practice-to-game ratios are a concern. One properly run practice is equal to several games when it comes to puck touches and ice time, yet "more games" often seems to be the mantra in youth hockey circles.

The trend toward specialization is another issue. Hockey is now a year-round sport for many; the three-sport athlete is becoming a dinosaur. Other than the prep school athletes I recruited, many of our recruits didn't play another sport in high school. Interestingly, while parents and others think that an all-hockey approach is the avenue to success, the majority of college and pro coaches believe otherwise. They see the benefits of carryover skills from other sports, fewer overuse injuries, and less burnout.

Moreover, Don Moorhouse and Roger Grillo, two noted hockey people mentioned previously, both have sons who grew up playing hockey and baseball. Don is now the radio voice of UMass Hockey, and Roger is the USA Hockey ADM regional manager for New England. It's only natural that they would be partial to hockey, but something interesting happened: Their sons became better baseball players. Evan Moorhouse was a catcher at Westfield State. Dominic Grillo pitched for the University of Rhode Island. Playing more than one sport turned out to be the right move.

We took part in the Whalers Hockey Fest in February. The opening line in the *Springfield Republican* game story written by Greg Cameron read, "Out of the Olympia and into the Great Outdoors." In an article for *West Point Magazine*, writer Jim Johnstone referred to the conditions as "North Country cold," and said the tailgaters reminded him of "ice fishing." Indeed, we played Army outside at UConn's Rentschler Field and lost 4–1. The Hartford Whalers-Boston Bruins Legends Game came after us, followed by an AHL contest with the Connecticut Whale and Providence Bruins. Many of our hockey alumni were there, too, as they watched from a warm luxury box high above the cold windswept rink. A bright sun glared from the sky and reflected off the ice and into the eyes of the players. The smeared eye black on their faces looked like war paint and helped mitigate the glare.

The goalies changed ends halfway through the third (lower sun) period.

Our six-foot-six gangling goalie Ryan Kerpan from Saskatchewan, who sometimes skateboarded to class, had the right attitude about the elements. "It kind of reminded me of being a kid out on the pond back home," he said in the *Republican*. "It was a little difficult with the wind and sun in your face, but I thought it was fun overall."

Dick Baker wrote about the game in the *Republican*'s affiliate MassLive. com. Baker began his article with, "This is not new for American International College hockey coach Gary Wright," and went on to talk about how I'd skated outdoors at Proctor Academy. (They now play indoors at the Teddy Maloney Rink.) And that my dad was my coach. He mentioned that current Proctor coach, Mike Walsh, played on the Springfield Indians Calder Cup–winning team in 1990. Hockey is a small world.

Springfield has always been a part of that world. In fact, Springfield's Barney & Berry Skates manufactured some six hundred thousand pairs a year by the early 1900s. An old advertisement depicting an outdoor game of hockey reads:

> It is not necessary to go far afield or afloat to get good sport. Nothing is more beautiful and exhilarating than a brisk spin or a lively game on the ice, and as the season for ice skating approaches we counsel all good sportsmen, young or old, to prepare for its enjoyment. A necessary adjunct to complete satisfaction is a pair of Barney & Berry skates.

Everett Barney, who himself skated on the frozen Connecticut River, was known as "the man who put America on skates." He died at the age of eighty in 1916 and was declared insane in his later years, a term more loosely applied in that era. Being involved as he was in hockey, it seems surprising that he would descend to the depths of the insane. Our unique sport, after all, is good for the brain!

Assistant captain Mike Little could surely skate. He lived in Enfield, Connecticut, and performed for the Springfield Pics when they were a level below the Junior Falcons. Rob Bonneau, a UMass Hockey alum, and Brian Collins (Kevin's brother) ran the Pics. They pushed Mike on me. I called former Catamount and Junior Falcons coach Mike McLaughlin to ask why Mike didn't make his team. He told me not to be concerned about it because the team's GM made promises to too many defensemen. Eric Lang and Trevor Large thought we had better prospects, but McLaughlin also spoke highly of Mike Little, so I took a chance on him. Some chance. He became an outstanding defenseman for us and eventually played professionally in the ECHL, AHL, and Europe.

"I'm pretty sure that Mike Little has the best stick-on-puck defending habits of anyone to ever play hockey," Mike Field, who coached our defensemen, said. "I'm kind of kidding, but not really. He was so good with his gap and stick that we had him do a 1-on-1 drill without a goalie in net. No one could score."

We rebounded to defeat Army 6–3 in the first round of the playoffs. The win sent us to play league-leader RIT, and they won 5–0 on Friday night. In the game's final minute, Taylor McReynolds, a highly penalized player, drilled freshman Blake Peake into the boards. He was penalized for boarding and accessed a game misconduct. I thought he should have been DQ'd and pressed the issue with the officials and the league, but the penalty stood. It was something I'd never done before. Even Blake told me to drop it, an indication of his toughness. I hoped Coach Wilson would sit McReynolds out the next night, but he was back in the lineup. We lost 5–1 before a sellout (2,100) crowd at the rocking Ritter Arena. Unlike the bustling bus ride back from Mercyhurst, the ride from Rochester felt more like a funeral procession.

Chapter 12

Battling the Big Boys

Our bus left the Olympia at 6 a.m. on March 1, 2012. We had a five-hundred-mile drive ahead of us to play the Robert Morris Colonials, a team near Pittsburgh, Pennsylvania, in the best-of-three first round of the Atlantic Hockey playoffs. We were the No. 10 seed in the twelve-team league, but we had reason to believe. Five of our losses came to teams from the big conferences, and we upset Brown 3–0, split with Mercyhurst and, importantly, logged a 2–0 shutout at Robert Morris (RMU). A home-and-home sweep over Army in late February offered optimism. We were making strides.

Ken McMillan interviewed me minutes after the Army sweep for an InsideCollegeHockey.com article, where he wrote that we "whooped it up in the bowels of West Point's Tate Rink last Saturday following a hard-fought win." I'm glad he didn't see my clumsy barrel jumps, but he did notice I gasped like a winded overweight hockey coach, which I was. In an otherwise euphoric moment, he asked me questions about wins and losses, and I answered first about the sweep: "It's a modest accomplishment, but it does have some significance attached to it. There's palpable progress here." And to another question I said, "We don't win as much as we'd like but it's not like, 'Hey, we're just moseying along and we're doing other good things so it's okay.' It's not okay."

We arrived for a 4 p.m. practice at RMU's Island Sports Arena. The lengthy bus ride provided plenty of time to plan the fifty-minute session. After goalie warm-up, we opened with the Greyhound Stretch, a lively two-way passing and timing drill that ends with each player receiving a stretch pass and attacking the net. We always started with it the day before a game.

Defenseman Chris Markiewicz felt that even though it was a quick and straightforward drill, "We knew that it was almost time for the game and everyone was in a good mood and excited."

The general manager of the Island Sports Arena is Dave Hanson, who played Jack Hanson in the iconic movie *Slap Shot*. He still wears his hair long for appearances with the Hanson brothers, like when they water-ski skate behind a Zamboni in various arenas. Former AIC player Mark Bosquet played Andre "Poodle" Lussier in the film. I've seen *Slap Shot* dozens of times. I love the film, but not that much. Most of my viewings came when our guys watched it on the bus. The frontal screen was right in my face, so I couldn't escape it. Still, I always enjoyed the film's classic scenes and hilarious lines.

The puck descended at 7:35 on Friday night and we were underway. Adam Pleskach scored his sixteenth goal to give us a 1–0 lead and Robert Morris defenseman Tyson Wilson tallied later in the period. Goals by Nate "Slick" Sliwinski and big Mike Penny put us up 3–1 after two. Things looked good. And, then they didn't. The Colonials collected four goals in the final frame to win Game 1. Our backs were to the wall.

Many of our players' parents were at the games. Grad assistant Casey Balog's young Pittsburgh cousins Erin and Matthew watched the whole series. They made black and yellow AIC signs and, of course, a colorful "GO CASEY" sign. Casey couldn't actually go anywhere, but they conspicuously cheered and waved their placards throughout the weekend.

We entered the third period of Game 2 with a 6–5 lead. The first two periods were a wild and woolly affair with eleven goals, and Coach Derek Schooley pulling goalie Brooks Ostergard early in the second, before putting him back in nine minutes later. Ben Meisner, who'd also been shaky in net, told me he was ready to go in the third. He delivered and stymied RMU the rest of the way. Jon Puskar made it 7–5, and we were headed to the deciding game.

Mike Field made an in-game adjustment in that second game when he tweaked the forecheck to contain RMU's set breakout. Early on, one of our guys got out of position and they scored off that breakout. Several minutes later we got caught in a line change, so someone chased their defenseman behind the net out of desperation, which disrupted their set breakout. Our players asked Mike if they could stay with that tactic. He agreed and later said, "I feel like the adjustment that our players made, and their ownership over whatever the result might be, helped us force a Game 3."

We made prior arrangements with the hotel for a possible third night and now we needed it. Rich Bedard flew in for the games, so he'd be staying around. I liked having my AD support us. Our coaching staff confirmed and scheduled the extra meals, meeting times, and checkouts with the hotel. Casey and Mike wore many hats, including those of traveling secretaries. "We now had additional logistical responsibilities," Casey said, "and we still needed to break down the game film."

Nielsson Arcibal was our captain. He was the son of a white mother and an African American and Filipino father, and two of his favorite NHL players growing up, besides Chris Drury, were Anson Carter and Jarome Iginla, "because they were good players who looked like me." Nielsson grew up in California and came to us from the USHL's Des Moines Buccaneers. He was a spark plug player. And fast as a Ferrari. Sometimes his emotions spilled over, like the time he got overly excited on the bench at Bentley, causing mild-mannered Casey Balog to tell him to "SHUT UP." He did, possibly figuring that if he upset Casey, he must really be acting up. Nielsson was having a strong senior year as we entered the Robert Morris series. He did everything for us, and would have been a league all-star if he scored more.

Nielsson received an inspiring text from his former AIC teammate Steve McLeod near the start of his senior year.

"You'll do great things," Steve wrote. And he told Nielsson that if he gained more confidence, he thought he had the ability to "take over" games. Steve's text to Nielsson was a nice gesture. He and Mike Penny became medical doctors.

I sat on the bus the next night as the team readied inside. Freshman Brandon Fagerheim hung out in the back. We were playing a Game 3 playoff rubber match and he wasn't dressing for the third night in a row. I checked in with him the day before. He wanted to play badly, but he didn't whine or cop a woe-is-me attitude. He stayed strong and ready if called on. That's what you look for as a coach.

The Colonials led 2–0 after two, and tallied early in the third to take a seemingly insurmountable lead. But we weren't done. Nielsson Arcibal, who centered the green line with Penny and Pleskach, scored to make it 3–1. And then he notched another to bring us within one at 3–2. We had a 5-on-3 power play opportunity with five minutes left, but couldn't capitalize. At

19:40, I called a timeout amidst a 6-on-5 goalie pull. We sent out the green line along with faceoff specialist Steve Mele, Jon Puskar, and defenseman Jeff Ceccacci. Coach Schooley called his timeout after seeing our faceoff alignment. At 19:49 Ceccacci took a point shot and Nielsson Arcibal scored off a scramble in front. He had tied the game 3–3 with a natural hat trick on a big icy stage. There are times when hockey has more drama than the theater.

However, two minutes into overtime, Robert Morris forward Brandon Blandina scored and simultaneously stuck a dagger in us. Back in the locker room, I expressed my admiration to the team for the high-compete level and will to win they showed throughout the series. And the comeback courage we displayed after losing the first game and being down 3–0 in Game 3. I thanked our seniors and, as was our custom, different team members spoke about our seniors and the season. And then the room turned still, until Jeff Ceccacci broke the ice when he rose up to get a drink of water.

AHA Commissioner Bob DeGregorio acted as league rep for our series, and we met near the locker room. Bob praised our play and Nielsson's performance in particular when he said, "It looked like he didn't want his college career to end." I asked if he'd say that to Nielsson, and he agreed. They talked for a short time. Nielsson's career was over, but he did "take over" the final period of his last game.

It would have been an even better story if Nielsson had scored in overtime. He didn't, nor did we take the series, but it was still quite a feat. When we met in downtown Springfield seven years after the game, he reflected back on his accomplishment. "The funny thing was, I felt like I had finally figured everything out just as my college career came to an end. I only wish I had scored more earlier." That's an interesting point, but there's a lot to be said for finishing strong.

That summer I spent my usual three weeks on sunshiny Lake Dunmore, which sits at the foot of the majestic Mount Moosalamoo. It's my favorite place in the world. I'm not the only hockey person on our section of the lake, as the Swett camp next door included Cub, Don, and Phil Swett, who all played at Middlebury College in the past. Phil later coached his son Bill at South Burlington HS in Vermont. Actress Cynthia Gibb rents the camp of our other next-door neighbor, the Shairs. She played Jessie Chadwick in the well-known hockey film, *Youngblood*. One of her lines was, "I think all hockey players should be able to read and write." Funny line, but it's just an antiquated stereotype now.

One of my seven nieces and nephews, Spencer Wright, my father's namesake, was often at the lake during my stay. When he was younger, he used to put on his hockey equipment and watch the Mighty Ducks hockey movie over and over. His parents would hear him doing the "Quack" chant in his sleep.

We opened with Penn State the next season. They were a new NCAA Division I program, and we were their first opponent. The game took place at their old rink, as the Pegula Arena was being built. A jam-packed crowd of 1,300 witnessed our 3–2 win, but it sounded like thousands in the cramped confines of the rink—until Jon Puskar scored in overtime. The twenty or so media members at the postgame press conference indicated how big-time Penn State is. We were lucky to have one or two reporters at home. Jim Ellefson, my brother-in-law, is a Penn State grad, but he cheered us on from his Vermont farm. A professor and published poet, he referred to our team as a "scrappy bunch of guys who never say die."

The next day we fell to Penn State 4–3 in Wilkes-Barre, Pennsylvania, where the Penguins' AHL team plays. The game was two hours from PSU, and yet 5,389 fans showed up. Then Union crushed us 8–0 at the Olympia. They were good and won the national championship a year later, but the lopsided loss stung.

The night had special significance to Springfield native Rick Bennett. He's remained loyal to his hometown and he had childhood friends at the game. When Rick and I scheduled the contest, I told him we could call it "Rick Bennett Night" to celebrate his return.

"Don't do that," he quipped. "I don't want the police to know I'm back in town."

We played at Quinnipiac on Election Night, Tuesday, November 6, 2012. Barack Obama had a big win and so did we, though his got more attention. Eric Lang, David Turco, and Matt Woodward, three of my former players coaching at Manhattanville College, came to the game, and we visited after. Matt Cassidy was initially not in the lineup, but I called him at the eleventh-hour to tell him he was dressing. "I'll be ready," he said. True to his word, he had the game-winner in our 2–1 victory. Ben Meisner had thirty-nine saves in the upset. The Bobcats moved on to a twenty-one-game unbeaten streak before losing to Yale in the national championship. The day after the game, former UVM teammate Peter Reynolds, who lived near Quinnipiac, emailed:

> "Dear Gary, great win! With the election and the hurricane, I lost track of the Quinnipiac schedule. I am pissed I missed it."

Whether we were preparing for Quinnipiac, Holy Cross, or whoever, one thing was certain. Chris Markiewicz, Steve Mele, and farm-boy-strong Adam Pleskach included "Pleshi-ball" in their pregame routine. The three close friends circled up after the team's dynamic warm-up to play this made-up game, named after Adam, that can't be found on Wikipedia. It's like hacky sack with modifications. The unpredictable ball featured six bumps to foster quick reactions. After it was passed around, you had to catch the ball cleanly with one hand, or receive a strike. Three strikes and you were out. Steve played fine, but Adam and Chris highlighted his losses, causing teammates to assume he was a bad player.

Army beat us 3–2 in front of a sold-out crowd on TK Night in early December. "TK" stood for Tom Kennedy, a former Black Knight player who was killed in action in Afghanistan. His family members were out on the ice for a solemn ceremony before the game. Coach Riley spoke and presented at the event. Both teams were on their respective blue lines. Adam Pleskach played a part in the proceedings as our captain. It was sad seeing Major Kennedy's young son standing on the ice in tears, but it also spoke of his love for his father, who must have been a great dad.

Rich Bedard later heard from Joe Hearn, whose son played at Army. Mr. Hearn wrote:

> I wanted to take a moment and commend your hockey team and staff for their incredible display of sportsmanship and respect by participating in TK night for the memory of a fallen West Point graduate and hockey player. Most amazing of all was at the end of a hard fought game that they lost by a goal, and facing a long bus ride home, they lined up at the blue line with their helmets off while the West Point school song was played. As a lifelong hockey person it was one of the most impressive things I've ever seen from an opposing team.

Boy, his words made me proud of my players.

We flew west on Southwest Airlines to play perennial power Air Force in late January. They had been Atlantic Hockey Champions and NCAA Tournament participants for four of the past five seasons. And they were quite hospitable. The visitor's locker room was stocked with shampoo, fluffy towels, black and white tape, rasps and files for stick blades, jugs of sports drinks and water, hard candy, and gum. We weren't great guests that night though, as we tied the Falcons 2–2. Pleskach and Markiewicz scored and Ben Meisner bailed us out fifty times.

The next night, Alexander MacMillan found the net in the first period. Ryan Timar tied it for Air Force in the second. The contest remained knotted 1–1 in regulation, which meant overtime. Richie Leitner scored a grand game winner at 0:18 of OT. We had beaten and tied the high-flying Falcons.

I ran into Blake Peake later at a store near our hotel. He was buying beer. We always drove home after a series, except when we flew. I didn't allow booze on the bus, but I left drinking after a series a gray area when we stayed over. I asked Blake about the beer and he said, "Getting three points at Air Force is so big that we're having a few beers in our hotel rooms. Plus, I'm twenty-three." I let it go and told him to tell guys to "keep the noise down." I mean, why not? I was so happy I almost started drinking again myself. Probably Coors Light, since we were in Colorado.

The *Colorado Springs Gazette* read "Falcons Lose To 11th Place Squad." (The headline zinged both teams.) "I don't want to take anything away from [AF goalie] Torf because he was good," coach Frank Serratore said. "Their guy [Meisner] was better. They had a good game plan and we got beat. Give the devils their due." Win or lose, I loved reading Frank's witty and straight-talk quotes.

A snowstorm postponed our upcoming series with Army, but we drove down on Sunday to make up one of the games, a 3–0 win for us. Then we swept Sacred Heart, which gave us a nation-leading six-game unbeaten streak. A tie with Holy Cross the following Friday extended it to seven games.

Army trailed 2–1 in the third period of the other rescheduled game at the Olympia, when a Cadet took a five-minute misconduct. I recall their captain, Cheyne Rocha, looked concerned about the call. He knew we had a potent power play. Our NCAA eighth-ranked PP then delivered on Adam Pleskach's goal. (We regularly switched between a 1–3–1 and an "overload" during play, as directed by our mid-points, Jeff Ceccaci and Chris Markiewitz, who quarterbacked the Snipers and Sharpshooters, respectively. Army assistant Eric Lang wrote: "1-3-1 PP unit is outright terrifying to defend—Looks like you guys expect to score every single PP.") Blake Peake later made it 4–1 off assists from Markiewitz and Pleskach. It was an all-captain connection.

Adam Pleskach was a preeminent player and captain for us. His skating style was not what one would call smooth, but he had the heart and game of a superstar. Mike Field eventually became the associate head coach at NCAA Division I Arizona State. He recruited Adam and Johnny Walker, who led the country in scoring at ASU. "Adam is a huge reason why I felt comfortable taking Johnny when other schools didn't," Mike said. "Both guys are ugly skaters but are elite competitors and have great instincts/shots. If I hadn't coached Adam, I never would have recruited Johnny."

Adam's assistant captains were Alberta natives Chris Markiewicz and Blake Peake. "It was an honor to be a captain at AIC," Chris said, "especially since you're voted in by your peers. Wearing a letter on your chest means a lot of things: leadership, responsibility, hard work, commitment, to name a few. It also means you are expected to show up and be those words every day."

We battled Bentley at the end of the regular season. After winning 2–1 at home on Friday night, we traveled to Bentley's off-campus rink on Saturday. Nicknamed the JAR (for John A. Ryan Arena), it's an "old barn" where even on the coldest days it feels chillier inside the rink than it does outside. We were down 3–1 halfway through the third when clutch goals by Jon Puskar and Brandon Fagerheim tied the game, and we entered overtime. I pulled Meisner with under a minute left, because we couldn't fall any further in the standings with a loss, but could pass Bentley with a win. We took a penalty at 4:48 of OT, so I put him back in. Coach Soderquist then pulled his goalie, perhaps hoping to win and get home ice if RIT beat Canisius (they didn't). The Bentley power play began, but we won the faceoff, and Blake Peake sent a long-distance puck into the unattended net with a second left. It was an improbable outcome, and pandemonium broke out on our bench.

The game changed so fast it took a moment before I knew we had won. Seth Dussault remembers being stunned, and then he saw the look on Bentley broadcaster Dan Rubin's face. "I think literally everyone in the JAR on both sides was making the same face," he said. "Just . . . stunning. That's the word."

The win ended our 2012–13 regular season at 12–15–6, and 8–3–3 down the stretch. We were slated for RIT in the playoffs. After the game, Bentley's doctor sewed five stitches into my bloodied face. I'd been hit by a puck in the first period ("Omigod, Gary," Mother wrote). And now I wouldn't have to wait at the hospital ER on a busy Saturday night back in Springfield. There are better ways to relish a breathtaking victory.

"The kids have been outstanding, win or lose," I said to Chris Lerch in his subsequent USCHO story. They've shown resilience, considering the adversity we've had in terms of wins and losses, so it's nice to see them get rewarded."

RIT swept us in two games, but our guys had much to be proud of once the initial sting of elimination waned. I often used John Wooden's expression, "The best way to improve your team is to improve yourself," when talking about team success. And, of course, there's our team mantra, "Come to Play. Make Plays. Keep Playing." We did that down the stretch when it counted most. Ceccacci, Meisner, and Pleskach were named to the league's All-Conference teams, but they had lots of help from their teammates, who were darn good players themselves.

The next two seasons weren't as strong as we hoped, considering our success the previous year. Graham Johnson returned as our full-time assistant, and Kyle Pobur had another year as GA. Mike Field had left to coach in the USHL the year before. Graham was a volunteer coach at Quinnipiac and assisted Norm Bazin at Hamilton. Kyle graduated with honors from Lake Superior State, where he played forward and defense for the Lakers. His versatility made him an asset as a player and as a coach.

Around this time, I wrote up a "Little Big Things That Help Us Win" poster in our school colors. It was framed and hung on our locker room wall. Here's a baker's dozen of the twenty-two categories:

- We need to win a hundred 1-on-1 battles to win the war (game).
- Tough players protect the puck and avoid turnovers.
- The message when you stop on the puck is that you care.

- Scoresheet plusses (+) are beautiful and minuses (-) are a blemish.
- A blocked shot can hurt, but mostly it hurts our opponents.
- Scouts watch how guys play away from the puck.
- The first player to help a 1-on-1 situation is our player.
- Short support is a speedy skate with a rewarding result.
- Goalies are our biggest asset, so play hard for them.
- O-zone changes are so unselfish, they're cool.
- Flip attacks flip out our opponents.
- Have patience with the puck like a pro.
- Put a little moxie in your hockey.

Our non-conference competition featured some of the biggest names in college hockey. We weren't afraid to play the so-called "big boys," and they jazzed up our schedule. We played at Michigan State (MSU) in early November of the 2013–14 season. The games were held on a Friday and Sunday because the Spartans had a home football game with rival Michigan on Saturday. We practiced that morning, and I gave our guys time to wander around the game-day campus. Cell service crashed with thousands of people on the grounds. I joined MSU fans in following the Spartan Marching Band from their warm-up area to the stadium. They didn't ask me to do any toots on the tuba.

We lost 5–4 on Friday night and 4–0 on Sunday. Friday's game was televised, and I did an interview from the bench during a first period time-out. It was a different experience compounded by our 2–0 deficit. Captain-elect Blake Peake put us on the board soon after. Alexander MacMillan later scored a no-quit goal at 19:54 of the third period on apples from Michigan natives Brandon Lubin and Jon Puskar to pull us within one.

Jon Puskar had ninety-six points in his career, so he just missed becoming our third D-I player to join the 100 Point Club. Jon could be a raging bull on blades, but he calmed down later in his career, without sacrificing his passionate play. In a USCHO.com article by Dan Rubin, Jon shared insight into the merits of the college hockey experience: "It's all about appreciating your four years to take full advantage of all your resources," Jon said, "whether it's on the ice with coaches, in the locker room with teammates, or in the classroom with professors. We have the chance to use all of these tools so we can help ourselves to be better athletes, students and people."

On the return flight, I wrote up a sheet labeled, "Coach Wright Comments on MSU Games." It's something our staff did to augment our ongoing evaluation of team members. More private matters were handled behind closed doors, while these comments were posted for all to see. It was a transparent way to hold everyone accountable. Players could get immediate feedback from us and also see that they weren't the only one being called out. The idea was that this format would help lead to better play. The five examples below are representative in that the comments are mostly encouraging, along with areas that need improvement:

- Whitney Olsen: Forward. Defenseman. Fourth Goalie. You gotta love that selfless versatility.

- Blake Peake: Solid effort and compete level. Nice goal, but two shots on net all weekend won't cut it.

- Jon Puskar: Played hard both games with positive bench presence. On own page on PP.

- Nate Sliwinski: High energy performer. Tenacious penalty killing. Improve overall positioning.

- Jake Williams: Nice goal. Good gap control. Led team in blocked shots.

We went to Maine a month later, the site of my first college coaching job. I got to see longtime friend Red Gendron and veteran hockey writer Larry Mahoney. We received a generous $20,000 guarantee to play Maine, even though we didn't take a flight. We stayed at the aptly named Black Bear Inn. My comp room included a Jacuzzi; they're apparently good stress relievers. I needed some relief, considering we were swept, but I passed and instead visited a Bangor bar with some of my old softball teammates after Friday's game. Shortstop Dennis Libby organized the outing. Despite losing earlier in the night, I had a fun time with my eternal teammates.

I made sure we cleaned the locker room when we moved out after Saturday's game. During my tenure as rink manager at the Alfond Arena, I observed how our opponents left the visitors' room. It was a mixed bag.

Innovator Charlie Holt at UNH, who "was the first college coach to use the center zone," according to former Bowdoin coach Sid Watson, helped his manager tidy up when UNH moved out. I took notice of that and did the same myself when I became a head coach.

We went on holiday break soon after the Maine series and hosted Air Force when we returned. Alexander MacMillan raced down the right side and rifled in a wrist shot early in overtime to give us the 4–3 win. Before the second game, broadcaster Seth Dussault, who gets as pumped as the players on game days, saw Frank Serratore in the Olympia lobby.

Seth waved from the snack bar and said, "Hey, Coach, how's it going?"

Coach Serratore said, "Well, after last night, [expletive] lousy, how about you?"

I'm sure he felt cheerier when the Falcons shut us out 2–0.

The Olympia was our home arena, but we did have an unusual rink on campus. President Vince Maniaci had an outdoor mini-rink constructed on the campus quad that our students could enjoy. He's not a hockey person per se, but he's got a keen imagination and a creative mind for marketing. In fact, when neighboring Springfield College copied his idea, he quipped, "We'll put hot tubs around ours and see if they'll do that." The rink added a winter wonderland look to our city campus and environs.

Our team played a 3-on-3 small game at the mini-rink, followed by a public skate with AIC students and staff. Everyone sipped on hot chocolate, and MassLive.com took footage and wrote about the activity. Seth Dussault stumbled out in an ill-fitting full uniform to drop the first puck. He was assisted by AIC employee and unofficial campus greeter Kevin "Moose" Panetta. Moose hosted another session where the first twenty-five student skaters got a free moose hat (don't wear them during moose hunting season). I blew the whistle every minute in our small game, as six new players leaped on the ice to play the puck and six others scrambled into a snowbank. They continuously appeared and reappeared like flash mobs in their colorful practice jerseys.

We staged a small game at the Olympia when we practiced on the day before leaving to play the Niagara Purple Eagles in the Atlantic Hockey playoffs. The game was called Safe House, and the cross-ice competition took place in one zone. Given the choice of playing a small game or working on defensive zone coverage (DZC), players will surely pick the former. After all, you rarely see anyone practicing defense on a pond. Playing a small game increases the pace because you decrease the space. Players have to make plays in traffic. The pace also picks up since these high-compete games are fun to play. The winners usually hold over-the-top celebrations. My players always asked "if we're playing a small game today." I often answered to the affirmative.

We didn't do the Dartmouth Drill that day, though it could have been on the docket since we were two days away from facing Niagara. I asked Dartmouth assistant John Rose once to suggest a new drill when we were out recruiting. He gave me this from Big Green coach Bob Gaudet: Two lines of players face the neutral zone along the boards of each blue, for a total of four lines. On the whistle, two 2-on-0s start simultaneously into the neutral zone, receive a coach's pass, and attack the far end. Each receiver goes down the wing and either shoots or creates a one-attempt rebound for his/ her partner. The two teams get a point for scoring off the shot and two points for a rebound goal. Play to fifteen points.

Defenseman Dom Racobaldo came to us from the Omaha Lancers of the USHL, and the Dartmouth Drill was his favorite. "It's a tough drill for goalies, but as a stay-at-home D-man it gave me a chance to have fun and score some goals! I still think about the 'Dartmouth' whenever I see a player shoot for a pad."

A sports psychology session took place in the locker room after the practice. Springfield College graduate students from their athletic counseling program worked with our team under the direction of Dr. Judy Van Raalte. After an initial introductory meeting, they met with us several times a season and always before the playoffs. Our players could also meet with them on a one-on-one basis. The "Best Stuff" sessions, as I called them, involved each of the grad students presenting to the team for five minutes. The short duration didn't infringe as much on our guys' time, and it forced the presenters to give a focused, "no fluff" talk. We felt fortunate to have these bright young individuals working with us.

Right before the Niagara game, I reminded our players that we split with them in January, "so we know how to win here." And I said that there's no better game to play in hockey than a playoff game. A USA Hockey poster hanging in the rink read, "All the talent in the world won't get you anywhere without your teammates." I cited it, along with a strategy I heard from NFL quarterback Drew Brees: "Start Fast. Finish Strong. Execute in Between."

We did start fast. Not on the scoreboard, but I knew right off that we were zoned in. Our shifts were short and sharp. Our bench comportment was poised and positive. Freshman tender Hunter Leisner was on his angles and looked confident in his crease as he made seven saves in the opening period. His counterpart, Jackson Teichroeb, stopped twelve pucks for the Purple Eagles. It was 0–0 after one. And then 0–0 after two. And 0–0 after three. We were headed to OT in this still scoreless game.

We'd keep playing until there was a 1 up on the scoreboard. So buzzing Yellow Jackets and flocks of Purple Eagles continued flying up and down the ice, thwarted by backchecking forwards, back-skating defenders and game-saving goalie stops. I sighed after Leisner's saves and silently cursed when we missed a scoring chance. Remarkably, the first OT remained 0–0. But at 4:43 of the second overtime, after eighty-five minutes of play, Niagara's Dan Kolenda tipped a shot past Leisner to win 1–0. Most of us on the AIC bench would have rather taken that shot to the head than have it end up in our net.

The sun still came up the next day, and unlike in our 1–0 OT playoff loss at Holy Cross a few years back, we were now in a best-of-three series. The hotel was near Niagara Falls, so we took the team to see the falls and walk around in the misty air. Rich Bedard came too. He usually only traveled to playoff games, and this time he came on the bus. (He also visited the spot where the stadium stood when he played professionally for the Niagara Falls Pirates.) We viewed the awe-inspiring falls from above, only a few yards from where the torrents of water tumble over the edge. Hockey is a game that honors toughness, but those daredevils who go over the falls in a barrel might be even tougher—or nuttier.

The lineup stayed the same for Game 2 except that we dressed Matt Cassidy for David Gandara at left wing on the blue line. They were both dependable players, but not quite good enough to be a lock in the lineup. Niagara (not the Falls) poured it on in the first period, with fifteen shots and three goals. They notched another in the second to take a 4–0 lead. We were in a bad spot. But we still had a chance. We outshot them 16–7 in the third and scored twice in a desperate attempt to win, or force overtime. We couldn't quite get it done, though, and lost 4–2. After the game, MassLive. com writer Thomas Baldwin spoke with Niagara coach Dave Burkholder, who said, "They were playing to keep their season going, and it's hard at any level to end someone's season." Some say it's like fighting for your life. That's hyperbole, of course, but when I saw the pained expressions on the faces of our players after the game, I could see why they fought so hard to play another day.

Rich Bedard retired soon after and was replaced by assistant AD Matt Johnson. I felt fortunate to have Rich as my athletic director, just as I enjoyed working for Bob Burke. Matt had been on staff for several years, so we knew each other well. He had been a successful women's soccer coach at AIC.

Matt Johnson later called me at Lake Dunmore to say that John Debonville had died suddenly. John was a close friend and appears in this book. Austin Orszulak phoned when he heard the sad news, and said that John sent him a nice note after he registered his first collegiate goal. That didn't surprise me. A popular professor at AIC, John directed the campus ministries, and often said, "We exist because of our students." Because he was an Episcopal priest, his funeral was held in Springfield's Christ Church Cathedral, and I spoke at it. I cited a line from poet Emily Dickinson in my talk: "That it will never come again is what makes life so sweet." A friend of John's daughter Katie asked who I was and Katie told her I was the hockey coach.

"A hockey coach reciting Emily Dickinson," she said in apparent amazement.

We opened the 2014–15 season with Union College, the defending NCAA Division I National Champions. Rick Bennett emailed to ask if I'd mind if they wore their "garnet" jerseys instead of home whites. At one point he wrote, "Well, back to the madness," in reference to the start of our hectic seasons. He concluded with, "I'll try my best to keep the circus before the game to a minimum. I respect you and your program and want to just play!!!"

I wrote back:

Thanks for your kind words. Wearing our whites is no problem. I like your 'want to just play,' line, but we are fine whatever the length of the ceremony, and in some respects it will be a neat experience for our players.

Union raised their 2014 national championship banner before the game. Freshman forward Johno May put us up 1–0 soon after the ceremony ended. His parents surprised him by flying out unannounced from Minnesota to watch his first college game. It must have been a big thrill for them, even though Union went on to win 7–3. The game was further verification that we were playing at one of the highest levels in hockey

A month later, we played the Michigan Wolverines, winners of a record nine national championships. Their athletic program is big, like their "Big House" football stadium. Four days before the game, I had to put down Ebbie, my aging black lab. I'd avoided the dreaded task for weeks, until it became clear that I could wait no longer. Sadly, our pets don't live as long as we do. I helped Ebbie into the car and drove to the vet, where Dr Lynn Dgetluck euthanized her. Even Lynn cried after, although she's done the procedure hundreds of times. I lost my best friend, who loved me whether we won or lost.

We took on Michigan at storied Yost Arena in front of 5,000 spectators each night. Recent GA Kyle Pobur came and took a panoramic picture of Steven Hoshaw, our captain, shaking hands under a pregame ceremony spotlight with his counterpart, Michigan's Andrew Copp. A policeman was assigned to our locker room. When I told him I'd go around to the bench, instead of walking on the ice, he suggested a police escort (like some FBS coach). "No thanks, I'm fine," I said. "I doubt many Michigan fans have heard of me, or AIC, so they can't be too concerned about us."

Just before the national anthem of the first game, the legendary Red Berenson surprisingly came to our bench to shake hands and welcome us to Yost. "You probably don't get to coach against many coaches older than you," the seventy-something Berenson joked. He was right about that. He and I were the longest-running D-I coaches at one college since Jack Parker retired. However, it felt like Red had a million more wins than me. (He also had six goals in an NHL game.) That gap grew when we lost 5–2, despite two goals by sophomore David Norris.

We converted on the power play early the next night. But the Wolverines bit back with three goals in three minutes. They bagged another in the second to go up 4–1, but we didn't blanch. We never did against big schools like Michigan, whose roster included ten NHL draft picks. Springfield native and (Bruce) Springsteen fan Austin Orszulak, who has attended over seventy of the boss's concerts, answered with successive rush goals. Both came off passes from linemate Johno May. Michigan later added two third-period tallies to win 6–3.

A quote from senior Matt Cassidy appeared in our game program the following week:

> Playing Michigan at Yost has been the highlight of my career. Everything from the history of the rink, the quality of the team, and the atmosphere the band/crowd creates is a perfect representation of what college hockey is all about.

Mike Towns had become our new GA. He captained the Adrian University hockey team, so he was but an hour from his alma mater when we played Michigan. Mike instituted our use of hockey analytics, such as Corsi, which tracks the sum of all shots, including off-target and blocked shots. It can be used as a team or line stat. If the green line attempts twenty-nine shots and our opponent tries twenty-one against them, their Corsi rating is a strong 58 percent (29/50). "The principle," Mike says, "is that in order to even attempt a shot you (a) need to have the puck, and (b) have it in the offensive zone." A book called *Stat Shot* by Rob Vollman covers hockey analytics in a way that's understandable to a broader audience. I've never been strong in math, so it helped me. Our Cornwall home was surrounded by farms when I was young, and one summer I told my parents I planned to become a farmer when my NHL career ended. "You'll have to know math to be a farmer," my father said knowingly.

We had a date with Dartmouth on Thanksgiving weekend. Their Hanover, New Hampshire, campus is forty minutes from Proctor Academy and borders Vermont, so my family got to see us play in a 3–2 loss. It was our second time competing against them. We had played Dartmouth in a memorable game back during the 2007–08 season. With a 3–2 lead in the third period of that game, and the puck in a scrum along the side boards of our zone, senior Chad Richardson yelled out, "Great game, guys," as the final seconds ticked off. But somehow Dartmouth's Jon Grecu wristed a last-second shot amidst a cluster of stick blades that fluttered past goalie Dan Ramirez at 19:59. The helmeted heads of my players hung for a moment, and then they got back on their horses and hustled through overtime. The game ended in a 3–3 tie, but we felt lousy about losing the late lead.

My mother continued to exclaim, "Oh no, oh no" during anxious moments of this second Dartmouth game. Meanwhile, my sister Lesley didn't confront any Big Green fans like the last time. (She had told a liquored-up Dartmouth student, who heckled Ramirez from behind our net, to "shut up." The student in turn bellowed, "Hey, Ramirez, your mother's here and she just told me not to yell at you.") Longtime college friends and teammates Herb Muther and Ken Yeates attended the game, as well as Proctor alums Tom Canfield, Doug Windsor, and Dudley Clark. All three played for my father. Dudley also came to see AIC goalie Jacob Caffrey; they met at Cardigan Mountain School when Jacob went there. Dudley taught and coached at Cardigan for many years. In his retirement, he drove the school's Zamboni and school bus; both were purposely parked outside the entrance to where his campus service was held when he later died. A New Hampshire license plate on the Zamboni said, "DUDLEY."

Green-liner David Norris soon told me that he was transferring to Arizona State for the second semester. They were converting from club to NCAA status. David's brother skated on their club team, and I believe his family had property in Arizona, so they were well acquainted with ASU hockey. I discussed the subject with our new compliance officer, Jessica Chapin, before she sent the permission-to-contact release form to ASU. Jess impressed me with how she handled the situation. I never heard from their coach Greg Powers, despite my efforts to convince David to stay. We had two games left with Bentley before the break, and David asked if he could still play in them. I said no. Good player or not, I didn't want him in the lineup if he didn't want to be on our team.

Graham Johnson left in the spring to take another job. He'd been my full-time assistant for three years, though we had a strained working relationship. He coached juniors for a couple of seasons and then became the head coach at Milwaukee School of Engineering, an NCAA Division 3 college.

Sixty candidates applied for the full-time position. Coach Towns and I did phone interviews with ten of the applicants, and we invited four of them to visit campus. Conducting exhaustive searches is one reason we've been able to hire so many promising young assistants. We decided on Steve Wiedler, the Curry College assistant. He was a dark-horse candidate, but he dazzled us during the interview process. He had good references, and I liked how he stayed loyal to Jeff Beaney, his Southern Maine coach, who was let go. I also liked an email he sent where he said,

> I've been thinking about AIC non-stop, and I know if I can get the chance to have an on-campus interview, I will leave no doubt in your mind that I am the man for the job.

I felt good about my staff for the upcoming season, and the recruiting went well. My thirty-second year at AIC would be underway in four months. I didn't know it at the time, but it would be my last.

Chapter 13

Endgame

I awake and roll over to see what time it is. The small clock on the night table beside my bed reads 8 a.m. I rub my eyes as if to scratch out the sleep, and then I get up. My mind continues to race from last night's 2016 season-ending playoff loss to Army. We arrived back at the Olympia after midnight and I keyed us in the backdoor of the closed building to drop off our equipment. (I often snuck out that door after a bad loss, and sometimes let the refs out the pseudo–escape hatch with me.) I also punched in a six-digit code to turn the security alarm system off and on. For me, it's a number to remember. For owner/rink manager Barry Tabb, the code represents the birth date of his daughter, Kelly, who died at a young age. Losing a game or a series is hard, but it's been said that there's nothing worse than losing a child.

Today feels like a Sunday, yet it's a Monday because the series went to Game 3. Thus, my Sunday fun routine of planning and outlining the upcoming week's practices at home is now disrupted. Not only that, but no matter what today is, there aren't any more practices to plan, or line combinations to consider, or team travel schedules to make. If there were, Arlene Pereira, the athletics administrative assistant, would already be calling me about the latter to say something like, "I need to order a bus for next weekend right now or else you won't have one." And I'd probably needle the always-organized Arlene about a bus she scheduled that never came a few years ago: "It'll be a travesty if we have to drive our own cars to a game again."

After stopping at the office, I'm hiking with Hobey at Fountain Park in Wilbraham. It's a 100-acre wooded oasis, surrounded by suburbia. Hobey is an active black Labrador mix with a white stripe on his chest that disqualifies him from Westminster's Best in Show competition. But he puts on a good show when we hike. A namesake of hockey hero Hobey Baker, my unleashed canine crashes through the underbrush, swims in the swamp, and futilely chases after rabbits and rodents. He sniffs everything in sight. I got him through a Paws4Rescue organization in Connecticut six months after Ebbie died. I don't know exactly where Hobey is right now as I walk down a trail, still consumed by myriad thoughts of the Army series, but he'll catch up with me before I arrive back at the car.

Today it's Fountain Park and tomorrow it could be somewhere else near my Springfield home. I even hike with a flashlight after work in the winter. I've come to enjoy these wilderness walks almost as much as Hobey. We are a determined pair of happy hikers, whatever the weather. The walks continue when our team is on the road. In fact, I often walk after games and, when we win, there's extra spring in my step. Sometimes I'll head back to the hotel before the bus leaves and get picked up as it passes by. Bobby Ferraris amusingly remembers that while he and my other assistants were seeking the "warmest spot in the rink," I'd be "on the Appalachian Trail in just a sports jacket."

Our students are on vacation, so the campus is quiet. Many of my players are scrambling to make arrangements to go home or to head south for spring break. A couple of seniors are looking to sign with pro teams for a few weeks, but they'll be back in time to complete their courses and graduate. Besides, the NCAA doesn't require second-semester seniors to be full-time students if they need fewer than twelve credits to graduate. Life goes on and plans have to be made following the suddenness of a season-ending loss, but for players and coaches, the agony of defeat can linger for a while.

Our staff hits the recruiting trail over the upcoming days. We've recently received a commitment from Kyle Stephan, a six-foot-two forward from the Wenatchee Wild of the British Columbia Hockey League (BCHL). The BCHL is generally considered the strongest junior league in North America next to the USHL. Mike Towns did most of the work recruiting Stephan, since Mike hails from that province. We are excited to have Stephan, although my excitement is tempered by thoughts that I may soon be leaving AIC. Recent developments sure seem to be pointing that way.

* * *

My departure has now been decided, and I'm walking over to meet with the team in the weight room where they are finishing up a workout. I want them to know I'm leaving before the school sends out an announcement. The short walk from my office to the gym is one I've made thousands of times before, but it's never felt quite like this. I'm about to meet with a team that will no longer be mine. And I'll soon be exiting a campus and a community that has been an integral part of my life for over three decades. I feel a sense of loss far worse than a lengthy losing streak.

Players gather around me in their sweat-soaked workout clothes and sneakers after I arrive in the weight room. Mike and Steve Wiedler are here too. I hold a yellow legal pad with a few talking points, and announce that I'm resigning from AIC, although some might call it retirement. I do know that I don't plan to coach in college again. I tell them it's a sad day for me, but I realize it's not necessarily a sad day for the guys who indicated they want a coaching change on the anonymous coaching evaluations. After a pause, I say that Mike and Steve will be running things until a new coach is hired. I let our players know that even though my assistants' jobs are now in jeopardy, I'm hopeful the new hire will retain them.

I thank the team for being always on time, even when carpooling twenty minutes through traffic to get to practice every day. I thank them for being good students and solid citizens on campus. And I acknowledge their effort, attitude, and discipline—and especially their will to win, however strong the opponent. I cite our road wins against Robert Morris and RIT and one-goal losses to Princeton, UMass Amherst, and UMass Lowell. "I wish we had won more," I say, "but we weren't losers, because we never quit or backed down to anyone. The games I just mentioned are proof of that."

I add that I'll miss coaching and working at AIC. And I let them know that I'll be in the office for a week or two if anyone wants to see me. I finish by wishing them good luck with their hockey careers at AIC and their future endeavors. After shaking a few hands, I head out the door and take a lonely walk back to the office.

AIC announces my resignation the next day. The *Springfield Republican* and USCHO run the story along with various other sports news outlets. It covers my years at AIC and mentions that we had a perfect NCAA Academic Rate (APR) of 1000 recently. The release notes that our team received the Atlantic Hockey Team Sportsmanship Award (lowest PIMs) for the third year in a row. AD Matt Johnson has some comments and the article includes a quote from me:

> My time at AIC has been enormously enriched by the people I've worked with on campus, our assistant coaches and the players I've coached. And by my coaching colleagues on the other bench. It has often been said that playing college hockey helps make college the best four years of your life. For me, that association extended nearly forty years (32 years at AIC). I only wish that my record had been better. Otherwise, it has been a wonderful run.

I carefully crafted that quote to get it just right. After I submitted it, public relations manager Candy Lash called to suggest I change the part about my record. She made a good point, since it does emphasize my losses, but I told her I want to keep it because that's the way I feel.

Over the next few days, I receive countless emails, texts, and phone calls. Some people call my cell, and others ring my office phone. I hear from college coaches, former players and assistants, and assorted hockey people. Even a couple of refs write me. I guess it's because I didn't get on them that much! I also hear from individuals going back to my earliest coaching and playing days. And UVM and Vermont Hockey School friends like Boomer Child, Mike Gilligan, Willie MacKinnon, and Ken Yeates. Former Sigma Nu brother and UVM teammate Tom McNamara sends out a group email saying:

> With all the free time on his hands, I imagine that Gary can now get back to honing his skills at more important pursuits like Whiffle ball, street hockey, and golf.

As a sportsaholic, I've always said that if someone will pay me a small salary to play those activities, plus pond hockey and softball, I'll give up my day job.

For all that, it's a text from Jon DeAndrade, a young administrator in our athletic department, that really hits me:

I just wanted to wish you well in your future ventures, and any time you want to go hiking at Peaked (Mtn.), you give me a call and we'll have both our dogs in the pond. Ha ha. You were such a pleasure to work with and I will always appreciate the fact that you were one of the only coaches who took time out of their day to speak with me when I was an intern, and made me feel included in this department. You're a great coach, but I'll remember you as an even better person.

I invariably tell our players that I hope they'll treat everyone the same. I want them to be as nice to the janitor as to the college president. Humility and humbleness are important traits for any person to possess. I share Jon's text not from a narcissistic standpoint, but because I want to practice what I preach. To this point, there's an observation Scotty Bowman once made on Wayne Gretzky in a *Sports Illustrated* article:

He was the kind of guy who'd get to know the clubhouse people, the stickboys. He treated everyone with respect. With older people it was always Mister. I'd say, "It's Scotty." But it was always Mr. Bowman. Even now. It's just the way he was raised.

The hockey office in the athletic annex (former TKE house) is like a second home to me. I'm going to miss it. It's homey with a fireplace in both my and my assistants' offices. Birch logs are placed in each fireplace, though they're no longer used for burning. There's also an old kitchen area, which now includes a computer, storage cabinet, and extra desk. My assistants' office doubles as a lobby and includes a Bryon Lewis–designed AIC Hockey logo on the carpet. I've spent countless hours in the office. I even come in on most Saturday mornings in the off-season, partly out of habit, and because I can work with fewer interruptions. This is where I meet privately with players, although I won't be holding my usual year-ending player-coach meetings now that I'm leaving.

I'm taking two weeks to wrap things up and clean out my office. I take down pictures and paintings, many of them hockey scenes, and remove a century-old brown-and-white photo of my grandfather, Stanley V. Wright, standing beside the plane he flew in WWI. I wonder if by some chance he met fellow flier Hobey Baker during the short time the Americans fought in the war. All those plucky pilots must have had nerves of steel considering that the Wright brothers (no relation) flew the first plane at Kitty Hawk barely fifteen years earlier. My grandfather came back from the war. Hobey Baker did not. Baker took a recently repaired plane up for a test run soon after the armistice, against the advice of his squadron mates, who saw no reason for him to tempt fate with the war over. Their concern was merited. The plane crashed.

I rummage through countless files, saving various papers and throwing others away. There are notes and letters that go back to when I started at AIC. They evoke memories. My big bookcase includes some 300 hockey books that I'm boxing up, including Anatoli Tarasov's *Road to Olympus*, former Brown coach Jim Fullerton's *Ice Hockey*, Howie Meeker's *Hockey Basics*, and *Hockey in Springfield* by Jim Mancuso. Large three-ring binders hold thirty-two years of AIC practices, drills I've collected through the years, and handouts from the coaches' convention and various other clinics. Several binders contain copies of magazine, newspaper, and online articles. In addition to hockey, the articles cover related subjects from the sports world and elsewhere. I've shared many of them with my players.

Today is my last day in the office. Mike and Steve have helped all week to lug boxes out to my car. I move them into my house with a dolly since my hips are headed for replacement. Our football coach, Art Wilkins, and athletic administrators Jess Chapin and Ben Rosenfeld are among the last to stop by. When I notice Jess becoming teary-eyed at one point, I pause to clear a small catch in my throat. It has been an emotional couple of weeks, and cleaning out my office and saying goodbye to people has accentuated the finality of my departure. Later in the day, after walking out of a now-empty office, I steer my old gray Chevy Cobalt onto Cortland Street. The athletic annex is in my rearview mirror. So is a forty-year coaching career.

The next week Eric Lang is introduced as the new AIC hockey coach. The event is held in the Athletic Hall of Fame Room. I don't attend, but I watch the video two days later. Matt Johnson announces, "We will now include two full-time assistant coaches on the bench, we will increase our scholarship offers to be more competitive with other D-I ice hockey programs, and we will commit more money to our equipment and recruiting budgets." I wish those critical improvements had been in place when I was coach, but no sense dwelling on it. Instead, I'm happy for the program and Eric.

The announcement doesn't take me by surprise. Eric and I have stayed in touch and I know he's been offered the job. He has been AIC's first choice all along. I recommended him highly to Matt Johnson, although the decision to hire Eric was obviously not mine. The fact that he played and coached at AIC is a big plus, and his success at Army and Manhattanville is impressive. He's also an exceptional recruiter. I tried to get him to come back to AIC as my full-time assistant in recent years, but it didn't work out for him financially with a big family, or otherwise. The other day, Eric asked me about Mike and Steve, and I spoke glowingly on their behalf. He's decided to keep both of them, which is great news; now they have to prove themselves to Eric, and I'm confident they will.

In the months after leaving AIC, I put my house on the market, schedule the first hip surgery in January, and make plans to move back to Vermont the next summer. It's a different life I'm living now. With extra time on my hands, I feel a little lost at times. My situation is compounded by a lack of mobility in both hips, a condition that's worsened due to my procrastination in having the procedure done. It precludes me from golfing and big hikes, although I limp along with Hobey on short walks. During this past season it got to a point where I could barely tie my skates. I clung close to the boards at practice, or waddled around the ice like a penguin. And I'm not talking about a Pittsburgh Penguin.

I've also started writing a book. It has been on my mind for some time, but my mother has been pushing me to go through with it. Indeed, penning this book has given purpose and structure to my retired life. It has allowed me to stay in touch with people, and it's kept me connected to the game. I almost feel like I'm living my hockey life all over again. I'm in the moment as I write about the past: skating on the pond at Proctor, trying to crack the lineup at UVM, coaching at AIC.

Now that I'm working on this book, I have decided to reveal that I didn't just resign from AIC as announced, but I was in fact, fired. I appreciate the administration's decision to call it a resignation (or retirement), which certainly looks better for me, and perhaps for the college. And it's true that I did retire from college coaching because I have no desire to coach at that level again, but my retirement was not voluntary. If I weren't writing this book, it would be easier and less awkward to leave my resignation as a personal choice, but unfortunately that's not the case. My story is more complete if I let it be known that the decision to leave AIC was not entirely my own.

My termination had nothing to do with any kind of unethical behavior. It was ultimately related to losing too many hockey games for too long a time. Certain higher-ups, my players, and some alumni had been disappointed with our lack of success and, by extension, my coaching. Winning minimizes problems, while losing maximizes them, but no players ever crossed me and we didn't have any on- or off-ice issues to speak of my last season, or during most years. But the losing is difficult on everyone, and guys can have less confidence in a coach when that happens. In the NHL, they often call it "losing the room" when explaining why a coach is let go. I know there was some of that in my case, but our work ethic and low penalty minutes over the past three seasons speaks to the discipline and structure of our program that remained even during the trying times.

I believe I became the country's second-longest active Division I hockey coach while at one school because my staff and I recruited good people who were diligent students and, most importantly, they graduated. Our hockey budget wasn't the biggest, but we competed hard on the ice and our team represented AIC in a very positive way. And I hired assistant coaches who doubled as educators. We assimilated ourselves into the entire institution, not just the athletic department. These qualities protected me for many years, but eventually the school made a change that was not easy for them to make since I know they felt good about me and the integrity of the hockey program.

My objective as a college hockey coach has always been to run a clean program and win hockey games. But there wasn't enough winning. My career won-lost record is on me; I chose this business, criticism comes with it. Accountability, too. It was AIC's prerogative to terminate my employment and I accept their decision without excuse. It hurts being let go and it's an unfortunate way to end a long career, but it's something I'm dealing with, as many others have had to. On the College Hockey News website there is an extensive list titled "All Time Coaching Changes by Year." In the last ten years alone, twenty-two Division I coaches are listed as having been fired (there may be more than that). If they change my status from "retired" to "fired," that will make it twenty-three, which means nearly 40 percent of colleges sponsoring D-I hockey have let their coach go during the past decade. It can be a tough business, which may be why so many of us are attracted to the risks and rewards of the profession.

I have a copy of a "Dear Colleagues and Friends" letter that the late Tim Taylor wrote when he was let go by Yale in 2006. I knew Tim fairly well, and spent time on the ice with him at summer hockey schools, but I was not in his inner circle by any means. A friend forwarded his email to me at the time. Coach Taylor was undoubtedly among the most knowledgeable hockey minds in the world and, as I mentioned earlier, he was head coach of our Olympic Hockey Team in 1994. In the letter he said that he always wanted to retire with three conditions:

> 1) To leave on my own terms. 2) That the program will be in great shape and poised for future successes, and 3) That I will walk away with my integrity and dignity intact.

He went on to say that No. 1 "has not happened," that No. 2 "is in place," and that with respect to No. 3, "I'm working very hard on it." You can feel the anguish in his words.

Like most of us, Coach Taylor hoped to exit on his own terms, but as *New Haven Register* sports columnist Dave Solomon wrote, "Unfortunately, that luxury is reserved for an extremely short list of coaching immortals." Solomon went on to say that Taylor "is a far more influential figure in Yale history than his record might indicate. Yet the ultimate examination of Tim Taylor, Yale hockey coach, still goes through 337–433–55, his career record after twenty-eight seasons behind the bench." I'm no Tim Taylor, but we are both examples of college coaches, who despite our subpar won-lost records, may have remained longer at our respective institutions because of our other attributes.

I came across a magazine named *Minnesota Calls* in the 1990s when I was at Bemidji State for the D-II national championship, as a member of the NCAA Division II/III Men's Ice Hockey Committee. Inside, there was an article called "Disorganized Hockey" by Barton Sutter. He talks about playing pickup hockey on ponds and also what he gleaned from organized sports in high school:

Mostly what I learned was how to lose, and because, as adults, what we often do is lose—parents, lovers, jobs, our fondest dreams—that was invaluable training.

Like people from all walks of life, I've had to learn how to cope with loss, due in part to my record as a college coach. And then I lost my job. Some of Sutter's other examples are still to come for me.

There are members of the press who can be inclined to define bottom-tiered programs with caustic words like "losing," "dormant," and "rudderless." These labels tend to paint teams with a broad brush, without the critic having a full understanding of the situation or challenges a particular college or coach faces. Or without realizing just how competitive and committed many players on that "losing" team really are. A key measure of courage is to endure defeat without losing hope. In essence, you only truly fail if you quit. I've coached all kinds of players in the past few years alone who are winners, not losers. A few examples would include recent captains like Nielsson Arcibal, Steven Hoshaw, Tom Mele, Blake Peake, and Adam Pleskach. Those guys would make any program better; their steadfast leadership would complement the culture of any hockey team. And there are many others I could name as well.

It's ironic that the quote I used to accompany my senior bio in the Proctor Academy yearbook comes from Ernest Hemingway in his book, *The Old Man and the Sea*. We read the story in English class, and I was struck by the line, "But man is not made for defeat. A man can be destroyed but not defeated." The wording was applied to the fisherman Santiago, who courageously battled a massive marlin before sharks ate it as he tugged it back to port. Looking back, I chose a kind of heavy quote, but to some extent it reflects the philosophical nature of the early 1970s, and my relative youth. It's pertinent and timely to my situation at AIC because it's about never giving up, a key component of competition—and life.

It's a Saturday in October, soon after the start of the first hockey season in over fifty years that doesn't include me as a player or coach, and I'm at Bruce Marshall's funeral service in Worcester, Massachusetts. He died unexpectedly in his sleep the other night. I sit with Larry O'Donnell toward the back of the crowded church. My former assistant, Glenn Stewart, who was on Bruce's staff at UConn, is seated several rows to our left. Andy Card sits nearby. He was the president of Franklin Pierce University until recently, where Bruce became head coach after leaving UConn. Card once served under President George W. Bush as chief of staff. I don't know him, but I'm impressed that he took the time to come to the service. Bruce must have made an impression on him, too.

Peter Belisle is speaking. He assisted Coach Marshall at UConn prior to becoming head coach at UMass Boston. He's talking about how Bruce was a "connector of people." How he often wrote thank-you notes by hand, and sent hockey T-shirts out to alumni, fans, and coworkers on campus, and how he connected friends and former players with job opportunities. Peter points out Bruce's prodigious fundraising skills and that he just "got stuff done." Then Peter croons a verse or two from Bruce's favorite singer Jackson Brown's hit song, *Stay*. My eyes start to well up as he sings a touch out of tune. But he's very much in tune with how much he misses Bruce and wishes he could have been with us longer.

Bruce is on my mind as I drive home on the Mass Pike, past the Western Mass landscape, its fall foliage painted with greens, reds, oranges, and yellows, the colors our forward lines wore in practice. The service was sad, but I'm glad I went. Twenty years ago, I didn't go to a funeral that I should have attended, and I've learned from that. Boomer Child had called back then to tell me that UVM teammate and Sigma Nu brother Jocko Clifford had died of a heart attack. He was only in his forties. I had a lot to do at work, so I decided not to go. Looking back, I don't recall any of those supposedly important work tasks that kept me from attending Jocko's service, but I clearly remember that I didn't go.

There can be smiles amidst the sadness. Remembering Jocko reminds me of the time he appeared on the UVM student radio station before a series with the Wisconsin Badgers. Duke Snodgrass, a Sigma Nu member, interviewed him on a late Sunday afternoon. Jocko didn't discriminate with his drinking habits, so he had a few before the radio interview. A bunch of us listened as he claimed he'd heard the Badgers were a dirty team, and he said that one of our forwards "hasn't shown me anything." (He used the player's name.) When Jocko got back to the frat house, he asked how we liked the interview. We told him it wasn't good and repeated what he'd said.

"OK, I'll just go back and do it over," he slurred.

"Jocko," we practically yelled in unison, "It's too late, you were on live."

The following summer, I moved back to Cornwall, Vermont, and I've been here for nearly eighteen months. Lake Dunmore is twenty minutes away. My retirement plans have always involved returning to my roots. I live in a small house called the Outpost that my father built about a hundred yards from his place on the twenty-acre property. He recently moved to nearby Leicester, Vermont, to live with my sister, Lesley, and her husband, Jim, now that he's in his nineties. A family currently rents my dad's house, which he also designed and constructed. Both houses feature beams and barn boards salvaged from decrepit old barns. He and his part-time help hammered in every nail. From the ridge where I live, I have a splendid view of the Green Mountains and the peaks of the Adirondacks.

Now that my hip replacements are done, I can return to golfing and hiking heights. I still stay in touch with hockey, occasionally making the two-mile drive (no lights) to watch Middlebury College games. And I've seen the Vermont men and women play. In fact, the UVM Hockey Alumni Weekend just got over. I didn't play in the alumni game, but I attended Saturday night's contest with Merrimack and got a "UVM Hockey Alumni/Brothers of the Gut" T-shirt. Ken Yeates and I visited the hospitality room, where it was nice to be among so many familiar faces, but we elected not to join the other alums in a between-periods ceremony at center ice. If they introduced everyone individually, which they didn't, I was afraid the large crowd might "who" me, as opposed to boo me—as in, *Who is that guy?*

In December, I watched AIC play Robert Morris at the Mass Mutual Center. I also watch them online. They are getting better fast with Eric, Mike, and Steve at the helm. (They'll be AHA champions in March.) I visited with the AIC staff outside the locker room after the RMU game, and Mike and Steve brought up a meeting I had with them during my last season. While holding up their top recruits list at the time, I said, "So one of these guys is way overweight, another won't pass the NCAA Clearinghouse, and a third practically leads his league in penalties. . . . Are you guys kidding me?" We all laughed about the tenseness of that moment, though they told me my point was well taken. Eric Lang says, I "coached the coaches" at AIC. I guess head coaches don't just coach players.

I also follow college hockey scores on the Internet and listen to UVM, Middlebury, and Norwich games on the radio. Cadets sportscaster George

Commo, who continues to work despite having Parkinson's disease, has provided expert play-by-play for a long time, and he plans to keep going. Radio probably lends itself better to baseball, but hockey is still compelling on the air if you listen with a little imagination. I used to hear the UMass broadcasts of my former player Don Moorhouse and his color man Brock Hines on nights my AIC team didn't play. Even now, I'll occasionally pick them up over the Internet. I've learned a lot listening to Brock's interviews with both coaches. So much so that when my AIC teams played UMass, and Brock interviewed me in the lull of our locker room during warm-ups, I always tried to educate the listeners with my answers.

The hockey books I've been reading tend to brighten up bedtime. I recently finished *Home Ice* and *Open Ice* by sportswriter Jack Falla. He was a hockey writer for *Sports Illustrated* and other publications. In both books, he talks frequently about his well-maintained backyard rink. (With respect to outdoor hockey, the author's wife, Barbara Falla, said, "Anybody can love summer, but to love winter you have to carry your sunshine around with you.") And he writes chapters (essays) about such hockey figures as Wayne Gretzky, Rocket Richard, George Vezina, Hobey Baker, the proverbial rink rat, and many more. My dog Hobey sleeps close by in his own bed, but when I read the "Searching For Hobey Baker" chapter, I didn't read it aloud to him for fear he wouldn't listen.

I'm now reading Ken Dryden's latest book, *Game Change*. It's a captivating yet tragic story about Steve Matador, the NHL player who was diagnosed with chronic traumatic encephalopathy (CTE) after his death in 2015. Matador suffered several concussions during his career that undoubtedly contributed to his untimely death. As with his first book, *The Game*, Dryden has now penned another masterpiece that might rank as the second-best book ever written about the sport of hockey. *The Game*, of course, is considered by many (and me) to be the best. In *Game Change*, Dryden focuses on the dangers of contact to the head, and calls out NHL Commissioner Bettman in particular to do more to protect players from reckless hits that can lead to life-threatening brain injuries. Tonight, I stay up late and finish the hard-to-put-down book. It should be required reading for everyone in hockey.

Game Change is of special interest to me on account of my longstanding views on harmful hits. I was often criticized by my players and others for not allowing enough hitting, though these accusations were rarely made to my face. Recent research on brain injuries has exposed the risks of participating in sports like hockey and football. In a way this information verifies that my fears were warranted all along. I have always espoused clean play and purposeful physical play, as well as legal checks that don't endanger an opponent. In other words, don't hit just to hit, or chase a hit for the sake of making a macho play or appearing on a highlight film. And especially don't target the head. Near the end of my coaching career, I cut back on overemphasizing the perils of bad hits, in part because I didn't want guys to play too tentatively, and it worked out fine. We still rarely took major penalties. Yet I continued to hold my players accountable in this area, and I expected the same from the opposing coach.

Many coaches we competed against did hold their players accountable. Union coach Nate Lehman once contacted me to say he was sitting out one of his student-athletes for the next game after he hit one of our players, Nick Grasso, from behind after the whistle. His player received a game misconduct, but Nate suspended him for another game. Bob Gaudet of Dartmouth emailed me several years ago to apologize for a two-minute penalty one of his players took. He wrote:

> It was definitely a major and I'm glad your player wasn't seriously injured. He had moved the puck and was not expecting to be hit with that type of force . . . that was inexcusable and not the way we play.

Dartmouth played BU next and I looked to see if Bob dressed that player. He didn't.

NCAA hockey exists in an educational setting, which is a big reason why fighting isn't allowed. Not so in pro hockey. Fighting has been reduced, but it's still around. Much of it is pointless, in my opinion, and if it's so necessary, why do players rarely fight during the all-important playoffs? For every fan that likes the fisticuffs, there's another who finds it off-putting. I don't know how you explain that behavior to a young kid who is taught that there are civil ways to resolve a dispute or to control anger. And if you want to fire up your team, why not go out and make a big play instead of punching someone in the face?

The late Red Kelly, who won eight Stanley Cups, along with four Lady

Byng Trophies, as a Hockey Hall of Famer for the Red Wings and Maple
Leafs, had another take on fighting: "I was the welterweight boxing champ
at St. Mike's (St. Michael's College School in Toronto); I could take care of
myself, but you're valuable to a team when you're on the ice."

Dryden includes a "fist to the head" as a concussion and CTE risk. Kevin
Collins, a Springfield resident, became a twenty-eight-year NHL linesman
after graduating from AIC, and said in a *Boston Globe* article:

> The game is so much better now. It's faster. It's more skilled.
> The competition is great. The players are in better shape. We
> don't need fighting. No one listens to me, but I recommended to
> the rules committee that maybe we should follow what hockey
> is everywhere. If you fight, you get disqualified.

Kevin Collins started officiating as a student at AIC. He and teammate
Dave Forbes were paid to work youth hockey games. Neither knew it then,
but in a few short years Collins would be calling Forbes offside in NHL
games. And then there was the time he led Boston Bruin Bobby Schmautz
to the penalty box following an altercation, and he had to strong-arm the
unruly Schmautz into the "sin bin." Schmautz started to come back after
Collins before his Bruin teammate Dave Forbes stepped in to prevent
him from accosting his friend and former AIC teammate. Kevin was later
inducted into the AIC and U.S. Hockey Halls of Fame.

I'm sitting on my screened porch while working on this book, as I do most
days. Dusk is turning to dark. Sometimes I listen to my favorite folk music,
like on Saturday mornings when WDEV's "Music To Go To The Dump By"
is on, and now I'm tuned into the nocturnal sounds of nature. Spring peeper
frogs are peeping, while beefy bullfrogs bellow out from our beaver dam
pond down back. A resident barred owl hoots with a "who cooks for you"
cadence, and I can hear coyote calls. Cows are mooing for their calves from
the pasture that abuts our property. These aren't the sounds of hockey rinks,
but this chorus of creatures complements my work, as I remember some
additional people and places that have touched my coaching experience
along the way.

I think about the players, who saw limited ice time, and often had to endure
healthy scratches, yet stayed positive and committed. They were important

team members whose worth couldn't be measured in goals, assists, or saves. (Manager Tony LaRussa said that he coached "core" and "complementary" players, and that he was able to give the players in the latter category everything but what they wanted most: playing time.) Being a fourth/fifth-liner in college myself has given me a unique perspective on the difficulties that these players face.

I remember Denis Budai, an inherently upbeat person, who came all the way from Yugoslavia to play in one game during his entire four-year career. He dressed on Senior Night in his last season. He told me at first that he didn't want to play in that game because, "I don't want to be like Rudy in the movie." I understood his reluctance, but he ended up dressing after we had a long discussion. I called him the "personification of perseverance" in his press guide bio.

There's Jim Agan, a Vermonter who was in and out of the lineup during his AIC career. And when he was in, he usually saw scarce ice time. He became discouraged at times, although you'd never know it if you saw him hustling in drills or hoisting up weights in the weight room. He stayed the course and graduated. He also received a championship ring his senior year, like everyone else on the 1990 team. Notwithstanding his limited role, he was one of the boys, then and now. Larry O'Donnell, in his own succinct way, says that Jim Agan "never played, never complained."

I recall Tomas Benovic, who spent much of his college career as a sixth defenseman. His senior year he evolved into a shut-down D, allowing us to match him against our opponent's top lines. I asked Adam Pleskach, now the captain of the Tulsa Oilers (ECHL), to name an unheralded AIC teammate that he especially respected. He named Tomas and talked about how he was the hardest worker in practice and in the weight room. Adam also admired his uplifting personality and said, "I am a better player to this day because Tomas always brought the battle level up in drills."

My thoughts turn to Connecticut native George Durso, a long-haired defenseman with mutton-chop sideburns who admired punk rocker Iggy Pop. George always sat calmly at the end of the bench until called on, and then he'd defend our end with a vengeance. And there's valedictorian Dean Yakura, presently playing for his eleventh professional team in nine years as a pro hockey player. That can be a red flag if an athlete keeps switching teams, but not in Dean's case. He's a coachable and team-first journeyman who has carved out a long career in the lower minors to continue playing the game he loves. He once turned down a position on my staff to keep playing professionally.

Thinking back on non-players Jimmy Sullivan and Phil Barnhart, both special-needs workers at AIC, makes me smile. Jimmy also subbed on our Coaches intramural softball team. Those two were among my favorite people on campus. When I somehow got named MAAC Coach of the Year once, they started yelling "Coach of the Year" when I came to lunch at AIC's snack bar, the Hive. After this went on for some time, I dropped by their table and asked them not to call me that anymore because "I received the award a while ago, and I've lost a lot of games since then."

Soon after, I said, "So do you guys think you can stop saying that now?"

They both nodded. I thanked them, and as I headed back to my table, Phil hollered, "OK, Coach of the Year."

There are all the officials, administrators, broadcasters, sportswriters, and fans, many of whom love the game as much as those of us who coach and play. David Sears, nicknamed "The Voice," had a number of sports broadcasting and announcing gigs and was the enthusiastic PA announcer at Middlebury College games. He'd always add a small anecdote like "from Cornwall," or "my boyhood friend" whenever he announced my name after introducing our starters. He would have been one of my neighbors now if he hadn't died a few years ago. His voice may be silenced, but I can still hear it in my head.

I fondly recall Sam Kim, who started applying for our GA position as a student at Boston College, where he worked off-ice on Jerry York's staff. He applied unsuccessfully on three different occasions. By his own admission, he didn't have the hockey "background or pedigree," to attract much attention, but he kept sending his résumé to "way too many places to count." His persistence piqued my interest and he eventually became our volunteer director of hockey operations while studying for his master's in sports management at UMass. That led to more opportunities, and he's now the video coordinator for the AHL's Bakersfield Condors. Sam's ultimate goal is to work in the NHL. He'll get there.

I smile at the thought of the four Holy Cross students who attended Crusader games decked out in referee shirts and black helmets. They tongue-in-cheek cheered for the officials and high-fived them as they exited the ice. The officials and everyone else were amused by the creative antics of these rare referee fans. I also recall Cornell fans holding up newspapers when our Maine starters were introduced, and the RIT student section shouting "eh" as they announced our Canadian starters.

I think of my former coaches. Dad now uses a walker, and when we take weekly rides on Vermont back roads, our talks often turn to Proctor hockey. Two years ago, I sat with Chris Norris when my father was inducted into Proctor's Athletic Hall of Fame. Jim Cross recently received the Hobey Baker Legend of College Hockey award, thirty-five years after he retired. Sometimes I wonder how I could be so fortunate that fate led me to these three wonderful coaches.

Bill Turner, AIC's first hockey coach, is someone I'll always remember. He joined our staff in the late 1990s, when he was almost eighty. I hesitated when he first approached me about volunteering, as he hadn't coached in thirty years and, at his age, I thought he might get hurt in practice. He was bowled over once, but gamely got back up on his worn-out skates. Hiring Bill proved to be the right move. He had kept up with the game by following the NHL, and his accrued wisdom benefited both players and coaches. He described his return to coaching as a "sentimental journey." Bill continued to skate with an old-timers' team called the Speed Limits, and each year they played in the Snoopy's Senior Tournament in California. One year he complained about his ice time.

Finally, I reflect not on any persons, but on a place. That would be Springfield, my longtime home and workplace until I moved back to Vermont. Like most cities, Springfield has its challenges, yet it's loaded with culture and a rich history. The old Indian Motorcycle building is next to AIC, and the historic Springfield Armory is on State Street. The Basketball Hall of Fame is downtown, and just across the Connecticut River, the Big E fair hosts a million and a half visitors each fall. Dr. Seuss was brought up in the city, Merriam-Webster's Dictionary is local, and Eddie Shore of old-time hockey fame once ruled the Springfield Indians with an iron fist. When John Dunham coached at Trinity College in Hartford, he said he had to recruit players willing to go to school in the city. I was in the same situation at AIC. It takes an intrepid person to experience a different and less cushy environment.

Besides Springfield, my hockey career, which began in Andover, New Hampshire, took me to Burlington, Vermont, and Orono, Maine. In all those places, I was fortunate to find wonderful people to work with. Social media makes it possible to stay in touch from great distances, so I am thankful that I can communicate with many of the people who have influenced my life, even if it's only on occasion. In a 1993 *New York Times* guest column, recently retired NHLer Doug Wilson said:

> Hockey is a special game played by special people, and I'm proud and grateful that I was a hockey player.

I now live a less exciting life than the one I became accustomed to in my coaching career. I don't go off to work every day, and the months seem to blend a bit, because there is no in-season, off-season or summer vacation now that I'm a retired hockey coach. Although weekends aren't as distinguished from the school or workweek as they once were, they still feel unique to me. I suppose it's because we've so valued them throughout our lives. Weekends can be the busiest and most intense time of a coach's life. Years ago, as we bused through the small towns of Western Massachusetts to play Williams College on a Saturday night, I thought of how wound up I felt about the game that night, yet the people in the homes we passed were relaxing or engaged in various forms of recreation. They didn't even know we had a game. Although I'll always miss the games, having weekends off is nice. And during hockey season, I get to be a fan and watch other teams play.

When MLB manager Gene Mauch retired, he was asked to reflect on his managerial career. He responded, "I always loved it, but I didn't always enjoy it." I feel the same way. There are headaches, such as conflicts with players, pressure to win, the grind of recruiting, and long work days that continue into the night. But there are many rewards in the coaching profession: mentoring young athletes, the competition, the people in the game, and living a rich hockey life on a vibrant college campus. Either way, I'm immensely thankful for the time I had in hockey. Willie Mackinnon wrote about Coach Cross and playing the sport at Vermont in the 1970s for a publication commemorating the first fifty years of UVM hockey. He ended by saying, "I would sign up for those four years again in a heartbeat." I would too, along with the rest of my career in the game, even with all the losses.

Winter's ice-cold arrival will come to Vermont in a few months. I love the four seasons, though winter will always be a favorite since it's hockey season.

This means I have no plans to retire in Florida. Today, Hobey and I are down at our beaver pond. He's splashing around and I'm guessing the pond will be frozen in about four months, as I gaze into the stream-fed water. At that time, I'm planning to skate for the first time in three years, now that I have two new hips. My coaching and playing days are over. So is most of my life on ice, but there's still time to resurrect my pond hockey career.

It is on this very pond that we played a neighborhood game some thirty years ago on a frigid December afternoon. People of all ages and sexes joined in. After competing for a while, we worked to set up a seven-year-old, who had been trying to keep up with us, for a goal. When it happened, the child was elated and everyone whooped it up. It was all quite simple: a kid shoots a puck between two boots, and a few witnesses share his joy. There were no spectators to cheer or boo, no reporters to cover the event, no scorekeeper to record the point—just smiles on half-frozen faces, frozen in time.

Acknowledgments

Many people have helped to bring this book to fruition. I am especially grateful to my mother, Nancy Means Wright, and Bruce Johnson, my longtime friend and colleague at AIC. They served as proofreaders, surrogate editors, and confidants. The fact that I have ready access to them, because of our already close relationships, is a big benefit. And they both appear in this book. Mother has published numerous books, and she first encouraged me to write this one. Bruce is a longtime college professor with a doctorate in education.

My niece Zelie Smith, and my mother's partner Llyn Rice, have provided much-needed assistance with their computer skills. Zelie grew up watching Middlebury College games and followed the St. Lawrence men's and women's hockey teams as an undergraduate. She was spotted at a few post-game parties.

I would also like to acknowledge Rootstock Publishing for publishing *Striding Rough Ice*. Co-publisher Stephen McArthur and creative team members Samantha Kolber, Marisa Keller, and Jim Higgins provided guidance and expertise throughout the process.

I was blessed with wonderful assistants during my coaching career, many of whom are presently coaching NCAA hockey. The following were involved with fact-checking and adding their AIC memories: Rob Abel, Bobby Ferraris, Frank Genovese, Mike Field, Greg Klym, Eric Lang, Jeff Matthews, Don Moorhouse, Richard Novak, Larry O'Donnell, Alex Smith, Patrick Tabb, Mike Towns, and Steve Wiedler. Field, Lang, Moorhouse, and Tabb also played for me.

I reached out to a number of my former AIC players, and most of them responded. The list is long, so hopefully I haven't missed anyone: Nielsson Arcibal, Mark Buckley, Chad Davis, Ben Ellsworth, Eric Forselius, Jay Johnson, Bryan Jurynec, Jeremy Leroux, Chris Markiewicz, Johno May, Ron Miller, Pat Moriarty, Peter Morris, Alex Murray, Tom Patty, Adam Pleskach,

Dom Racobaldo, Vezio Sacratini, Bill Teggart, and Paul Ventre.

Maine hockey alums include Gary Conn and Brian Hughes. Jack Semler, the head coach when I assisted at Maine, chipped in with his thoughts and memories, especially during our drive down to the Cape for a golf outing with several past players.

Former Rice High School players who shared stories and jogged my memory are Paul Averill, Bob Boucher, Chris Furlani, Tim McKenzie, Tom Rocheleau, and Jeff Royer.

I am also indebted to past UVM hockey players and teammates for contributing: Tom McNamara, Herb Muther, Will MacKinnon, Tim O'Connell, and Ken Yeates.

I wish to thank three UVM Sigma Nus, who are on an email chain/ group text with me. Peter Beekman, Chris Wallace, and Tom Wheeler think hockey year-round. And sometimes too early in the morning. I know, I get their texts.

Proctor Academy hockey players Jim Hoyt, Dave Roper, Jon Randall, Peter Williams, and Doug Windsor added to the "Proctor Pond" chapter. They all played for my father, Spencer Wright. Donald Wright, my brother, who also skated for Proctor, supplied me with a treasure trove of memories. He also confirmed stories that reach back to a time when we were little tykes barely out of double-runners.

Other contributors include AIC hockey alum and former NHL linesman Kevin Collins and childhood friend Evan Snyder, who shared many of his recollections of pickup hockey at Proctor. Cindy Bolger provided feedback after reading the manuscript cover to cover. UMass Boston bench boss Peter Belisle weighed in on the late Bruce Marshall, while Babson coach Jamie Rice answered several of my questions. Bill Beaney told old hockey stories during our weekly walks on Cider Mill Road.

Finally, other people and institutions that I wish to thank include the staff at the historic Springfield (Massachusetts) Central Library, where I was able to peruse old Springfield Republican, Boston Globe and Boston Herald articles. Nich Hall at UVM and Lauren Smith from Proctor Academy supplied photos for the book. And then there's Seth Dussault, from the AIC Athletics Communications office. Seth is almost a walking library himself when it comes to hockey, particularly AIC Hockey. As I said in the book, "He's one of those unique people who help make college hockey great."

About the Author

Gary Wright recently retired from a thirty-two-year head coaching career at American International College (AIC) in Springfield, Massachusetts. His 1990 team won the ECAC East championship, and he was named MAAC Coach of the Year following AIC's first season in NCAA Division I. He previously served as an assistant at the University of Maine and as head coach at Rice Memorial High School in Burlington, Vermont. A graduate of the University of Vermont, Wright was a member of the Catamounts hockey team.

Wright has directed a YMCA summer camp and a National Youth Sports Program for inner-city youth sponsored by the NCAA. He also ran his own hockey school, Kids on Ice, and authored a book titled *Pass The Biscuit: Spirited Practices for Youth Hockey Coaches and Players*. He has been inducted into the Proctor Academy Athletics Hall of Fame and the AIC Athletics Hall of Fame.

He lives in Vermont, and his interests include golfing, music, and hiking with his dog, Hobey.

 **Also Available from Rootstock Publishing:**

All Men Glad and Wise: A Mystery by Laura C. Stevenson
Alzheimer's Canyon: One Couple's Reflections on Living with Dementia by Jane Dwinell and Sky Yardley
The Atomic Bomb on My Back: A Life Story of Survival and Activism by Taniguchi Sumiteru
Blue Desert: A Novel by Celia Jeffries
Catalysts for Change: How Nonprofits and a Foundation are Helping Shape Vermont's Future by Doug Wilhelm
China in Another Time: A Personal Story by Claire Malcolm Lintilhac
Collecting Courage: Anti-Black Racism in the Charitable Sector Edited by Nneka Allen, Camila Vital Nunes Pereira, & Nicole Salmon
An Everyday Cult by Gerette Buglion
Fly with a Murder of Crows: A Memoir by Tuvia Feldman
Hawai'i Calls: A Novel by Marjorie Nelson Matthews
Horodno Burning: A Novel by Michael Freed-Thall
The Hospice Singer: A Novel by Larry Duberstein
I Could Hardly Keep from Laughing: An Illustrated Collection of Vermont Humor by Don Hooper & Bill Mares
The Inland Sea: A Mystery by Sam Clark
Intent to Commit: A Novel by Bernie Lambek
A Judge's Odyssey: From Vermont to Russia, Kazakhstan, and Georgia, Then on to War Crimes and Organ Trafficking in Kosovo by Dean B. Pineles
Junkyard at No Town: A Novel by J.C. Myers
The Language of Liberty: A Citizen's Vocabulary by Edwin C. Hagenstein
A Lawyer's Life to Live: A Memoir by Kimberly B. Cheney
Lifting Stones: Poems by Doug Stanfield
The Lost Grip: Poems by Eva Zimet
Lucy Dancer Story and Illustrations by Eva Zimet
No Excuses by Stephen L. Harris
Nobody Hitchhikes Anymore by Ed Griffin-Nolan
Pauli Murray's Revolutionary Life by Simki Kuznick
Preaching Happiness: Creating a Just and Joyful World by Ginny Sassaman
Red Scare in the Green Mountains: Vermont in the McCarthy Era 1946-1960 by Rick Winston
Safe as Lightning: Poems by Scudder H. Parker
Striding Rough Ice: Coaching College Hockey and Growing Up in the Game by Gary Wright
Street of Storytellers by Doug Wilhelm
Tales of Bialystok: A Jewish Journey from Czarist Russia to America by Charles Zachariah Goldberg
To the Man in the Red Suit: Poems by Christina Fulton
Uncivil Liberties: A Novel by Bernie Lambek
Venice Beach: A Novel by William Mark Habeeb
The Violin Family by Melissa Perley; Illustrated by Fiona Lee Maclean
Walking Home: Trail Stories by Celia Ryker
Wave of the Day: Collected Poems by Mary Elizabeth Winn
Whole Worlds Could Pass Away: Collected Stories by Rickey Gard Diamond
You Have a Hammer: Building Grant Proposals for Social Change by Barbara Floersch